LIBRARY OF HEBREW BIBLE/ OLD TESTAMENT STUDIES

466

Formerly Journal for the Study of the Old Testament Supplement Series

TOUCHING THE HEART OF GOD

The Social Construction of Poverty
Among Biblical Peasants

William Robert Domeris

t&t clark

NEW YORK • LONDON

T & T Clark International, 80 Maiden Lane, New York, NY 10038

T & T Clark International, The Tower Building, 11 York Road, London SE1 7NX

T & T Clark International is a Continuum imprint.

Library of Congress Cataloging-in-Publication Data
Touching the heart of God : the social construction of poverty among biblical peasants / William Robert Domeris.
    p. cm. -- (The library of Hebrew Bible/Old Testament studies ; #466)
  Includes bibliographical references and index.
  ISBN-13: 978-0-567-02862-4 (hardcover : alk. paper)
  ISBN-10: 0-567-02862-3 (hardcover : alk. paper)
  1. Poverty in the Bible. 2. Poor--Biblical teaching. 3. Bible.
  O.T.--Criticism, interpretation, etc. I. Title. II. Series.

BS1199.P64D66 2007
  221.8'3625--dc22

                                    2007001800

06 07 08 09 10   10 9 8 7 6 5 4 3 2 1

Printed and bound in Great Britain by Biddles Ltd., King's Lynn, Norfolk

CONTENTS

ACKNOWLEDGMENTS

The genesis of this book took place in the Chapel of Mary Magdalene (Hillbrow, Johannesburg)—dedicated to the spiritual care of teenage prostitutes. It was there that I began to realise the complexity of poverty. This awareness grew through my interaction with World Vision in Africa and here in the poverty-stricken Eastern Cape. Eleven years in the making, the book is indebted to several people. First and foremost I must pay attention to Norman Gottwald, for his helpful insights and constant encouragement. Secondly, my thanks go to the University of the Witwatersrand (Johannesburg) for making my sabbatical in Berkeley possible. The editorial assistance of Mary Stevens, Andrew Mein and Duncan Burns has been invaluable in ensuring a more readable volume, I dedicate this book to my wife Shona and my daughter Kima.

ABBREVIATIONS

AB	Anchor Bible
ABD	*The Anchor Bible Dictionary*. Edited by David Noel Freedman. 6 vols. New York: Doubleday, 1992
AIACCP	Archaeological Institute of America Colloquia and Conference Papers
AOS	American Oriental Series
ATANT	Abhandlungen zur Theologie des Alten und Neuen Testaments
ATR	*Anglican Theological Review*
BA	*Biblical Archaeologist*
BAIAS	*Bulletin of the Anglo-Israel Archeological Society*
BARev	*Biblical Archaeology Review*
BASOR	*Bulletin of the American Schools of Oriental Research*
BBET	Beiträge zur biblischen Exegese und Theologie
BiBh	*Bible Bhashyam*
BN	*Biblische Notizen*
BTB	*Biblical Theology Bulletin*
BurH	*Buried History*
BZAW	Beihefte zur ZAW
CahRB	Cahiers de la Revue biblique
CBQ	*Catholic Biblical Quarterly*
Coll	*Collationes*
CR:BS	*Currents in Research: Biblical Studies*
CTM	*Concordia Theological Monthly*
Dda	*Dialoghi di Archeologia*
ErIs	*Eretz Israel*
EvT	*Evangelische Theologie*
ExpTim	*Expository Times*
GNS	Good News Studies
Hen	*Henoch*
HUCA	*Hebrew Union College Annual*
IDB	*The Interpreter's Dictionary of the Bible*. Edited by George Arthur Buttrick. 4 vols. Nashville: Abingdon, 1962
IEJ	*Israel Exploration Journal*
Int	*Interpretation*
IRT	Issues in Religion and Theology
JANES	*Journal of the Ancient Near Eastern Society*
JBL	*Journal of Biblical Literature*
JBQ	*Jewish Bible Quarterly*
JNES	*Journal of Near Eastern Studies*
JNSL	*Journal of Northwest Semitic Languages*
JSOT	*Journal for the Study of the Old Testament*
JSOTSup	Journal for the Study of the Old Testament: Supplement Series

JSS	*Journal of Semitic Studies*
JSSEA	*Journal of the Society for the Study of Egyptian Antiquities*
JTSoA	*Journal of Theology for Southern Africa*
NEA	*Near Eastern Archaeology*
NGTT	*Nederduitse gereformeerde teologiese tydskrif*
NICOT	New International Commentary on the Old Testament
NIDOTTE	*New International Dictionary of Old Testament Theology and Exegesis.* Edited by Willem A. VanGemeren. 5 vols. Grand Rapids: Zondervan, 1997
NTT	*Norsk Teologisk Tidsskrift*
OBT	Overtures to Biblical Theology
OLA	Orientalia lovaniensia analecta
OrAnt	*Oriens antiquus*
OTE	*Old Testament Essays*
OTL	Old Testament Library
OTS	*Oudtestamentische Studiën*
PEQ	*Palestine Exploration Quarterly*
Qad	*Qadmoniot*
RevB	*Revue biblique*
RHPR	*Revue d'histoire et de philosophie religieuses*
SBLDS	Society of Biblical Literature Dissertation Series
SBLMS	Society of Biblical Literature Monograph Series
SBLWAW	Society of Biblical Literature Writings from the Ancient World
SBT	Studies in Biblical Theology
SJOT	*Scandinavian Journal of the Old Testament*
SSN	Studia Semitica Neerlandica
SWBA	Social World of Biblical Antiquity
TA	*Tel Aviv*
TBT	*The Bible Today*
TDNT	*Theological Dictionary of the New Testament.* Edited by Gerhard Kittel and Gerhard Friedrich. Translated by Geoffrey W. Bromiley. 10 vols. Grand Rapids: Eerdmans, 1964–1976
TDOT	*Theological Dictionary of the Old Testament.* Edited by G. J. Botterweck and H. Ringgren. Translated by J. T. Willis, G. W. Bromiley, and D. E. Green. 8 vols. Grand Rapids: Eerdmans, 1974–
ThWAT	*Theologisches Wörterbuch zum Alten Testament.* Edited by G. J. Botterweck and H. Ringgren. Stuttgart: W. Kohlhammer, 1970–
TS	*Theological Studies*
UF	*Ugarit-Forschungen*
VT	*Vetus Testamentum*
VTSup	Vetus Testamentum, Supplements
YNER	Yale Near Eastern Researches
ZAW	*Zeitschrift für die alttestamentliche Wissenschaft*
ZDPV	*Zeitschrift des deutschen Palästina-Vereins*

Chapter 1

Tackling the Giant

1.1. *Introduction*

The Hebrew Bible retains the echoes of many voices including the poor. Job writes:

> Like wild donkeys in the desert, the poor go about their labour of foraging food; the wasteland provides food for their children. They gather fodder in the fields and glean in the vineyards of the wicked. Lacking clothes, they spend the night naked; they have nothing to cover themselves in the cold. They are drenched by mountain rains and hug the rocks for lack of shelter. The fatherless child is snatched from the breast; the infant of the poor is seized for a debt [pledge]. Lacking clothes, they go about naked; they carry the sheaves but still go hungry. They crush the olives among the terraces; they tread the winepresses, yet suffer thirst. The groans of the dying rise from the city, the souls of the wounded cry out for help. But God charges no one with wrongdoing (Job 24:5–12; translation by Pope 1965, 161)

A window opens in Job onto the life of the poor. Denied proper provisions and in the absence of a fully functioning system of reciprocity, the poor scavenge for food, for some edible plant in the wild or some left-over in the refuse of the wealthy. Their full day of labour is rewarded with just enough to fill a corner of an empty belly. Cold and rain are the companions of the poor and even the rock faces deny them protection. Shame and abuse go hand in hand. The bully-boy sentiment of oppression peeps through in the humiliation of the poor, and God seems not to care. Behind this graphic portrait stands the reality of an economic system still only partly understood but one which will occupy our attention for the remainder of this book.

Poverty is an extremely complex social phenomenon, one which at the dawn of the twenty-first century, we do not yet understand fully (Narayan et al. 2000). Several decades ago, Rossi and Blum wrote, "The poor are different: On this, there is consensus." Beyond this consensus lies a host of questions: How are the poor different? How do these differences arise, and what maintains them? (1968–69, 36). To these questions one may add: How should one define poverty? Then there are the questions which are at the heart of this book: What does the Hebrew Bible say about poverty? How do these insights enable us to combat poverty today?

All too often poverty is randomly combated. The poor are rarely given a voice to speak and when they do, their responses seem not to fit our questions. Or perhaps it is the reverse. We ask the wrong questions. We ask about the solutions to poverty and they speak about hungry children crying in the night (Fenyves, Rule and Everatt 1998). We ask about opportunity and they speak about the endless trials of looking for work. We ask about the future and they speak about the present.

Nobel Laureate and Archbishop Emeritus, Desmond Mpilo Tutu, once described a visit in the 1980s to one of Apartheid's "solutions" in the form of a Black squatter camp, on the edges of a White city. He reported his conversation with a little girl who lived with her widowed mother and her sister.

> "Tutu asked, 'Does your mother get a pension or a grant?'
> 'No' she replied.
> 'Then what do you do for food?'
> 'We borrow food' she replied.
> 'Have you ever returned any of the food that you have borrowed?'
> 'No.'
> 'What do you do when you can't borrow food?'
> 'We drink water to fill our stomachs.'" (cited in Webster 1986, 94)

The naivety of the little girl contrasts strangely with the horror of the situation that she describes. Her innocence serves to throw into relief the fact that for many people, poverty is a shameful existence and one that is eventually capable of destroying a person's sense of self-worth and dignity, which should attend them as members of the human race. Theirs is a world apart, rarely spoken of, but omnipresent.

The choice which has led a select group of people, over the course of the centuries, into a life of voluntary poverty, is a noble calling. Their decision to share in the world of the poor is a courageous endeavour. But even then, they are able only to glimpse, as through a mirror darkly, the stark horror which the poorest of the poor inhabit as their private world. Voluntary poverty should not become the criterion by which to understand all poverty, nor should it be allowed to colour our perception of it (Gutierrez 1973, 288–91). Few people choose poverty. The majority of the poor have poverty thrust upon them. The poor do not exult in their lack of worldly possessions. They are not, by virtue of their situation, somehow closer to God than are the rich. The fate of the poor, which leads some to grovel in the streets, in the garbage of the well-to-do, is hardly a noble or spiritual calling.

Poverty has been studied for a wide variety of reasons, and from a number of perspectives. Studies of macro-economics deal with problems like third-world debt, famine in Africa or Asia, and the growing disparity between the wealth of the first world and the poverty of the third world (e.g. Øyen, Miller and Samad 1996; World Bank 2000). Other studies have been concentrated at the level of micro-economics, focussing upon individual communities and their specific needs and concerns (e.g. Key Indicators 1995; McAllister 2005; Robinson 2005). The discussion of theoretical issues has become increasingly more commonplace (e.g. Sen 1977, 1981, 1999; Schram 1995; Atal and Øyen 1997; Maxwell 1999). All too often, faulty definitions (or even an absence of definition) have in the past lead to an oversimplification of the problem of poverty and to simplistic solutions. Today, most authors no longer simply assume an understanding of poverty, its dimensions and origins, and there is increasing awareness of the diverse nature of poverty.

Poverty exists in our world in a variety of forms and in varying degrees of severity. What is poor in Lesotho or India, and poor in the suburbs of Berkeley, California are literally worlds apart. Even within a particular community, the concept of "the poor" may have different meanings, depending upon the individual's own position and preconceptions. Worldwide poverty displays a broad-based spectrum of meaning, a kaleidoscope of subtle, but deeply felt nuances, of a world within worlds. It is this dark world, inhabited by the poor that I will attempt to sketch within these pages, by drawing on the ethnography of the Hebrew Bible (hereafter HB) and the witness of archaeological and anthropological data. Clearly, poverty often operates along time-worn lines, so that in the full understanding of such processes lie the fundamentals (guiding principles) required for the solution to contemporary poverty. But in acknowledging any such resonances with the present, we should not be blind to the presence also of the differences created by time and culture. In this, the choice of an interpretative model and a workable definition of the complex system we call "poverty" are critical

In the biblical mind, "poverty is a social idea and not just an economic category" (Soares-Prabhu 1991, 156). The poor are "a sociological group rather than a religious group" and "may be defined not by their spiritual attitude of dependence on God but by their sociological situation of powerlessness and need...not necessarily economic need" (1991, 156–57; cf. George 1977, 6). These are not some elite group of the "spiritual poor"—a notion that is even less clear than real poverty and "leads to comforting and tranquilizing conclusions" for the non-poor (Gutierrez 1973, 289–90).

1.2. *The Purpose of this Book*

There are four main objectives in writing this book. The first objective is to show that it is possible, given the various forms of evidence (archaeology, ethnography and comparative social theory), to compile a reasonably accurate description of the peasant poverty of ancient Israel. In the words of the anthropologist Geertz, I will set out to create "a thick description" (1973).

The second objective is to use the theory of the social construction of poverty to interpret the ethnography and archaeology of Israel in the first millennium B.C.E. In this work, I set out to reconstruct the peasant history of Israel, flagging particular economic milestones evident from the primary and secondary sources. Once we have a solid understanding of the precarious nature of peasant livelihood in Israel over the centuries, I will develop an understanding of the various human interventions over time, and posit the possible impact on peasant survival modes.

The third objective is to show that the conditions of peasant poverty worsened from the period of the divided monarchy (Iron II) into the post-exilic period (Persian and Hellenistic times) and beyond (Roman times). What some scholars (Coote 1981; Gossai 1993; Lang 1985; Premnath 1988) perceived to be a process entirely contained within the Iron Age, was instead spread across the centuries. A process of progressive deterioration in the well-being of the poor of Israel was rightly surmised, but the time-scale was wrong. The world of the HB and that of the New Testament were economically light years apart.

I will conclude with a model of the social construction of poverty, which makes use of the twin concepts of power/powerlessness and honour/shame and which is designed to be directly applicable to the world of the HB.

The fourth objective is to encourage meaningful programmes for dealing with poverty that includes the poor in the evolution of their own coping strategies. To achieve this end, I conclude also with five key principles of poverty, which sum up the major insights into the way in which poverty is manifested. The rationale, in using the Bible, is to encourage those people who take the Bible seriously to seek not just the amelioration of poverty in their communities, but its eradication.

1.3. *Methodology*

In attempting a description of poverty, especially the poverty of a community millennia removed from one's own, the choice of an adequate methodology is essential. How does one encompass a topic which

includes Biblical Studies, ancient Near Eastern history, peasant economics, Hebrew semantics, archaeology of the Near East, anthropology,
political studies and sociology? To avoid writing an encyclopaedia of
poverty in ancient Israel, I have elected to follow a model drawn from
the Philosophy of Science (Wylie 1989), which allows me to incorporate
evidence from a variety of sources without appearing too eclectic in the
process.

The primary data for this study come from three main sources. The first
source is written material (ethnography) of which the HB is the major
component. The study of poverty in the Bible is a well-travelled path, and
I have been able to drink from a rich variety of wells on the way. There
are a number of academic studies which seek to give an overall picture of
poverty in the HB (Bammel 1968; Boerma 1979; Hauck and Kasch
1968; Kutsch 1978; Van der Ploeg 1950; Schwantes 1977; Wolf 1962a,
1962b).

More detailed studies fall into three basic categories. The first category is that of the semantic study of poverty (e.g. Kuschke 1939; Wittenberg 1986; Pleins 1992; Domeris 1997 [various]). The second category is
that of the theological study of poverty (Coggins 1986–87; Hobbs 1988–
89; Gillingham 1988–89; Haan 1991; Hoppe 1987; Whybray 1988–89;
Gowan 1987, and see bibliography cited therein), including studies from
the perspective of liberation theology (see Araya 1987 for further references). The third category is that of the sociological study of poverty in
the HB (Von Waldow 1970; Levenson 1976; Lang 1985; Hoppe 2004).
Considerable attention has also been paid to the teaching of the New
Testament, with regard to the teaching of either Jesus or the early Church
on wealth and poverty (Hamel 1989; Malina 1987; Moxnes 1988;
Schmidt 1987; Schottroff and Stegemann 1986; Hengel 1986).

Studies of the HB already have a clearly established set of methodologies, which need no discussion. What is necessary is to address the issue
of dating. In the face of the debate about the historicity of the biblical
sources, my starting point is a position somewhat closer to the Minimalists (Revisionists) than to the Maximalists or Traditionalists (cf. Dever
2000, 1191). The terms are constant, but the parameters keep changing.
In essence, the issue is how much of the pre-exilic account of the origin
and history of Israel is reliable as an economic and historical document
(cf. Grabbe 1997; Gottwald 2001)?

Thompson (1992, 1999), Lemche (1993, 1998) and P. R. Davies
(1992) leave little space for the earlier (pre-critical) studies of the history
of Israel common until the late seventies, by subscribing to a Hellenistic
or Persian dating for the majority of the texts of the HB. Similarly, Linville (1998) considers that the biblical history of the monarchy reflects a

concern with the insider–outsider issues of the colonial Judahite community of Persian times (but cf. Mullen 1993). Gottwald concurs that the Persian Empire consequently receives a most favourable treatment (2001, 111), but asks why the sources reveal so little of their own time and so much of the earlier periods (2001, 96–97, 158–72).

From my perspective, Gottwald makes a helpful distinction when he differentiates between biblical information that is "information about specific persons, places and events" and "information about social and cultural structures and processes" (1997, 21). The latter is more likely to be considered authentic by both sides—Minimalists and Traditionalists. He then states his confidence in "the capacity of the biblical sources to give us trustworthy scenarios of the political life of ancient Israel beginning with tribal times, despite their sketchy, sometimes distorted, detail and their preoccupation with religion" (2001, 246). While not as generous as Gottwald (2001) in my selection, nevertheless I believe there is good reason to suggest that material available for a reconstruction of the economy of the Iron Age may be found in the ethnography of the HB. Interpreting the texts remains a challenge and the choice of model is vital, for the evidence rests in the interlocution of text and empirical finds.

Other written sources include cognate material from the rest of the ANE, including the adjacent Mediterranean societies (Greece and Egypt) adduced primarily for their comparative value and not because I believe that Israelite society perfectly mimicked these societies. Of these texts, the most important for our purposes are the letters making up the El Amarna correspondence, for their valuable insights into the nature of Canaanite peasantry.

The second source is the archaeological data, especially those drawn from the field of the Archaeology of society (cf. Levy 1998). Here, in the dust and debris of ancient mounds, lie the raw data for reconstructing the economy of ancient Israel and Judah. Interpreting the data requires inevitably a choice of theories, which means that I shall enter various debates including that of the origin of Israel. With one exception, I shall follow the emerging consensus; this exception is our decision to opt for the Lower Chronology over against the Higher Chronology. I do not think that this choice has any major impact on the overall argument of this study but it allows critical emphasis to be placed on the oblique role of the Assyrians in the history of the peasants of Israel and Judah.

The third source of data for this study is the collective peasant studies, drawn from anthropology and sociology, which have application for the peasants of the ANE (e.g. Lenski, Lenski and Nolan 1991). Because peasantry follow certain broad patterns, one can safely make some deductions for the peasants of Israel and Judah. Nevertheless, I have hesitated even to do this, unless there was some additional primary or secondary evidence near at hand. I have utilised material drawn from the classical worlds on the same basis. For example, I make extensive use of the Mediterranean materials of Gallant (1991) who studied ancient and modern Greek peasants and created some useful computer models. I also have used the work of Carney (1975), De Ste. Croix (1981) and Kautsky (1982) all of whom offer useful interpretative overviews, but which still require testing against the hard data drawn from the archaeology and ethnography. In addition to these studies, I refer to studies dedicated to the peasants of Iron Age Israel/Judah (Hopkins 1985; Dar 1980, 1986; Borowski 1987) and to their counterparts in New Testament times (Hamel 1989; Oakman 1986).

Holding these disparate sources together is my model based on the writings of Wylie (1989). Dever (1994), faced with the variety of models in use, called for an epistemology for relating biblical and archaeological data. Wylie (1989), a philosopher of science, offers just such an epistemology. Simply put, Wylie proposes that archaeological and ethnographical evidence should be tested against different models. For example, such evidence as exists for early Israel, both from archaeology and relevant texts, should be applied to the proposed models, with the test being what Wylie calls a "tightness of fit" (1989, 3–10), meaning a reasonable fit between data and theory. A good measure of fit, according to Wylie (1989, 17–18), is when all the available evidence is able to be fitted into place in support of the chosen model. What follows is in the words of Gottwald "a project of critical imagination" (2001, 158).

1.4. *The Heart of God*

In the HB lies a wealth of insights into the world of the poor. Its pages overflow with unique insights, novel economic perspectives and radical observations. The poor of the HB lived cheek by jowl with the spectre of starvation, the ghoul of disease and the monster of oppression. As we immerse ourselves in these pages, one cannot fail to be moved by the cries that come to us across the centuries. In listening to the echoes of these cries, my hope is that the reader will come to know more deeply the pain of poverty, and to become more aware of the treacherous web of its social construction.

The Western world has become highly successful at hiding poverty, concealing its more obvious signs by sweeping the poor into the dismal corners of society. In the third world, or two-thirds world, poverty cannot be hidden. It has assumed gargantuan proportions, bringing in its trail a deep sense of hopelessness and helplessness (World Bank 2000). Famine, starvation and astronomical debt follow in the wake of so-called Aid Packages, along with corruption, greed and bloody power struggles. We seem to be no nearer to solving the problem of poverty than were our ancestors and, in some countries, even further away. Perhaps, since the first world has the resources to end global poverty, it is really a question of whether or not there is the will to bring this about (Sachs 2005).

In a graphic portrayal of poverty, Araya writes

> Poverty is not innocent or neutral. Poverty is lethal. Material poverty is life historically menaced, thwarted, and destroyed, for the primary sources of the real life of the poor are menaced by the permanent nonsatisfaction of their basic needs: employment, food, housing, good health. Life is being annihilated, either slowly, by oppressive structures, or quickly and violently, by repressive structures.... Poverty is the expression of the true necrophiliac essence of an institutionalised system built on the death of the poor for the benefit of the elite, whose wealth is continually increasing at the expense of the increasing poverty of the masses. (1987, 22)

"Do you know where hell is?" enquired a seventeen year old girl, trapped in a vicious cycle of drugs, poverty and prostitution, "I live in it!" (personal communication). Real poverty is hell on earth—"What we mean by material poverty is a subhuman situation...a scandalous condition inimical to human dignity and therefore contrary to the will of God" (Gutierrez 1973, 291). To speak about poverty is to touch the Heart of God.

Chapter 2

Naming the Poor

2.1. *Poverty Defined*

Poverty is more than a simple process of some people having less than others. The very complexity of the phenomenon of poverty (Øyen 1997, 123) has led to multiple attempts to find a meaningful definition (cf. Schram 1995; May 1998; Maxwell 1999). Such definitions struggle to do justice to the widely differing manifestations of poverty and to the multiple processes which undergird it (cf. MacPherson and Silburn 1998). "At its simplest poverty refers to a basic lack of the means of survival; the poor are those who, even in normal circumstances, are unable to feed and clothe themselves properly and risk death as a consequence" (MacPherson and Silburn 1998, 1). The difficulty of this definition is not a lack of clarity, but the sheer volume of people it applies to both today in the Two-Thirds World and in the world of the HB. The requisite response is to seek some identifiable measure of comparison across such widely differing localities.

2.1.1. *Minimum Subsistence Levels*

Subsistence needs have been deemed to be measurable in economic terms, which has led to the creation of such measures as the "breadline" or "minimum subsistence levels" (Maxwell 1999). While useful as an analytical and comparative tool, such measures have increasingly come up for criticism (Ruggles 1990; Streeten 1995). They fail to take into account details like the seasonality of peasant poverty, or the availability of edible plants for which to forage in rural areas (Norton, Owen and Milimo 1994, 93). Subsistence levels, while a critical tool in the fight against poverty, incline one to think of the poor as simply those who are economically deprived, leading to purely economic solutions (food and clothes), while ignoring the human element of freedom and dignity (cf. Novak 1996; Sen 1999).

Øyen writes:

> The most common trap in poverty research has been to treat poverty as a
> homogeneous phenomenon.... The need for a simple political instrument,
> and the dominance of income as an indicator of poverty, have helped turn
> a very complex phenomenon into an over-simplified picture of poverty as
> a gradual and almost uni-dimensional economic phenomenon. (1997,
> 126–27)

Instead poverty is multi-dimensional and socially relative and demands
various responses from the simplest level to the most complex.

2.1.2. *Absolute and Relative Poverty*

The foremost distinction is between absolute and relative poverty (World
Bank 1978, 1980). Absolute poverty is defined as a condition of life so
characterised by malnutrition, illiteracy, disease, squalid surroundings
and high infant mortality so as to be beneath any reasonable definition of
human decency (World Bank 1978, 111). Relative poverty is the misdistribution of assets, income and power (Øyen 1997, 127). The definition
thus moves away from access to the basic necessities for survival to the
question of access to material or non-material needs that can open up
paths to a better standard of living. A third level of the definition might
include access to social goods and participation which gives the individual better control of his/her own life situation (1997, 127).

2.1.3. *A Basic-Needs Definition*

A refinement of the subsistence definition has led to what is called "a
basic-needs" definition (MacPherson and Silburn 1998, 6), which recognises a wider set of necessities than just food and clothing, including adequate housing, clean water and minimum education. The rural African
poor, for example, face a number of specific barriers that prevent them
from increasing their economic productivity (Key Indicators 1995, 18–
19). These include factors such as time-consuming tasks. For example,
the daily collection of water could take up more than three hours per day
and the fetching of firewood consumes at least one hour per day. Notably,
80 percent of the people who fetch the water and firewood are women.
Thus, women in the vast majority of poor rural African households are
forced to spend more than four hours a day (or more than one day per
week) collecting water and firewood (Key Indicators 1995, 19).

Another barrier to economic productivity is the health of the poor. The
disease pattern among the poor is striking, with

> the higher prevalence of diseases of poverty among the lower income
> groups, including tuberculosis, diarrhoea and fever. In addition, the much
> higher rates of mental disability among the poor are an indication of the

poor mental health facilities as well as the likely influence of violence and trauma on many poor people. (Key Indicators 1995, 22)

The lower the person on the scale, the higher will be the incidence of the disease and disability, both mental and physical. Poor children are especially vulnerable, being the victims of both disease and under-nutrition, resulting in stunted growth (1995, 23).

2.1.4. *A Multi-faceted Issue*

Each definition, from the simple survival notions to the complex social structuring, has something to add to our understanding of poverty, and to our proposed means of addressing poverty (Øyen 1997, 129).

> Our concept of poverty determines our definition and our definition determines our measures. What we choose to measure, and how, gives us the problem we choose to confront and thus shapes our policy.... Unless and until the poverty problem is adequately conceptualised, defined and measured, countless millions will continue to suffer. (MacPherson and Silburn 1998, 17)

Conversely, there are those who argue that "it is the social scientists—alongside the politicians—who are unable to define the phenomenon, but it is a social reality, the way millions of people experience it that emphasizes its existence...and forces one to deal with it" (Tsiakalos and Kongidou 1991). Truth lies on both sides of this debate.

Samad sums up, "Poverty...is neither an economic nor a purely social problem, but is multi-faceted, with economic, social, political, cultural and demographic dimensions. It is a condition as well as a process..., a cause and an effect" (1996, 34).

2.2. *Poverty as a Social Construction*

MacPherson and Silburn write:

> By now it is clear that the attempt to construct an absolute and presumably universal definition of poverty is fundamentally flawed, both in theory and practice. Poverty analysts are driven remorselessly to accept that poverty has to be understood as a socially constructed concept with powerful qualitative and normative components. As such it is inherently a relative concept. (1998, 7)

In grappling with such a socially constructed concept, I have chosen to base my model on the theory of the social construction of poverty. Simply understood, this means that poverty is the end result of a process in which external elemental and societal forces are operative. My task here, in this work, is to discern those forces that operated in ancient Israel, and to describe their impact in the lives of the peasant poor.

Theories that deal with the social fabric of poverty have to do with those forces that act either to cause or to perpetuate poverty, ascribing these either to internal or external origins (Øyen 1997, 127). On the one hand are the internal forces, which serve to create and to sustain poverty. On the other hand there are the forces external to the poor, which serve to work against any escape, on their part, from the clutches of poverty. Øyen then gives examples of a class-dominated society, a religious or military monopoly of politics, absence of a voting system and the "informal majority consensus stereotyping poor people as incompetent" (1997, 128). Sen describes such societies as denying the poor the fullest expression of the freedom necessary for the meaningful development of the individual within a complex society (1999). In the same vein, Townsend adds exclusion of the poor from participating in "the elaborate social demands and customs which have been placed upon citizens of that society," such as "access to diets, amenities, standards, services, and activities which are common or customary" (1993, 36).

The world of the poor is a world set apart and defined by the non-poor as intrinsically different, and inferior. Øyen reminds us that "the poor are marginalised from civil society, but causes and manifestations of poverty are woven into the way social and economic structures are organised in the world of the non-poor. Therefore, poverty cannot be understood as a phenomenon isolated from society at large" (1997, 123). This is not to say that individually each of the non-poor are "to blame" for the poverty of their society, or conversely that the poor are individually all the "innocent" victims of a brutal system. But the fact is that there is a system operating, whereby a certain group of the population are labelled as "the poor," not by themselves but by the non-poor. Few people opt voluntarily to join this world, and the mere fact of the inability of the poor to leave that world at will means that it is in many ways a social prison—a place of marginalisation (Øyen 1997, 123) and a place surrounded by barriers.

My premise for this book is that poverty is indeed a social construction, not least for the biblical poor; an imposition on the poor by the world of the non-poor and the deliberate creation of a subset within society, through the initial processes of labelling and demarcation, and the subsequent processes of disempowerment, oppression, marginalisation and alienation. This is a map of the processes of poverty, which will engage the mind on the journey through time into the heart of peasant poverty in ancient Israel.

2.3. *The Power of a Name*

To be poor means more than just experiencing an absence of wealth or possessions. It is to occupy a specific place within the social ordering of society. To call someone "poor" is to make a value judgment: it is to create two groups, us and them; to say, that they (the poor) are somehow different from us (the non-poor) and because there is such a small step between difference and value, to imply that they are therefore inferior, lacking in certain values and deviant. A boundary line is drawn, with "us" on one side as the normative group, and "them" on the other as the different or strange. Once such a line is in place, it becomes easier and easier to stereotype those on the other side, even to demonise them, as sources of evil. The line prevents contact, prevents relationships, without which rumour and suspicion are free to grow. So the poor become the lazy, the drunkards, the addicts, the failures, the unintelligent, the rejected, the shamed, the immoral and, most telling of all, the God-forsaken.

Labels, following Labelling Theory (cf. Johnson 1995, 151–52), are the names that one group uses to demarcate insiders and outsiders (Halliday 1985, 164–67). The power of the label depends upon the extent to which it may become normative for the broader society. These, oft-times shameful, labels are initially abhorred by those who experience them as oppressive. Even though over time they might come to accept them as a necessary evil, the pain of the shame still remains.

Labelling is a response to assumed deviance, as Johnson makes clear,

> The core idea of labelling theory is that the social response to deviance can profoundly affect how people are perceived and how they perceive themselves as well as the resources and opportunities that are then made available to them…. To the extent that societies try to control deviance by backing people into a corner and forcing upon them a deviant status and limited opportunities, they actually promote deviance. (Johnson 1995, 151)

Here in a nutshell are the component parts of the social construction of poverty—labels, limited opportunities and deviant status.

Poverty labels signal areas of possible exploitation within the economic domain, by separating out those with economic power (the non-poor) from those without. The powerful control the dominant labels and symbols, allowing them to draw the lines, and create the orders within their domain, and to lump completely disparate groups into seemingly homogeneous parties, often without invoking any basis in reality, or only the most general of bases (Matthews and Benjamin 1991). No group identity or class consciousness binds the poor together. They are unified only by virtue of their place within the thinking and perspective of the dominant class.

2.4. *Hebrew Terms for the Poor*

Socio-linguistics speaks of over-lexicalisation, in that labels tend to pro-
liferate (Halliday 1985, 164–82). In place of the comparative paucity of
words for poverty and wealth in the English language, Biblical Hebrew
contains a veritable treasury of terms. The various terms for the poor in
the HB emerged as the descriptive names foisted on the poor across different cultures, societies and regions. They would have been the labels
used by the non-poor to demarcate those perceived to be different from
them; to draw the line, the boundary within the social ordering, marking
out poor and non-poor.

The struggle is not only in the finding of English equivalents, but
in understanding the finer nuances of difference or similarity from one
Hebrew term to the other. Words as signifiers are as much informed by
their context as they, in turn, inform that context. Both by grouping the
terms generally within semantic domains, of wealth or poverty, and by
exploring the individual instances of a term, we are able to gain some
sense of the breadth of the composite picture, even if the finer details
may continue to elude our gaze.

The eight Hebrew terms, making up the main part of the semantic field
of the poor in the HB (Domeris 1997a, 1:228) are *ebyôn* (61 times), *dal*
II (48 times), *miskēn* (6 times), *ʿānî* (37 times), *ʿānāw* (81 times) and *rwš*
(11 times) among others (cf. Botterweck 1977, 1:29). To these, we should
add *mwk* ("poor"; 5 times) and *dkʾ* ("crush"; 18 times) in accord with the
NIDOTTE listing (Domeris 1997a, 1:228). The numbers in brackets refer
to the listing in *NIDOTTE* (1997).

2.4.1. ʾEbyôn *(#36): Those in Economic Need*
Kuschke (1939, 53) relates the term *ebyôn* to the root meaning "want,
desire, request, be willing," or better "to lack or to be in need"
(cf. Gillingham 1988–89, 16), although there remains some uncertainty
(cf. Botterweck 1974, 27–28). He renders the term as "needy" along the
lines of a constant or urgent deficiency (Kuschke 1939, 53), and others
have tended to follow suit (e.g. Botterweck 1974). The sense pertains of
those who are "completely dependent on others for their daily survival"
(Domeris 1997a, 1:228).

The term *ebyôn* is used 61 times in the HB, and is found in all three
parts of the canon. In the Prophetic corpus (cf. Pleins 1992, 5:403–4), the
word *ebyôn* is used 17 times and its usage there is typical of the rest of the
HB, for we find that these people lack homes (e.g. Isa 14:30); are hungry
and thirsty (e.g. 32:6–7); are abused by the powerful (e.g. 29:19); and
suffer injustice (e.g. 32:7) and economic exploitation (e.g. Amos 2:6).

Pleins (1992, 5:404) disputes Kuschke's reference (cf. 1939, 53) to a patient or pious endurance, but the evidence brought to bear by Botterweck (1974, 37–38) is convincing. The parallelism found in the various Psalms of Lament clearly extend the meaning of *'ebyôn* beyond the dimension of poverty, into the realm of one's reliance and need for God (Pss 86:2; 40:17 [16][1]; 69:37 [36] and see further examples in 1974, 38).

2.4.2. Dal *(#1924): The Poor Peasants*
Carroll (1996, 1:951) renders the verb *dll* I (#1937) as "small, helpless, powerless, insignificant or dejected" and draws attention to the Ugaritic cognate, the root of which means "to make poor, to oppress." Cognates abound in the various Semitic languages, of which the Old Assyrian and Old Babylonian are most instructive, since the cognates mean "obligation to work, work, and compulsory labour" (*CAD* 3:173–77; see Fabry 1978, 3:208–15). From the Middle Babylonian period onwards, the term takes on the more general notion of labour, including both forced and free forms (Fabry 1978, 3:210). Pleins relates the term *dal* II (pl. *dallîm*) to the poor peasant farmer (1992, 5:405), which is a generally accepted position (cf. Carroll 1996, 1:951) and includes the idea of forced labour (Coote 1981, 24–32; Domeris 1997b), rather than considering it a general term for the "wretched" (as in Andersen and Freedman 1989, 310).

The noun *dallâ* II (#1930) is used 5 times, to refer to the "poorest people of the land" left behind in Judah after the deportation of the ruling elite to Babylon in the sixth century (e.g. Jer 40:7; 52:15–16). Pleins (1992, 5:406) speaks of "poor farm labourers" (cf. *CAD* 3:173), who now become liable to work the fields and vineyards of their Babylonian overlords (2 Kgs 24:14; 25:12), but the term "peasants" suffices, since it carries a due sense of obligation to some more powerful personage (Wolf 1966, 1–17; Saul and Woods 1971; Bundy 1988, 4–13).

2.4.3. Maḥsôr *(#4728): The Shameful Poor*
Maḥsôr derives from the root *ḥsr* (#2893) which carries the sense of diminish, decrease or lack and may be rendered as "want" or "lack," a sense that is shared by its cognates in other Semitic languages (Meier 1997). Leaving Proverbs aside, *maḥsôr* is used in Deut 15:8, where it has the sense of lacking provisions (so also Judg 18:7; 19:19, 20; Ps 34:10). One might then, on the basis of these 5 instances, render the term as "the needy," with the further understanding of being dependent

---

1. The verse numbering of the Hebrew Bible is followed throughout this volume. Numbers in square brackets refer to the verse numbering used in English translations.

on the good will of others. It is the latter notion of dependence that lies at the root of the choice of this term by the compilers of Proverbs.

Of the total of 13 occurrences of *maḥsôr* over half of these occur in Proverbs (8 times). Pleins (1992, 5:407) renders the *maḥsôr* as the "lazy poor." But while the noun is used in contexts of poverty arising from laziness (cf. Prov 6:11; 14:23; 21:5; 24:34), it is also found in situations of poverty that result from excessive living (21:17), or even poverty that comes from a lack of generosity (11:24; 21:5; 24:34). Given the diversity of the three causes listed here, one could as easily have spoken of the miserly poor as the lazy poor. Taking into account the didactic nature of the book of Proverbs, with the sages addressing their young (male) students, one may make certain deductions. First of all, the students are deemed to be members of the elite, and so unlikely to be in danger of real poverty. However, while their lives differ radically from the lives of common peasants, there is still some danger that extended bouts of laziness or excessive living might impact upon their economic well-being (cf. Wittenberg 1986).

There is another dimension to the term *maḥsôr*, for it is not poverty in itself that is feared by the wise, whose wealth in land probably precluded that possibility, but rather the shame of being poor, of being considered unable to care for one's family and even worse, of becoming dependent on the good will of others. In the HB, shame and honour are important dimensions for interpreting poverty (Malina 1981; Bechtel 1991; Domeris 1995). To be numbered among the *maḥsôr*, then, at least in Proverbs, is to be found in that state of being shamefully unable to provide for one's dependents and reliant on the charity of others. Hence, one can say that the *maḥsôr* are indeed the shameful poor.

2.4.4. Miskēn *(#5014): The Honourable Poor (Ecclesiastes)*

The term *miskēn* is only used in Ecclesiastes (4 times) to describe the poor in situations where poverty is seen to be better than some other state. The related term *miskēnut* (#5017), used only once (Deut 8:9), has the sense of a lack of material goods. The Arabic cognate has the sense of a poor person, or a peasant (Domeris 1997d, 2:1001). Pleins defines the term as "poverty is better" (1992, 5:407), but I would emphasize again here the idea of honour (see Domeris 1997d, 2:1001–2), seeing the *miskēn* as the opposite of the *maḥsôr*—where one is shamed by circumstance, the other achieves honour. For Ecclesiastes, the poor may at times be considered worthy of honour in spite of the fact that normally poverty carries overtones of shame. The teacher is emphasizing to his pupils the necessity of seeking honour no matter what one's economic or power status may be.

2.4.5. Rwš *(#8133): The Powerless Poor*

Primarily a Wisdom term, *rwš* and its cognate *rêš* ("poverty"; #8203) occurs some 22 times in the HB. This term is defined according to Pleins as "economically poor, of modest means, beggar" with the sense of "someone who is politically and economically inferior, frequently referring to someone who is lazy" (1992, 5:407). I would challenge the aspect of laziness especially since the root *rwš* may be defined as "to become poor, oppressed, and weak" (Domeris 1997j, 1085). The root and its various derivatives (used 31 times in all) denote destitution, and on several occasions there is a link with oppression. Indeed, only once is the connection between *rwš* and laziness made explicit (Prov 10:4). In other instances, poverty is linked with injustice (13:23), social alienation (14:20; 19:7) and powerlessness (18:23; 22:7). Paradoxically, Pleins sees such instances as factors in the life of the poor rather than as constituent elements of poverty, while elevating laziness to the level of principle cause (1992, 5:407–8), which is clearly not the case. Rather it is the reverse; laziness is the exception, and injustice is the principle cause. Injustice leads to alienation and powerlessness. Sœbø (2004, 13:424) concludes that *rwš* "serves to establish a sharp contrast between the 'poor' and the 'rich.'" Second Samuel uses *rwš* in Nathan's parable to refer to the poor peasant who then suffers abuse at the hand of the landlord (2 Sam 12:1, 3, 4). In Eccl 4:1 (cf. 5:8 [7]) the connection with oppression is again obvious (Domeris 1997j, 1085 *pace* Pleins 1992, 5:408).

Underlining the use of *rwš* throughout the HB is the sense of powerlessness, which makes it an ideal term for contrasting with the rich and powerful (Prov 10:4; 13:8; 14:20; 18:23; 22:7; 28:6). The sharply contrasting power-relations expressed here highlight the sense of being overpowered and the general disadvantages and shame experienced by the poor. Peasants, under patronage, have expectations about the level of care and provision they might duly expect from their patrons or the wealthy people of their community. We are dealing here with clients and not beggars (*pace* Pleins 1992, 5:408). It is not just any rich person who is targeted, as the term "beggar" presupposes, but that specific individual who is seen to be in some way responsible for the particular poor person. Giving to the *rwš* is a token of true righteousness (Prov 28:27), a living-out of the expectations of the community—an obedience to the laws of reciprocity.

Shame and honour are again key ideas here. Proverbs takes issue with those who would shame the poor. Mocking the poor (*rwš*) is tantamount to mocking God (Prov 17:5), while in the eyes of God the upright *rwš* are more honourable than those of perverse speech (19:1), evil deeds (28:6) or a liar (19:22). All people are equal in God's eyes for he made them all whether rich or poor (17:5; 22:2; 28:27; 29:13). *Rwš* is also used figuratively of David's state in a love song (1 Sam 18:23). In the Hymn scroll from Qumran (1QH), *rwš* is one of the terms used to depict the sects dependence on God (1QH 5:14). In the Rabbinic writings, *rwš* is used of a person on death row, indicating "a sense of misery and lack of hope" (*Num. R.* 10 on Prov 31:7; see Domeris 1997j, 1086) and clearly powerlessness.

2.4.6. ʿĀnî *(#6714): The Oppressed Poor*

The link between poverty and oppression is nowhere clearer than in the term *ʿānî* which is found 80 times in the Hebrew canon. The term is related to *ʿānâ* II (#6700) meaning bowed down, afflicted (so BDB 776) and probably comes from the same root (Pleins 1992, 5:411; Dumbrell 1997, 3:454–56; Gerstenberger 2001, 233). Pleins takes the sense of "economically poor; oppressed, exploited; suffering" as the preferred reading of *ʿānî* (1992, 5:411). Similarly, Gillingham deduces that it has a "clear association with physical poverty," and adds that there is both the sense of "outward deprivation but also inner humiliation" (1988–89, 17). She notes that the verb *ʿānâ* is used in Deuteronomy of sexual humiliation (Deut 21:14, 22, 24, 29). The views of Pleins and Gillingham challenge the traditional rendering of *ʿānî* (cf. Dumbrell 1997) as normally implying humility or meekness. Quite correctly, in their view, such a rendering is secondary rather than primary. The notion of being meek or humble is arrived at only by extension of the core meaning, namely, the state of being oppressed and down-trodden. To be humble is to be like those who are oppressed and put down.

Exiles, individuals in times of trial and the poor are all victims of what they perceive as oppressive behaviour, and so understand themselves to have been pushed down or, in a very negative sense of the word, humbled—forcibly humbled would be a better expression. So, a statement that "It is the nature of Yahweh to dwell with the lowly and contrite of heart" (Dumbrell 1997, 3:459; cf. Ps 74:19) should not be understood as a commendation of meekness, but rather as an underlining of God's "preference for those who are poor and oppressed" and is perhaps to be read in the light of the events of the Exile (1997, 3:459).

2.4.7. ʿĀnāwîm *(#6705): The Poor as an Identifiable Group*

ʿĀnāwîm is usually considered to be the plural of a presumed singular *ʿānāw* and is found some 24 times in the HB. Pleins, however, argues that *ʿānāwîm* should be seen as the plural of *ʿānî* (1992, 5:411–13), which has much to commend it. Pleins subtitles the term "a political movement of the pious poor" (1992, 5:411) on the basis of the work of Lohfink (1986), who believed that the *ʿānāwîm* were not simply a group of pious poor but that they also had a political agenda. There are unfortunate negative overtones attached to the term pious, suggestive of a false piety, but one might substitute a synonym like religious or spiritual, and think in terms of social movements which combined a strong religious commitment with a clear social agenda. Alternatively, the word might mean no more than some collection of oppressed poor.

The term *ʿānāwîm* is found in the Prophetic and Wisdom writings and falls within the broader context of oppression and injustice. In the Wisdom material, *ʿānāwîm* is found 13 times in Psalms. The contexts detail hunger (Ps 22:26 [27]), suffering (69:32 [33]), landlessness (37:11) and in several instances focus upon God's relationship with and rescue of the poor (e.g. 25:9; 34:2 [3]). Taken as a whole, there is nothing here to suggest that the *ʿānāwîm* are different from the rest of the poor (*pace* Pleins 1992, 5:412) or other victims of oppression. The consistent use of the plural suggests that the poor are here being understood as a body, or, in contemporary terms, "class" of the poor—an identifiable group, but one which has merited the attention of the God of Israel.

2.5. *The Semantic Domain of Poverty by Genre*

The fullest explication of the Hebrew terms for poverty requires that one should consider the terms not just in terms of the roots, but also in terms of literary genre as in the various theological dictionaries (e.g. *TDOT*, *NIDOTTE*), hence the following subsections. Frick offers a useful table of usage, in which he stresses the way in which usage enables us to reconstruct the shape of the underlying ideology (1994a, 83–84). Unfortunately, due to the complex nature of the history of production for each of these three genres, no definitive chronological deductions can be made, except to suggest that each genre contains a cross-section of chronological referents. The following is only a general indication and is not meant to be exhaustive or to deal with every book within the genres.

2.5.1. *The Pentateuchal Usage*
In the Pentateuch, the terms for poverty are *dal* (Exod 23:3; 30:15; Lev 14:21; 19:15), *ʾebyôn* (Exod 23:6, 11; Deut 15:4, 7, 9, 11; 24:14), and *ʿānî* (Exod 22:25; Lev 19:10; 23:22; Deut 15:11; 24:12, 14, 15). Let me elaborate on these latter three in turn in addition to some lesser known terms.

I begin with *dal*, which is used in various contexts in the Pentateuch. For example, *dal* is used as the adjective to describe Pharaoh's vision of starving cattle (Gen 41:19), which for Carroll "suggests weakness, need and powerlessness" (1996, 1:951). In the legal texts, the rights of the *dal* are protected (Exod 23:3; Lev 19:15; Deut 1:17), while their economic status brings a concession within the Levitical code—they may substitute doves or pigeons for lambs in the ritual cleansing marking the re-admission of diseased people back into the community (Lev 14:1–32, esp. 21–22). The *dal* are still subject to the half-shekel tax taken during a census (Exod 30:15), which has led Fabry to argue that the *dal* is a "free and full citizen" (1978, 3:219). Fabry calls the tax (Exod 30:15) an "inspection fee" and on the basis of Exod 30:15 and the absence of the *dal* from Lev 25:6, suggests that the *dal* in fact owned property. By contrast, some scholars argue that the *dal* was an Israelite without property (Hentschke 1963, 13; Gillingham 1988–89, 16; cf. Jer 39:10). "Peasant" is probably a safer rendering than either of these two suggestions, given the complex nature of property ownership in the HB, hence the elaboration of *dal* is one "who is perpetually caught up in the struggle to make a daily living by hard work, who in this constant grind has to give up his independence to a large extent" (Fabry 1978, 3:219; cf. Von Rad 1960, 135)—a comprehensive description of peasant poverty.

The second term is *'ebyôn*, which is used nine times, usually in contexts of physical need (e.g. Exod 23:11; see also Humbert 1952, 4–5), leading Pleins to think that *'ebyôn* are "landless wage labourers living on the very edge of existence," "the beggarly poor" (1992, 5:404). Pleins, therefore, presupposes that these people were a class of landless beggars rather than simply poor peasants, which the text does not warrant. In support, he refers to Deut 24:14–15, which he argues explicitly links *'ebyôn* and day labour (1992, 5:404). In fact, Deuteronomy uses the composite "poor (*'ānî*) and needy (*'ebyôn*)" and not *'ebyôn* on its own, so one needs to be cautious here. Moreover, there is no necessary link between wage labour (the hired man) and the position of being landless. Peasants frequently offer themselves as hired labourers to augment their subsistence agriculture, especially in difficult times.

The composite "poor and needy" in Deut 24:14, I suggest, refers to some form of contract labour, with daily rations; the majority of both *'ānî* and *'ebyôn*, probably, were impoverished peasants whose lands were unable to sustain them and their families for the whole year. These people are vulnerable to abuse and dependent on the community for their well-being. Not surprisingly, the *'ebyôn* along with the *'ānî* feature in the legal codes as those in need of protection (e.g. Deut 24:10–13, 17) and in the prophets (e.g. Ezek 18:12) as the objects of oppression.

The third term, ʿānî, is used seven times, in laws regarding lending to the poor (Exod 22:25; Deut 15:11; 24:12) and provision for labourers (Deut 24:14–15) or those without food (Lev 19:9–10; 23:22). Pleins concludes that ʿānî refers to "someone who has no real estate and little to eat" (1992, 5:410). There is a curious tendency in Pleins' writing to suppose that hunger implies an absence of land, whereas given the difficult agrarian situation in Israel (see below), peasants with land regularly went hungry. Given the root meaning, and the association with labour, I should preferably think of the ʿānî as poor peasants, leaving the issue of land aside. That they are needy and vulnerable to exploitation and oppression goes without saying.

Terms used less frequently include the verb *mwk* ("to be or become poor"), which is found only in Leviticus (25:25, 35, 39, 47; 27:8), and *mahsôr*, which is found only in Deuteronomy (Deut 15:8). The term *miskēnut* (#5017), used only once (Deut 8:9), has the sense of a lack of material goods. The legal material fits rather well the composite picture of peasantry.

2.5.2. *The Prophetic Usage*

The Prophetic texts use a spread of terms including *dal*, *ʾebyôn*, *ʿānāw* or *ʿānāwîm* and *ʿānî*. Underlying most, if not all of these terms, is the threat of oppression. The *dallîm* are seen as vulnerable to abuse especially in the courts (Botterweck 1977; Isa 10:2; Amos 2:7) and in the economic milieu (Amos 4:1; 8:6). They may be taxed (Amos 5:11), which, along with the continued obligation on them to offer sacrifices, suggests to Carroll that they "are not totally destitute" although "they do suffer economic hardship." Carroll agrees that "the term refers to poor peasant farmers" (1996, 1:951) thus aligning with the legal material.

The word *ʿānāwîm* is used seven times all within the broader context of oppression and injustice (e.g. Amos 2:7; 8:4; Isa 6:1; 29:19). Zephaniah 2:3 may be an exception (cf. Pleins 1992, 5:411). So also the word *ʾebyôn* is used 17 times in contexts of oppression, injustice and violent abuse (cf. Pleins 1992, 5:403–4). Finally, *ʿānî* is used 25 times and so is the most common of terms for the poor in the prophetic texts. Pleins (1992, 5:408–9) details three contexts in which the *ʿānāwîm* are found: economic oppression (e.g. Isa 3:15; Ezek 18:12), unjust treatment in legal decisions (e.g. Isa 10:2) and victimisation through deception (e.g. Isa 32:7). All three contexts illustrate the sheer abuse of power by one group over another.

The combination of terms is instructive. *ʿānî* is used in conjunction with *ʾebyôn* (e.g. Isa 14:30–32), with *ʿam* II ("people"; #6639 [e.g. Isa

3:15]) and with *dal* (Isa 26:6), most probably to imply a category of victims of oppression. In Deutero-Isaiah and Trito-Isaiah, *'ānî* is associated with the Jewish exiles in Babylon (e.g. Isa 41:17; 66:2), again with the emphasis on oppression (Pleins 1992, 5:408–9). The more common rendering in English as "humble" or "contrite in spirit" (e.g. Isa 66:2; cf. Dumbrell 1997, 3:458) does inadequate service as a signifier of people who are actually poor and oppressed (Pleins 1992, 5:409). In effect, such translations do a disservice to the literal poor by confusing their poverty with an attitude of mind.

Amos, in particular, uses a spread of terms for the poor (*dal*, *'ānāw*, *'ebyôn*, *'ānî*). His combination of terms is interesting. So *saddîq* (righteous or innocent) and *'ebyôn* (poor or needy) are used together (e.g. Amos 2:6), although they are not obviously synonymous expressions. Andersen and Freedman (1989, 309) speak in terms of the righteous poor. This might seem to imply some sense of endemic goodness in being poor. I would prefer to give *saddîq* its legal sense and to think in terms of innocent people unjustly condemned, rather than imputing either innocence or righteousness in a generic sense to the poor. The ones who are righteous (innocent) in God's eyes are those people who have been falsely accused and oppressed through an unjust legal system. Considering the harsh conditions of the Israelite peasants, and their vulnerability to exploitation, it is easy to understand Amos's linking of *dallîm* and *'ānāwîm*. The "humble destitute" (as in Andersen and Freedman 1989, 309) scarcely does justice to the extremes of peasant poverty in the face of oppressive structures. Instead, one might think in terms of "oppressed peasants."

Jeremiah also uses several terms for the poor, including *'ebyôn* (20:13; 22:16), *'ebyônîm* (2:34; 5:28), *dallîm* (5:4; 39:10) and *'ānî* (22:16). Like Amos, Jeremiah locates the poor in contexts where injustice and oppression are evident. Not surprisingly, there are several references to the fatherless (5:28), widows (49:11) and the alien (7:6), often together (7:6; 22:3; cf. Lam 5:3; Gowan 1987). Similarly, Ezekiel implies a situation of oppression when he uses the combination *'ānî* and *'ebyôn* (16:49; 18:12; 22:29) to describe the poor and needy, along with several references to the marginalised, widows (22:7, 25) and in combination with them, the fatherless and the aliens (22:7). The underlying message of the prophets is one not just of poverty, but of the oppression of the poor. The peasants of Israel are facing more than the simple struggle of peasants worldwide. They are facing a collapse of social structures with endemic oppression, violence and injustice.

2.5.3. *The Wisdom Literature*

In the Wisdom texts, *ʿānî*, *ʾebyôn*, *ʿānāw* or *ʿānāwîm*, *dal*, *rwš*, *miskēn* and *maḥsôr* are the terms used to describe poverty. A range of contexts are evident in which, once more, oppression predominates. The most common term in the Wisdom texts, *ʾebyôn*, is found mainly in the Psalms (23 times), most often in contexts of suffering at the hands of the violent or wicked (Ps 109:16). God's protection for the poor is a notable theme (e.g. Ps 35:10; see also Botterweck 1977, 1:38–40). In Proverbs, *ʾebyôn* is used four times, three of which are in Prov 30–31, and the context is once again that of real poverty.

The second most common term is *dal*, which is used in Job (6 times), Proverbs (15 times) and Psalms (3 times), usually in contexts where the vulnerability of the poor to oppression is underlined (e.g. Prov 22:16; Job 20:19), or where God's role as protector of the poor is envisaged (Prov 14:31; Job 5:16). As in the Prophetic texts, *dal* is used of peasants who are suffering oppression. In Job 5:16 and 20:10, for example, *dal* is used in the context of injustice. In Job 20:19, *dal* is contrasted with the rich, in the context of oppression. The view that *dal* fell into disuse in the inter-testamental period (Fabry 1978, 3:215) is dismissed by Pleins (1992, 5:406) on the basis of the occurrences of the term (11 times) in Sirach, where once again oppression predominates.

The third most common term is *ʿānî*, which is used 16 times, appearing in Proverbs (8 times), Job (7 times) and Ecclesiastes (once). Pleins (1987, 63–67) highlights three contexts in Proverbs, namely, that of charity to the poor (e.g. 14:21), the terrible situation (oppression) of the poor (15:15) and the comparison of the poor with other groups (e.g. the arrogant in 16:19). Psalms demonstrates a similar range of meanings for the term *ʿānî*, from basic poverty to societal oppression (e.g. Pss 9; 10; 74:19) but may carry a corporate meaning referring to the physical affliction of the whole nation (9:13; 10:12; 18:28; 68:11; 74:19). For the most part, *ʿānî* speaks of the individual or group who have experienced some form of "material deprivation…illness, threat of death, verbal abuse, persecution, oppression and exile" (Gillingham 1988–89, 17).

Notably, the word *ʿānî* may also be used in the sense of humility or depression of spirit (Pss 22:25; 25:16; 34:7; 88:16; 102:1). Renderings, however, like "the humble afflicted" (Dumbrell 1997, 3:459) undercut the abuse of power basic to the core meaning of *ʿānî*, as evident in Job who highlights the miserable existence suffered by the oppressed. They are driven into hiding (24:4), their children are taken as pledges (24:9), and they are murdered (24:14).

Other Hebrew terms for the poor include the term ʿanāw, which Gillingham (1988–89, 19) understands as implying either physical poverty (Pss 76:10; 147:6; 149:4) or spiritual brokenness (22:27; 25:7–9, cf. v. 3). Such spiritual brokenness, taken literally, is more inclusive than the common expression of spiritual poverty is assumed to cover, and may be used of those who lose their spirit (dignity or self-worth) through some abuse of power, as well as those who lack a spiritual centre for their being. The notion of oppressed people (Ps 34:1–6) in danger of losing the spirit of human dignity is very real (Soares-Prabhu 1991, 155–56). All these features are readily identifiable by anyone who has come close to real poverty, and underscores the authenticity of the matrix of biblical poverty.

The term ʿanāwîm is found thirteen times in Psalms, in contexts that include hunger (Ps 22:26 [27]), suffering (Ps 69:32 [33]), the need for land (Ps 37:11) and God's rescue of the poor (e.g. Pss 25:9; 34:2 [3])—all of which describe real poverty and the vulnerability of the poor to abuse. The term miskēn is only found in Ecclesiastes (4 times) to describe the poor in situations where poverty is seen to be better than some other state, representing perhaps the naivety of an idealist perspective or simply the consequence of living in a shame/honour culture.

The combination of terms for the poor in the Wisdom literature is instructive. The linking of ʾebyôn and dal, for example, suggest that they both share the sense of physical poverty and probably also a peasant context (Domeris 1997a, 1:230). Further signs of the connection between poverty and oppression are especially evident in Job where defence of the poor at the hands of the strong is a notable theme (cf. Pleins 1992, 5:404; Botterweck 1977, 1:35). For example, the twinning of ʿanî and ʾebyôn rendered as "poor and needy" (e.g. Job 24:14; Ps 72:13; see Domeris 1997a, 1:230) is instructive. In Job 24:4, ʿanî and ʾebyôn are used within a context of violent oppression, and in v. 14, they are the objects of murderous actions. ʾEbyôn also occurs in parallel with those in trouble (Job 30:25). Other indications of the presence of oppression abound. The ʿanāwîm (Job 34:28; cf. 24:5 where people are desperately searching for food) are part of the larger group including the dal (poor peasants) and the fatherless (Job 29:12), all of whom cry to God for help in the face of human abuse and suffering.

In the Psalms, oppression and chronic poverty are never far away. The combination of ʾebyôn with ʿanî (15 instances) is an expression which Gillingham connects with oppression generally or, in her terms, to the results of "the malevolent actions of others" (1988–89, 17). ʿAnî and ʾebyôn are also paired in Prov 30–31, showing an understanding of the "concrete suffering" that in the view of Pleins is "unique in Proverbs"

(1992, 5:409). This comment is in line with Pleins' view that "the Proverbial tradition lacks the comprehensive and rather concrete social justice vision for the *'ānî* that we find in the legal and prophetic materials" (1992, 5:409). Actually there are a number of other instances of concrete suffering, as Pleins own examples (e.g. Prov 15:15) show (cf. Washington 1994).

Yrš is found in Prov 30:7–9 with a strong connection with real poverty, so that its sense appears closer to *rwš* than to its own root (Lohfink 1990, 6:373). Other combinations of terms continue the link with oppression. For example, *'ebyôn* is used with *dal* three times in Psalms (72:13; 82:3–4; 113:7) in the context of actual physical poverty (Gillingham 1988–89, 16). Generally, across the Psalms, the picture of material poverty is vividly portrayed (35:10; 86:1, cf. v. 14; 40:18, cf. vv. 3, 15–16; 69:34; 70:6; 140:13). The poor experience hunger (132:15), increased risk of death (37:14; 72:13; 109:16), legal condemnation (109:13), oppression (72:13–14) and troubles (34:6[7]; 41:1[2]). Finally, they are in real danger of being forgotten and losing hope (9:18[19]). This brief survey indicates the strong linkages which the Wisdom genre envisaged between poverty and oppression.

2.5.4. *The Historical and Other Writings*
The historical books (1 and 2 Samuel, 1 and 2 Kings, 1 and 2 Chronicles, Ezra and Nehemiah) have very few references to the poor. Five words are used, namely *'ebyôn*, *dal*, *dallâ* II, *rwš* and the niphal of *yrš*. In the other writings (Ruth and Esther) *dal* and *'ebyôn* appear.

Yrš appears with *dal* in the Song of Hannah with a sense of endemic poverty (1 Sam 2:7–8). *Rwš* is used four times of the peasant in Nathan's parable (2 Sam 12:1–4). *Dallâ* II is used in the reference to the poorest of peasants who are allocated to work the land under the Babylonian governors (2 Kgs 24:14; 25:12; cf. Jer 39:10; 52:15–16). In Ruth 3:10 rich and poor (*dal*) are compared and in Esth 9:22 there is a reference to giving gifts (charity) to the poor. Pleins suggests that the relative absence of poverty from the extensive work of the Deuteronomistic Historian is indicative of his reluctance to deal with poverty, especially as a contributing factor leading up to the Exile (1992, 5:404).

2.6. *Conclusion*

The rich variety of Hebrew terms adds colour to the picture of the poor in the HB, but all too often this is diluted in the modern translations. For example, in Ps 10 following the NIV, the term *'ānî* ("oppressed poor") is once translated as the "weak" (v. 2) and twice as the "helpless" (v. 9), while Dahood (1965, 60) renders each instance correctly as "the afflicted." The examples might be multiplied a hundred times, with the result that the full portrait of the poor is often obscured in translation. Thus, the face of real poverty is lost in the vague and amorphous world of the weak and helpless. While creative translation is to be encouraged, such a venture should not be developed at the expense of the voice of the poor, as faint as this may be.

In the HB, the poor are contrasted with a wide variety of agents, including the unrighteous, the wealthy, the powerful and civil and religious leaders. This means that the semantic domain of poverty is tied to several other domains, including wealth, power, honour and righteousness. To limit the biblical understanding of poverty to economics is to fail to hear what the Bible is saying about the different dimensions of poverty, as this book will make clear.

Understanding the varied dimensions of biblical poverty requires as a precondition an understanding of the economy of Israel in both the pre-exilic and post-exilic periods. Previous studies of poverty have failed in this precise task and this study seeks to correct this omission. Since the economy was an agrarian one, I begin with a study of the agrarians of Israel and in so doing take the first steps in the affirmation of what might be called the peasant tradition in the HB. This involves going back to the initial process that would culminate eventually in the emergence of the divided monarchy—Israel and Judah—and then following the journey through into the post-exilic period.

Chapter 3

THE ECONOMIC NATURE OF ISRAEL

3.1. *The Historical Roots of Biblical Poverty*

"Poverty is like illness. It shows itself in different historical situations, and it has diverse causes" (Wilson and Ramphele 1989, 14). The purpose of this chapter is to outline the early origins of the agrarian society of Israel/Judah, born from a peasant womb, and already troubled by the perennial problems of agriculture in the Near East. Long before the existence of the states of Israel and Judah, the ancestors of the peasants of Israel struggled to maintain their livelihood in what was described as a "land flowing with milk and honey." The reality was very different—soil and climate combined to make this so. Israel's peasants simply continued this selfsame struggle with the elements, and with the added complication of an increasingly oppressive political and economic situation. The roots of biblical poverty reach back far behind the social conditions of the eighth century, behind even the origins of early Israel.

3.2. *Reconstructing the Origins of the Historical Israel*

Levy and Holl (1998, 8) write that "the central motif in the archaeological history of Palestine is its location on the periphery of major states and civilisations of the ANE." Caught in the rip-tide of the greater states, tiny Israel was thrown about from its earliest times, as a minor item on the agenda of the great nations—so that even its origins are obscure. Indeed, few questions are as vexed and perplexed as the quest for the historical Israel. The comfortable academic consensus, which prevailed for most of the twentieth century, has been overthrown (Marcus 2000; Gottwald 2001; Finkelstein and Silberman 2001; Dever 2001). Early Israel—that is Israel before the time of the monarchy, which traditional thinking referred to as Israel in the times of the Judges—we shall speak of as Proto-Israel (so Dever 2000).

Understanding the origins of Israel has long been a particular occupation of HB scholarship. I shall use Wylie's (1989) model drawn from the archaeology and the Philosophy of Science, for finding the best fit between the evidence and the model. Wylie argues that one needs to test all the available evidence including ethnography (texts; cf. Hayes 1987, 5–9) and archaeological finds (cf. Ben-Tor 1992a; Finkelstein 1998a) against the selected historical reconstructions (cf. Lemche 1991; Coote and Whitelam 1987; Whitelam 1996) and contemporary sociological models. A good measure of fit, according to Wylie (1989, 17–18), is when all the available evidence is able to be fitted into place in support of the chosen model.

The historical reconstruction, which I have chosen to employ, argues that the later Israelites and Judeans were the direct descendents of the peasants of the El Amarna texts. This is not a new perspective, as I shall show. What have not been fully developed before are the implications of such a connection for the understanding of peasant poverty in Israel. In dealing with both issues, I shall draw upon the various forms of evidence starting with the ethnography.

3.3. *Ethnography*

The ethnography relevant to the origins of Israel, aside from the HB, is limited mainly to three sources: the El Amarna texts, the Stele of Merneptah and the account of Shishak's invasion. I shall treat the first two here, leaving Shishak's account for our discussion of the early monarchy and then look briefly at the HB accounts.

3.3.1. *The El Amarna Tablets*
The El Amarna tablets are the correspondence between various individuals in Cisjordan, often rulers of the various city states and the kings of Egypt. They form a useful window into the peasant economy of Canaan and the petty intrigues of the leaders of the various city-states and may be dated to the middle of the fourteenth century B.C.E. or some two hundred years before the invasion of the Sea Peoples (Hess 2000). They also serve to provide a backdrop for the context in which Israel arose. In spite of their clearly political nature and bias, as emphasised by Liverani (1983), a few vital items may be discovered. What is interesting is the concern expressed regarding the relationships between ruler of a city-state and the peasants (*hupsu*) and the allusions to the poverty of the peasants. In the poverty of these peasants lies the roots of biblical poverty.

The dangers posed by enemy forces for the internal situation of the city-states like Byblos and Jerusalem (cf. Chaney 1983, 72–83) are another element. Rib-Iddi of Gubla (Byblos) writes to the king of Egypt about the encroachment of the Sa.Gaz people and their chariots (EA 74:17–32; 87:21). His concern is that "There is no grain for our support. What shall I say to my peasants? Their sons, their daughters have come to an end" (EA 85:10–13) and he appeals to the king to send grain ships from Egypt (EA 85:17). In another letter Rib-Iddi inquires "From whom shall I protect myself? From my enemies or from my peasants?" (EA 112:10–12). The reason apparently is that the peasants intend to desert (EA 114:22). Rib-Iddi refers the king to a parallel situation, where the Sa.Gaz people conquered a city following the desertion of the peasants (EA 118:37–39).

As the tale progresses, one finds that times become increasingly difficult, leading to Rib-Iddi's complaint that "there is no grain for my provisions, and the peasants have departed for the cities where there is grain for their provisions" (EA 125:25–30). Later, he writes "now the country is conquered, for the people have deserted in order to take the country for themselves, and there is no one to guard the city of Gubla" (EA 129:33–38). The fear of those people who are in the process of taking the country for themselves certainly sounds like a peasant revolt is in process. Landsberger's cogent study of peasant unrest is useful here (1973). Rib-Iddi warns the king of Egypt that there is a great deal of gold and silver in the temples of the city, which the enemy will capture (EA 137:61–63). As the end of the story unfolds, we find that he has quashed an internal revolt (EA 138:39)—but as this is the last letter from Rib-Iddi the remainder of the story is left untold.

In another set of letters, this time from Abdi-Hiba of Jerusalem, a similar tale unfolds, but this time it is the Apiru who are the threat (EA 286:56). Abdi-Hiba cries out that "if there are no archers the land of the king will desert to the Habiru [Apiru]" (EA 290:22–24). Once again, the threat of a peasant revolt and desertion to the enemy is clearly a real one.

The El Amarna tablets clearly imply that the majority of the population of Late Bronze Age Cisjordan were peasants. Proto-Israel may have been among these peasants or may have been located at the periphery, perhaps in the ranks of the Apiru (Bright 1980, 111). Since there is nothing to indicate the economic, ethnic or political nature of the Sa.Gaz or the Apiru in these tablets, the assumption that they are nomadic or even semi-nomadic is entirely conjectural. The link between Hebrew and Apiru is often raised along with a suggestion that these are both ethnic signifiers and so refer to a specific and distinctive people who are in competition with the other peoples of Canaan (cf. Halligan 1983).

A more credible view is that the Apiru were a social class (Gottwald 1979, 389–485; Loretz 1984, 252–63; Na'aman 1986a). The precise nature of the social class, given their bad press in the El Amarna correspondence, is rendered variously as "outlaws" (Weippert 1971, 58–65) or "parasocial elements" (Rowton 1977). The best identification comes from Chaney (1983, 77–83) who described the Apiru as "social bandits," following the work of Hobsbawm (1965, 13–29; 1969, 11–115; 1973, 142–57). Hobsbawm had concluded that "social banditry is universally found, wherever societies are based on agriculture (including pastoral economies), and consisting largely of peasants and landless laborers ruled, oppressed and exploited by someone else" (1969, 15).

Building on the work of Hobsbawm and the El Amarna texts, Lemche and Chaney individually argue that the ancestors of Proto-Israel would have been numbered among the population as part of the broader peasant environs of Cisjordan (Lemche 1997; Chaney 1983, 77–83). In other words, the ancestors of Israel were peasants, probably following a sedentary lifestyle, or living in close proximity to such a lifestyle.

3.3.2. *The Stele of Merneptah*

Dated to about 1207 B.C.E., the stele of Pharaoh Merneptah locates "Israel" as a settled entity within Cisjordan (Hasel 1995). The presumption of most writers is that there is a relationship between the later nation of Israel and the stele (cf. Görg 2001). The text claims that Israel was eradicated ("Israel is laid waste; his seed is no more"; cf. Whitelam 2000, 18–22), but such a claim is not inconsistent with the propaganda purposes of such monumental steles. Ahlström (1991) and Hasel (1995, 55–61) take the term *prt* ("seed") to refer to agricultural produce (grain), so suggesting that Israel is an agrarian entity rather than a city-state or a semi-nomadic people.

The precise geographical location of the group (or groups) is unclear. If Israel is the parallel coda to Canaan rather than the fourth element in the south-to-north sequence, the Central Highlands would be a strong possibility (Ahlström and Edelman 1985). Alternatively, Hjelm and Thompson (2002, 15–18) consider a location within the boundaries of later Philistine controlled territory. This is in agreement with Singer's view, that the Pharaoh was concerned with turning the route between Gaza and Aphek into an Egyptian controlled route (1988, 5–8). It also suggests that Proto-Israel was forcibly dislocated from its lands in the Coastal Plains and took refuge in the Central Highlands ahead of the Sea Peoples' invasion (in line with Mantovani 1988; Dever 2000, 1191).

Gottwald concludes that the stele, along with the archaeological sur-veys (cf. Finkelstein and Lederman 1997) substantiates the existence of "a population of cultivators and herders, at least some of whom bore the name Israel, lived in the regions of Canaan where the state of Israel subsequently arose, and furthermore that the biblical character of this population as politically decentralized and socially linked in village and kin arrangements is authentic" (2001, 164). In essence, Proto-Israel was a nation of sedentary agrarians, and I shall argue, peasants.

3.3.3. *Indigenous Texts*
The HB is in itself a complex and over-layered document, difficult to date but filled with various pieces of information. Recovering the history of the biblical poor requires that one reads the Bible against the grain (Mosala 1989; Domeris 1991b). Such a reading assumes that the interests of the biblical writers are often, if not always, identical with the ruling elite—the non-poor of the time. It means searching the text, a text lay-ered with the debris of historical and ideological deposits, for clues about the plight of the poor. We need to recognise that the people of the Bible employ what Wyatt (2001) calls "a mythic mind," in so far as they framed their history in myth—"a universal meaning-giving strategy." This does not imply that the account is devoid of historical reality, but rather that its full meaning lies outside of the realms of history.

The role of the biblical text has itself become a site of struggle with some scholars (e.g. Davies 1994) suggesting that the Persian period (late sixth and early fifth centuries) is the most likely location for the re-creation of the literary Israel—from her roots through to the late monar-chy and Exile. Thompson (1995) takes an even more extreme view when he argues that the HB came together only in the Hellenistic period. A more conservative position connects the Deuteronomic History with the ideology and superstructures of Josiah's reign (Naʾaman 1995). For pur-poses of this work, I will opt for the *via media* of Davies.

Leaving aside the vexed question of the dating of the biblical material, one can make some general comments about the texts pertaining to the ancestors of Israel or Proto-Israel (so Dever 2000). The origins of the people of Israel, according to the Bible, are associated with various tradi-tions, suggesting a multiplicity of origins and raising the question of why all these sources were preserved (cf. Gottwald 2001, 246–52). The Exodus account is the best known, and since some of the Shasu trekked from Egypt into Sinai and thence to Canaan, they may well have authored the epic tale (Giveon 1983–84). Whatever its origins over the centuries, the Exodus has served as a powerful legitimation myth (cf. Gottwald 2001, 163).

3.4. *The Political Context of Canaan at the Change of the Eras*

The primary evidence for the origins of Israel consists of the archaeological data from the Middle Bronze into the Iron Age, coming from the
excavations of the major urban areas and the various archaeological
surveys conducted both in Transjordan and Cisjordan. In particular,
attention has been paid to the ceramic indicators for the Late Bronze
Age, Iron I and Iron II. Traditionally, Iron I was dated from 1200 to 1000
B.C.E. (Mazar 1990), but the newer "low chronology" suggests 1150
B.C.E. to 925 B.C.E. instead (Meyers 1997)—these lower dates are the
ones we will use within an accepted variance of 25 years on both dates.
Using the "Lower Chronology" I will argue that the twin states of Israel
come into existence during Iron II (post-925 B.C.E.), with the origins of
Proto-Israel coming at the end of the Bronze Age.

3.4.1. *The End of the Bronze Age*
A date of about 1200 B.C.E. marks the end of the Bronze Age in Cisjordan (Freedman 2000). Ussishkin (1995), based on the destruction level
of Late Bronze Megiddo, opts for a more precise 1130 B.C.E., with a
variance of 25 years either way. What brought about the change of the
era? Various factors were involved. Probably, the end of the Bronze Age
had less to do with shortages of tin and copper (for making bronze) than
with the cultural transition that swept through the eastern Mediterranean
at this time (Chaney 1983; Coote and Whitelam 1987). Nevertheless, a
change in technology obviously played a role. The earliest remnants of
iron working are commonly found in proximity to Mycenaean ware, suggesting a possible Aegean origin for the technology (Muhly 1984).
Widespread access to the new Iron technology most likely brought in its
wake economic, political and ideological changes (Mirau 1997). Climatic
change may also have had something to do with the social and political
upheavals at the end of the Late Bronze, as in the transition from Early
Bronze to Middle Bronze (Stiebing 1994; Drori and Horowitz 1988–89).
Finally, for Canaan, the turn of the ages was concurrent with the collapse
of Egyptian sovereignty over the land, which from a reading of the El
Amarna texts was apparently accompanied by widespread peasant unrest.

3.4.2. *The Collapse of Egyptian Rule Over Canaan*
As Egyptian control faltered, Bienkowski (1989) argues that some of the
marginal areas of Cisjordan declined (cf. Knapp 1989), while other more
strategic areas flourished, as evidenced by the continued presence of
luxury items (cf. Liebowitz 1989). Egypt struggled to keep open the

trade routes with Europe and Asia, but the cracks appeared in the antiquated colonial administration. The Egyptian response was to increase tribute, which placed additional burdens on an already disenchanted peasant population (Bienkowski 1989). Cisjordan was itself fractured by other destabilising factors, including the encroachment of Apiru and Sa.Gaz, mentioned in the El Amarna texts (Albright 1975, 98–119; Stiebing 1983; Hopkins 1993). The same texts mention problems in harvesting crops and collecting firewood and water (EA 149:75–76; 154:11–18) and the collapse of the city-states (cf. Bunimovitz 1998, 327). The door opened for Israel to begin its long walk into history.

Singer's reconstruction (1988) of Egyptian rule over the coast of Palestine in the Late Bronze Age suggests that it lasted through the successive reigns of Ramses II, Merneptah and Ramses III (1304–1166 B.C.E.). Domination of Ashkelon, Gezer, Megiddo and Lachish was vital to the process of Egyptian domination. Aside from Shishak's later invasion, the death of Ramses III (1166 B.C.E.) marked, to all intents and purposes, the end of Egyptian sovereignty over Cisjordan (Singer 1988, 8–10). A time of political upheaval followed. A cartouche of Ramses III was found in the destruction level of Lachish, suggesting a destruction date for the city of 1150 B.C.E. by some unknown hand (Ussishkin 1987, 28–34). Gezer was destroyed, probably by Shishak in about 918 B.C.E. (Dever 1985)—this being the last attempt at Egyptian domination. Shishak probably also destroyed a group of fortress-like structures, of unknown provenance, in the Negev desert, which had lasted barely half a century (Cohen 1985, 56–68). Without Egyptian domination, Canaan was open to a new dispensation for her people.

Between 1175 and 1150 B.C.E., the Sea Peoples (including the Philistines) invaded the Coastal Plains (Dothan and Zukerman 2004, 48–53). Megiddo fell to the Sea Peoples in about 1130 B.C.E., bringing to an end Egyptian control of that area and preparing the way for the Sea Peoples to settle there (Ussishkin 1995; Finkelstein 1995, 213–22). Their pottery has been found throughout the Coastal Plain and into Galilee, especially the Jezreel Valley, Beth Shan and Tel Dan (Stern 2000). The presence, in particular, of the Philistines is indicated by the transition from Mycenaean IIIC ware to locally made Monochrome ware (Finkelstein 1995, 222–39), but it is only in the eleventh century that the Monochrome Canaanite pottery finally gave way to the true Bichrome Philistine ware (Finkelstein 1998b; cf. Dothan 1998).

Iron I (1200–1000 B.C.E.) marked the time of internal transition of population. The general movement of populations was from west to east and not east to west—the direction gleaned from the tradition of the

Joshua invasion (Mantovani 1988). With the advent of the Sea Peoples, the indigenous population of the Coastal Plains migrated into other parts of the land. There appears to have been a significant influx of people wishing to escape Philistine controls (Broshi 1974)—an insight rarely given its full value. The Central Highlands became home for many of these new settlements (Fritz 1987, 99), including communities of Proto-Israelites (Dever 2000).

The Philistines had an initial "technological and demographic edge over the people of the highlands" as shown by their artefacts (Finkelstein 1997, 236).The red slip which would mark the later Israelite pottery of the Iron Age makes its gradual appearance in Philistia in the late twelfth and early eleventh centuries (Mazar 1998), strengthening our idea that Proto-Israel were sedentary peasants resident in that area before they were forced out by the Philistines. The peasants fleeing the coastal low-lands carried with them various innovations, including the use of iron and ceramic traditions. The innovative burnishing (polishing) of pottery, dated to the mid-tenth century (Holladay 1991), would become another marker of Israelite pottery.

3.4.3. *Shifting Population*

Dever speaks about a shift in settlement type during the transition from Bronze Age into the Iron Age, leading to declining urban centres gener-ally and the increased population of the hill country (2000, 1191). He cites possible figures for the Central Highlands from about 12,000 per-sons at the end of the Bronze Age to about 75,000 by the eleventh century B.C.E. (2000, 1191). These figures may be too high for the carry-ing capacity of the region, but, nevertheless, we should think in terms of a significant population increase (in excess of the normal birth-rate). Gottwald suggests a more feasible total of some 400,000 persons for the whole divided monarchy (mid-eighth century), which includes substan-tial lands outside of the Central Highlands (2001, 190).

Whatever figures one uses, the fact is that the Central Highlands experienced a major increase in population in Iron II. Moreover, the data clearly indicate that these people were sedentary farmers and not semi-nomads (cf. Whitelam 2002). Everything about them suggests continuity with the peasants of the El Amarna texts. Mantovani (1988), as shown above, speaks of the predominant population movement in Iron I as being from west to east, not east to west, involving indigenous peasant groups. The compulsion to move probably came from the breakdown in Egyptian rule and the ensuing menace of the Sea Peoples (Mantovani 1988). This view explains the migration of the ancestors of Israel far more succinctly than many of the other more complex explanations (see below).

Bunimovitz and Yasur-Landau state that "a migrant group can identified by pottery [only] if their cultural background is conspicuously different from the one into which they entered" (1996, 93). In the case of Proto-Israel, the continuity of the ceramic typology indicates that the "new" inhabitants of the Highlands were culturally the same as the older indigenous peoples of both Cisjordan and Transjordan (cf. Coote and Whitelam 1987).

3.5. *Lines of Continuity*

In terms of Wylie's "tightness of fit" (1989), all the evidence suggests that the later peasants of Israel were in direct continuity with the original inhabitants of Canaan—specifically the peasant inhabitants. Hopkins deduces that the settlement in the Highlands

> represents a movement along the pastoral–agricultural continuum in response to increasing demands for subsistence and social production. The increased number of Highland inhabitants could not be supported by the Late Bronze Age economy. The shift to a more intensive exploitation regime relieved these pressures. (1985, 272; cf. Mendenhall 1970, 107)

Similarly, Coote and Whitelam conclude that

> Israel originated during the third and fourth quarter of the thirteenth century with the shift in land use and settlement patterns of the Palestinian highland and dry land margins. The shift occurred mainly in response to changes in the economy of the eastern Mediterranean area associated with a drop in trade during the thirteenth century…or later. (1987, 116, 119)

For Coote and Whitelam, it was the collapse of trade that played a critical role in the crippling of both peasants and urban elite and the rise of social banditry (1987, 119–25), thus setting in motion the settlement of the Central Highlands and consequently the basis for the nation of Israel. This is a rather tenuous argument and so Whitelam (2000), in a later article, switches focus to the agrarian renewal which marked Iron Age Israel following the devastation at the end of the Bronze Age. This reordering of the rural areas led in time to the growth of towns and cities in Iron Age II (Whitelam 2002, 1:400–15) and the relocation of large numbers of peasants including the ancestors of biblical Israel. I have suggested (in line with Broshi 1974; Mantovani 1988; Dever 2000, 1191) a simpler answer—a mass migration ahead of the invasion of the Sea Peoples (cf. Whitelam's "devastation"), which led to the settlement in the Central Highlands (cf. Whitelam's "agrarian renewal").

3.6. *The Quest for Proto-Israel*

The prevailing opinion among archaeologists is that the basic continuity with minor cultural variances between the earlier Canaanites and the later Israelites can be accounted for in terms of one of three different models: geographical separation (Mazar 1992), meaning a new group of people (of the same ethnicity) coming from a neighbouring geographical region; chronological separation, implying a change from peasants to semi-nomads and back again and which took place over the centuries from Middle Bronze to Iron Age (Finkelstein 1999); and cultural evolution (Bloch-Smith and Nakhai 1999, 101–27; Bloch-Smith 2003), implying changes over time to stable a community. Of these opinions, I find the third to be the best "fit" for the following sets of evidence.

3.6.1. *Skeletal Evidence*

The primary data, regarding ethnicity, are those of the physical remains of the people themselves. Smith examines skeletal and especially cranio-facial evidence in Cisjordan and concludes that the only evidence for the advent of a new population group comes from the Middle Bronze II (1998, 69). The new group, however, did not settle into the whole land and some cities like Lachish reveal continuity with the previous group from Middle Bronze right into the Iron Age (Smith 1998, 71). Jerusalem shows signs of both groups (new and old) but this is based on a very small statistical sample.

Generally, from the Middle Bronze II onwards, there are fluctuations in all measurements, suggesting greater heterogeneity in the peoples inhabiting Israel (Smith 1998, 73). What is clear is that many of the inhabitants of the cities of Iron Age Israel carried the skeletal features of their Canaanite ancestors from the Middle Bronze Age—a clear argument for cultural continuity.

3.6.2. *Ceramic and Other Markers*

Initially, arguments in favour of a new ethnic group were based around the biblical text and certain of the existing archaeological data. Innovations such as the so-called four-roomed house (Shiloh 1970, 1973), plastered cisterns and underground silos, terrace farming and the so-called collared rim jar were cited as evidence in favour of the advent of the ethnically distinct Israelites (Fritz 1987). Fritz, however, had noted in passing the presence of three- and four-roomed houses (also called pillared-houses) at Tel Qasileh, which can be identified on the basis of the pottery, as a Philistine settlement (1987, 94) but did not consider that it posed a problem for his theory. More cracks were quickly to appear.

Further study and a much greater database has revealed that these so-called innovations are not confined to the Central Highlands; nor are they uniquely Israelite in origin (Whitelam 1986, 60; Mazar 1992, 289–90; Gottwald 1993, 175; Chaney 1983, 59–60; Hopkins 1985, 148–50). Indeed, pillared dwellings have been traced to the Middle Bronze II (Emeq Refaim) that are remarkably similar to the Israelite four-roomed houses (Eisenberg 1989–90, 89). Schaar believes that the four-roomed house may be understood as an adaptation of two earlier house-building traditions dating back to the Early Bronze Age (Schaar 1991, 81–97). Moreover, the architecture and culture of Iron Age Moab, as revealed in the survey of 450 sites, strongly resembles that of the Central Highlands, including collared rim jars and four-roomed houses (Miller 1989). Overall, in speaking of ceramic indicators, Bunimovitz and Yasur-Landau conclude that there is "virtually no difference between 'Canaanite' and 'Israelite' pottery" (1996, 96). Not surprisingly, Whitelam (1986, 60) could already at that time speak of the growing consensus "that the emergence of Israel was indigenous to Palestine, whether the result of a peasant's revolt or not."

The consensus has grown. Mazar adds that "there is nothing in the archaeological record to suggest that the settlers came from outside of the Land of Israel, as stated in the Biblical traditions" (1992, 296). He elaborates, "The settlers had no traditions of their own in the realm of architecture, pottery, crafts, and art" (1992, 295; cf. Dever 1993; 2005). For Dever, the Israelites who descended from the "the hill country settlers comprised a motley collection of urban dropouts, displaced peasant farmers, [and] refugees from various strata of decaying Canaanite society" (2000, 1191). He concludes that "today all archaeologists and most biblical scholars are agreed upon some variation of an 'indigenous origin' model for the Iron I people of central Cisjordan" (2000, 1191; cf. Gottwald 1983; Whitelam 1986, 1996; Holladay 1998; Finkelstein 1997, 1998a; Dever 2005).

More finely, opinion remains divided between a narrow view—Proto-Israel is contiguous with one strand of the inhabitants (specifically a group of semi-nomadic inhabitants of Cisjordan—[so Finkelstein 1988, 1997, 1998a]) or the broad view, namely, Proto-Israel is a composite peasant category containing elements of several groups (Dever 2000, 1191; Miller 2004, 64–68). Put differently, Proto-Israel was either to be found in the ranks of the semi-nomadic settlers of the land or to be numbered among the sedentary peasants of Canaan. Pastoralism and sedentary farming are both common threads throughout the HB stories (cf. Whitelam 1986). Which leaves the question of which view has the "tightest fit" (cf. Wylie 1989) in the light of the archaeological data?

3.7. *The Agrarian Nature of Israel*

One thing was always clear from the archaeological evidence. Proto-Israel found its home mainly in the highlands, while the Sea Peoples became established primarily in the coastal lowlands. On this basis, one can draw a clear line between the Israelites and the Philistines (Finkelstein 1993, 110–15) and we have given reasons to suggest that the advent of the former caused the relocation of the latter. If they were originally peasants, as attested by the El Amarna letters, then the likelihood was that they would become peasants again. But was there a transitory period as Finkelstein (1988, 1997, 1998a) suggests, in which Proto-Israel adopted the more transitory lifestyle of semi-nomadism?

In her discussion of this general issue, Grigson (1998) offers four definitions (based on Khazanov 1984) for modelling Proto-Israel as an agrarian entity. These are nomadic pastoralism, semi-nomadic pastoralism, agro-pastoralism and mixed farming. Although Grigson rejects all but the last one, I shall examine each in turn as a possible model, weighing up the arguments of Grigson and others.

3.7.1. *Nomadic Pastoralism*
The first of Grigson's models (1998) is nomadic pastoralism. In this model, no cultivation is practised, but wild foods may be gathered. Continuous, total transhumance is found with sheep, goats and camels and which is linked to settled zones for access to water, pasture and the supply of plant foods. This was the model which dominated thinking about the founding mothers and fathers of Israel for most of the twentieth century, until it was soundly refuted by Gottwald (1978; 1993, 174–75). Grigson (1998, 264) likewise rejects the applicability of the model for Proto-Israel, arguing that such pastoralism is found only in Arabia and not in the Levant and concludes that "there is no evidence that full-scale nomadic pastoralism was practiced in the Levant from the Chalcolithic to the Iron Age" (1998, 259). Grigson's conclusion appears sound so this leaves the other three forms to consider, namely, semi-nomadic pastoralism, agro-pastoralism and mixed farming.

3.7.2. *Semi-Nomadic Pastoralism*
Semi-nomadic pastoralism involves a model in which plant cultivation is minimal and almost entirely separate from animal keeping. Sheep and goats are kept with some cattle and seasonal transhumance is practised by some of the population (Grigson 1998, 264). Some forms of pastoral activities are clearly attested in the evidence of the host of new settlements (Proto-Israelite) which abounded in the Iron Age in the Central

Highlands (Callaway 1976; Hopkins 1985; Coote and Whitelam 1987; Dever 2005). The question is whether the evidence from these settlements fits with the long-term practise of sedentary agrarianism (so Holladay 1998; Dever 2005) or with semi-nomads settling down (so Fritz 1987; Finkelstein 1998a).

Over the years, various scholars have argued for some form of co-existence between a semi-nomadic Proto-Israel and the Canaanite peasants. Rowton (1977), for example, developed a model of community that he described as dimorphic and parasocial, namely, two communities living in close proximity—one sedentary and one semi-nomadic. Fritz developed a symbiosis model, which argued that Proto-Israel lived in close contact for centuries with the sedentary Canaanites and so were hardly intruders on the scene (1987, 84–94; cf. Mazar 1992, 296). Finkelstein believed that the sedentary population of Cisjordan of the Middle Bronze Age adopted a pastoral lifestyle through the uncertain times of the Late Bronze Age, until the advent of the Iron Age enabled them to re-settle their original homelands (1988, 1998a). Of the sites in the Central Highlands, nearly half (116 of the 254) of those occupied in Iron Age I had previously been occupied in the Middle Bronze Age but abandoned through the Late Bronze Age (Broshi and Finkelstein 1992). Of these three models, only that of Finkelstein has remained a contestant and even this is now under serious attack.

Scholarly opinion has swung decisively against the view that Proto-Israel was semi-nomadic by nature. The vast majority of the studies of the new settlements argue for a sedentary model (Mendenhall 1962; Campbell 1976, 3–45; Callaway 1976; Miller 1977, 252–62; Gottwald 1978, 1979; Chaney 1983, 50; Frick 1985; Whitelam 1986; Coote and Whitelam 1987; Dever 1991, 87–90; 2005; Grigson 1998, 259; Holladay 1998). As Sasson's study of the pastoral component of three sites in the Highland area concludes, ancient herds could not "supply the necessary requirements of energy and protein for the local inhabitants" (1998, 47), therefore they must have planted crops (1998, 47–51). Structures such as cisterns, forts, towers and terraced fields point to a long established tradition of sedentary agriculture and so cannot be considered to be evidence of the settling-down of pastoral nomads (Rosen 1988, 58–59). The notion of the semi-nomadic origins of Israel evaporates before our eyes.

3.7.3. *Agro-Pastoralism*

Agro-pastoralism or semi-sedentary pastoralism (Grigson 1998, 264) is when plant cultivation and animal-keeping are only partially integrated.

Agro-pastoralism may indeed be a useful model for Proto-Israel according to Finkelstein, who finds evidence for existence of these pastoral
groups in cemeteries and open cult places not related to nearby settlement sites (1988, 341–45), in the oval and linear layouts of the villages
(1988, 238–50) and in the ratio of faunal material of sheep/goats to cattle
(1988, 356). Its relevance, however, even in the view of Finkelstein is
limited to Proto-Israel and suffers from the same problems as those that
attended the model of semi-nomadism. This leaves Grigson's clear preference, namely, mixed farming.

3.7.4. *Mixed Farming*

Under the model of mixed farming, plant and animal-keeping (including
sheep, pigs, goats and cattle) are completely integrated. Archaeological
data from the Highland villages show precisely this pattern. Aside
from terraced fields and other sedentary evidence, there are signs of
sheep, goats and cattle, which are kept in roughly equal numbers (cf.
Finkelstein 1985; Hellwing 1988–89). There would be a very limited
movement of animals away from the primary household, which rules
against semi-nomadism. Pigs make up only about 10 percent of any
Near Eastern faunal assemblages (Zeder 1996). There is a gradual decline
in the keeping of pigs from the Chalcolithic Age onwards (Grigson 1998,
251; Hellwing and Sadeh 1985) and therefore the absence of such
remains should not be taken as a key indicator for Proto-Israel (Knight
2001).

I accordingly adopt the model of mixed farming for Israel and Judah
during Iron II (following Hopkins 1985, 245–50; Holladay 1998, 386–91;
Grigson 1998, 249–63). Holladay (1998, 386) concludes that the archaeological data support the view that the general economy of the time of the
monarchy was a "system of mixed peasant agriculture," which included
cereals, arboriculture, viticulture and small domestic flocks and herds.
Herds provided diversification and risk-spreading. This is in direct continuity with the earlier evidence for the peasants of the Late Bronze Age.

Mixed farming continued to be the dominant form of the economy to
the end of the millennium and beyond that into New Testament times (cf.
Oakman 1986; Hamel 1989). For much of this time "Judah was more
isolated topographically and had a smaller population and a stronger
pastoral economy" than Israel (Gottwald 2001, 165; Finkelstein and
Lederman 1997). Nevertheless, both were sedentary economies with
strong roots dating back to the Bronze Age and the trials and tribulations
of the El Amarna period.

3.8. *Conclusion*

The balance of evidence suggests that the village population of Iron Age Israel were agrarians who practised a mixed form of agriculture, which included some pastoral activities. In spite of Finkelstein's assertions (1998a) this was probably true also for Proto-Israel. The general trend favours a continuous pattern reaching back into the Bronze Age and a strong link between the inhabitants of the Highland villages and the original peasants of Canaan. This meant that the conventional difficulties faced by the later peasants of Israel reached back for centuries before the rise of the monarchy. Poverty did not suddenly appear midway through monarchic Israel as an idealist state collapsed. It had always been present within the fabric of the ANE peasant way of life. Poverty was common in both the El Amarna period (Late Bronze) and in the Iron Age and it would become worse over the centuries due to the politic-economic interference of the non-poor.

In the next chapter I examine the rise of the respective states of Israel and Judah and why one can speak of peasant poverty. I will also begin to observe the ways in which the political economy undermined the already precarious peasant existence and drove the marginalised deeper into poverty. Oft-times carrying the brunt of the blame for the poverty of peasant Israel, the states of Israel and Judah, while hardly innocent bystanders, are most accurately to be understood as contributing factors in unbalancing the scales in a delicate game of peasant risk and survival. While foreign tribute undoubtedly played a role, the stage was already set; long before the separate monarchies of Israel and Judah came into existence, peasant poverty had begun to play its ominous role, and would plague the land for millennia to come.

Chapter 4

THE EMERGENCE OF THE STATES
OF ISRAEL AND JUDAH

4.1. *Understanding Peasants*

Peasant studies from all quarters of the world substantiate the view that peasantry is a distinctive phenomenon (Silverman 1986, 125) and that excepting the reality of local change, peasants through time and place have a great deal in common (Redfield 1956, 25). Indeed, a peasant in ancient Greece often has more in common with a peasant in twentieth-century Africa than with a fellow citizen living in a nearby city. Halstead shows convincingly that there are strong continuities between the ancient and modern peasants of the Mediterranean (1987)—which allow for the cautious use of comparative material (cf. Gallant 1991).

Among biblical scholars there is a wide range of meanings attached to the word "peasant." For example, Lang uses the term peasants to imply Israelite agriculturalists that were neither share-croppers nor tenant farmers, but owned their own land (1985, 86). Hoppe (2004) uses "peasant" interchangeably with "farmer," who may or may not have tax or other obligations to the ruling elite of their day. Chaney (1983, 74 n. 31) opts for Landsberger's definition of peasantry as inclusive of "all low status cultivators." None of these definitions is helpful for our purposes.

Several other terms have been offered as descriptors for the agrarians in Israel, including serfs and share-croppers (Premnath 1988), although the norm is peasants (Chaney 1983; Gottwald 1986). Meillassoux (1991, 89) distinguishes serfdom, which was common in Feudal Europe, from sharecropping according to the manner in which the peasant surplus was extracted. In the case of a serf, the surplus was set as a rental in kind or coin. Whatever the weather or the fertility of the soil, the rental remained constant. By contrast, in share-cropping, the peasant paid a percentage of the crop with further charges for equipment and resources (Premnath 1988, 51), and so was less vulnerable to the weather (Meillassoux 1991, 89). In essence, serfdom and share-croppers are simply a variation of peasants. The Asian Mode of Production with large state labour projects found in Egypt and Mesopotamia (Pixley 1987, 3) is not applicable to Israel (Holladay 1998, 391).

I return, then, to my quest for a definition of peasant that would be applicable for ancient Israel and Canaan. The one key indicator for peasantry appears to revolve around the demands made on peasant surplus. Wolf states that "Peasants...are rural cultivators whose surpluses are transferred to a dominant group of rulers that uses surpluses both to underwrite its own standard of living and to distribute the remainder to groups in society that do not farm but must be fed for their specific goods and services in turn" (1966, 3–4). Shanin writes about peasants across cultures, that "The peasantry consists of small agricultural producers who, with the help of simple equipment and the labour of their families, produce mainly for their own consumption and for the fulfilment of obligations to the holders of political and economic power" (1971b, 240). In Chayonov's theory of peasant economy, the emphasis is on the peasant household as both a productive and a consumptive group (1986; cf. Saul and Woods 1971, 105; Bundy 1988, 9). Common to all these definitions is the notion of the peasant surplus and the demands exercised upon it. I conclude that peasants (including the peasants of Israel) are agrarians who rely on the labour of their family and who are obliged to share their surplus with a number of non-agrarians (Wolf 1966, 1–17; Saul and Woods 1971; Bundy 1988, 4–13). What remains of the surplus is divided between the needs of the family until the next harvest, seeds for planting, contributions to local festivals and making loans to neighbours (Carney 1975, 198).

4.2. *The Shape of Peasant Society*

In speaking of the history of power, Mann (1986, 50) suggests that social inequality has its roots not in the differences, real or imagined, between individuals so much as in the inequalities of nature, such as degrees of fertile or barren land. While standing as distinct from those other groups that benefit from its surplus, peasantry is itself not monolithic. Such differentials among peasants led in time to degrees of power and rank. Villages in ancient Israel would have been composed of families and associations of families, and these would fall naturally into further divisions, with some families seen as poorer or as less important than others. So much is apparent from the comparative work of Lutfiyya in Baytin, a modern Jordanian village (1966, 32–35, 106–7). The result was the same for both ancient Israel and modern Jordan—an unequal distribution of power and resources among the peasant communities. Gottwald (1986), for example, draws attention to an initial increase in difference between one peasant and another concluding that "although the full breach seems not to have developed until the 9th–8th centuries" he finds its origins earlier.

The rise of the united monarchy, under David and Solomon, has long been blamed for the emergence of a stratified society in Israel (Mendenhall 1975; Coote 1981; Frick 1985, 1–70; Gottwald 1986). Gottwald writes that it was "during the united monarchy [that] the vast majority of Israelites became peasants" (1986, 78–79). He refers to the collapse of the judicial system (cf. 2 Sam 15:1–6) and the tax system of Solomon, which created opportunity of upward mobility for some agrarians (1986, 82–83; 2001, 113–18). Similarly, Lemche (1996, 108–17) suggests a change from a what he calls a patronage system (peasantry) for the Late Bronze Age to a village-based tribal system in Iron I and back again into peasantry in Early Iron II. The move back to peasantry was then seen to be a direct consequence of the changing economy stemming from the emergent state of Israel/Judah (cf. Gottwald 2001, 94–96; Mettinger 1971, 87; Fritz 1996, 189). So much of this is based upon the premise of an idealist period in the initial stages of the settlement in the Central Highlands or some form of power vacuum for which we have no evidence. The impression that poverty was essentially a problem created by the monarchy of Iron Age Israel and Judah deserves to be challenged especially in the light of the New or Lower Chronology.

4.3. *The New Chronology and the United Monarchy*

The tenth-century Karnak inscription of Shishak's invasion of Canaan (ca. 924 B.C.E.; cf. 1 Kgs 14:25–28; 2 Chr 12:1–12; cf. Clancy 1999) seems to suggest that the separate kingdoms of Israel and Judah are not yet in existence (so Ahlström 1993, 12–16). Revised assessments of the tenth-century demographics in western Palestine and new understandings of the settlement patterns for the Hill Country have challenged the very existence of the united monarchy (Thompson 1992; Davies 1992; Ahlström 1993; Lemche 1998). What this implies is that the less formal structure that preceded the independent states of Israel and Judah lasted longer than the traditional chronology had previously allowed. Now new understandings of the rise of statehood for Israel/Judah date the full transition to the period of the divided monarchy.

Dever, following the Higher Chronology, has argued for a dramatic population increase from the twelfth to the tenth century (Iron I) localised in relatively few urban centres in the Central Highlands (1997, 178–84). The Lower Chronology, the preferred view of this work, together with general surveys and the renewed excavation of urban areas, suggest that the populations of Israel and Judah increased substantially from the ninth century onwards (Finkelstein and Lederman 1997). Broshi (1993) gives some overall estimates for Cisjordan based on data from excavations and recent surveys, ranging from about 65,000 for 1200 B.C.E. to about 150,000 for 1000 B.C.E. and to 400,000 for 734 B.C.E. Of this latter number, Judah made up about a quarter (110,000) with the majority of people living in villages (Gottwald 2001, 190), and Philistia half that again (50,000).

Several cities (Samaria, Jerusalem, Ashdod and Ekron) reached considerable size (over twenty hectares) in Iron II (1000–586 B.C.E.). The number of village sites in the Central Highlands also increased with the number growing from 254 to 520 (Broshi and Finkelstein 1992) during the same period. In Transjordan, Edom's history begins in the main in the ninth century or later, with only some faint indications in northern Edom for Iron I (cf. Bienkowski 1992; Finkelstein 1992). All this suggests that the ninth century B.C.E. is a critical moment for the political Cisjordan.

Finkelstein's three-stage evolution to statehood for Judah and Israel (1996, 1998a, 2001) offers a useful model for our purposes: Stage one is the informal tribal system or heterarchy of Judah and Israel lasting to the middle of the ninth century B.C.E.; Stage two is the rise of the Omride dynasty; and Stage three is full statehood in Judah, which occurs about a century later. Critical to this model is the archaeology of the cities of Israel and Judah and the rise of urbanisation in Iron II (Dever 1987, 1998a, 1998b).

4.3.1. *A Tribal Heterarchy*

Following the traditional chronology, Israel under the judges (Iron I) was a chiefdom (Frick 1985, 71–97). In choosing a more precise definition various anthropological terms have been offered including "dimorphic" society (Frick 1985), frontier society and segmentary society (e.g. Rogerson 1986). The last is now seen to be flawed (so Fiensy 1987); the problem stems from the uncritical adoption of Evans-Pritchard's study on the Nuer of Africa. Evans-Pritchard's 1940s research among the Nuer is now considered by anthropologists to be highly questionable because he appears to have used nineteenth-century models and comparative North American data in an uncritical fashion (Fiensy 1987, 80-83). A more valuable descriptor comes from Gottwald (2001, 171) who suggests the concept of heterarchy. This would mean that some regions had the status of developed chiefdoms and others had far less structured formats; to my mind this model is preferable. This heterarchy, following the Lower Chronology (Finkelstein 1991b, 47–51), would have lasted from the eleventh into the ninth century, including the time traditionally called the period of the united monarchy.

The heterarchy allows for a power-elite, reminiscent of Thompson's description of eclectic bands composed of "relatively few adventurous men grouped around a prestigious leader, on a warpath…not yet aristocracy as a separate class, but live off booty and the gifts and bribes leaving agricultural work to others" (1965, 48–60). In unfortified villages, as in the Central Highlands, the possibility of raids and banditry would have been high. As a result of such raids, it is likely that Israel's cultivators continued to resemble their peasant ancestors paying their surplus to a new breed of exploiters as their ancestors did in the city-states of the El Amarna correspondence (so Chaney 1983, 78–79). Holladay (1995, 377) refers to archaeological evidence of mighty men found in the presence of inscribed arrow heads from Phoenicia (dated to the twelfth century by Davies 2002), which he believes points to some form of paramount chieftainship or formal organisations. A simple reading of the vivid narratives about David is not inimical to this idea (cf. Chaney 1983, 83; cf. Gottwald 1986, 91) and explains their long-time appeal.

Following the HB, David functioned variously as chief and social bandit (Chaney 1983; Finkelstein 2001, 110–12). For example, we have the account of two factions that appeared under opposition leaders (Saul and David) with different towns supporting their favoured leader (Neufeld 1960, 34–37; Soggin 1977, 340–80). David, effectively a minor chief in the heterarchy that was Israel/Judah, had his base in the fortress of Ziklag, where he had settled with his mercenary band, composed of refugees from justice and starvation (1 Sam 27:6; Neufeld 1960, 28–29; Chaney 1983, 78–79). Such a chief would be judged in terms of his success in obtaining and distributing resources (Chaney 1983, 79), as a warrior and charismatic person (Harris 1979) with the attendant tales of his courage.

David's move to Jerusalem simply continued his status as chief (Na'aman 1996a, 17–20) and in the absence of archaeological indicators to the contrary, that was probably true also for Solomon and his immediate successors (Wightman 1990; Knoppers 1997; Gottwald 2001, 181–85). From the second half of ninth century (ca. 840 B.C.E.) we have the Tel Dan inscription (an Aramean Victory stele) referring to "kings of Israel" of the "house of David" (Na'aman 1996a, 23–27). Is this a reference to the dynasty of Beth-David (Kallai 1993; Halpern 1994; Dever 1997) or not (Lemche and Thompson 1994)? The evidence seems to favour the notion that the house of Omri used the Davidic name to legitimate their dynasty. Further than this we cannot go.

For Gottwald (2001, 173–74), the united monarchy represented the "liminal zone" between chiefdom and fully fledged ANE statehood. "Instead of a 'leap' to statehood, one should rather say that the traditions imply 'eroding' tribalism in tandem with 'creeping' or 'incremental' statism" (2001, 174). Commenting on David's role, he writes, "it is plausible to posit incipient and early state formation that was launched as a 'power grab' by a popular Judahite military chief who for a time was able adroitly to balance the disparate groups in his realm while operating from a newly founded capital uncompromised by tribal rivalries" (Gottwald 2001, 184). Meanwhile, the agrarians of the Central Highlands continued to use their surplus to satisfy the demands of a variety of persons and protection rackets—an informal system of peasantry was already in existence.

4.3.2. *The Rise of the Omride Dynasty*

Dever uses Central Place Theory in his study of urbanisation in Iron Age Israel (1998b). This leads him to speak of a settlement pattern with a focus upon large central places with extended nodes; he includes cities, provincial towns and villages (1998b, 418), to which Gottwald adds military-administrative sites (2001, 187–89). Following Fritz (1995), Dever saw the Iron Age II urbanisation in Israel as revival of the typical Middle and Late Bronze Age patterns (1998b, 418). For the peasants of Israel, could they have remembered, it was a return to the familiar pattern of the past, a replay of their place within the boundaries of the city-states of the El Amarna period.

Archaeologically speaking, the process of statehood effectively began for Israel in the Iron Age II period, but was attributed originally to the reign of Solomon (Frick 1977, 100; Mendenhall 1983, 99). Following the Lower Chronology, it was not until the early ninth century, with the rise of Omride political and economic powers, that urbanisation as a key indicator for statehood is clearly evidenced for the northern kingdom of Israel (Finkelstein 1996, 1998a, 1998c, 1998d, 2001). I shall briefly examine the archaeological data from the key sites, laying out the grounds for such a conclusion.

4.3.2.1. *Jezreel.* Jezreel has one of the best exposures of stratigraphy enabling other sites like Megiddo and Hazor, where earlier expeditions have destroyed much of the upper levels, to be re-dated to the period of the Omride dynasty. The monumental four-chambered gateways, for example, found at Jezreel (cf. Ussishkin 2000), Jerusalem (E. Mazar 1987) and Megiddo were originally considered as Solomonic and dated to the mid-tenth century (cf. Yadin 1975; Milson 1986). They are now consid-ered to be later (divided monarchy) following the Lower Chronology and based on the Jezreel stratigraphy. Barkay stresses the continuity with Canaanite patterns in that the gateway is "an improved version of the four-chambered gateways common in Cisjordan and Syria since the Middle Bronze Age" (1992, 308).

4.3.2.2. *Megiddo.* The detailed study of the Iron Age pottery from Megiddo (Finkelstein, Zimhoni and Kafri 2000) and the thorough analy-sis of the various strata (Finkelstein and Ussishkin 2000) has led to a complete re-evaluation of the site and its history. Originally dated to Solomon's reign (tenth century) including the famous "Stables of Solo-mon" (Ussishkin 1994), the dating has since been changed to the ninth century in line with the pottery at Omride Jezreel (Finkelstein, Zimhoni and Kafri 2000; Oredsson 1998; Finkelstein 1998c; Finkelstein and Ussishkin 2000).

4.3.2.3. *Gezer and Dor.* Finkelstein has proposed that the monumental gateway at Gezer belongs to the ninth century or later (2002, 263–93) again on the basis of the better stratigraphy obtained at Jezreel. One should probably include also the four-chamber gate from Tel Dor rather than look for a tenth-century date as initially proposed following the Higher Chronology of the excavators (Stern, Gilboa and Sharon 1989).

4.3.2.4. *Hazor.* The traditional dating of the city, Hazor, is based on Ben-Tor and Ben-Ami's finds (arising from their 1990s excavation), which suggest a tenth-century date and an implied association with Solomon's united monarchy (1998, 5; cf. Ben-Tor 1993, 2000; Gottwald 2001, 90–91; see 1 Kgs 9:15 which includes Hazor among Solomon's fortified cities). Instead, Finkelstein (1999; Finkelstein and Silberman 2001) argues for an early ninth-century date, linking the rebuilding of Hazor with the Omride dynasty and the general urban renewal which attended that time and to which the archaeology gives credence.

4.3.2.5. *Samaria.* All indications are that the history of Samaria is inte-gral to the history of the northern kingdom. Since Samaria had a gap in occupation from the Early Bronze period until Iron II (the early ninth cen-tury B.C.E.), this is the earliest date one might venture for the origin of the state of Israel. So when Omri established his capital city here, this was the first truly Israelite state-centre (Olivier 1983). Traces of several ter-raced olive and vineyards indicate its use as a state-centre for processing such products (Stager 1990). The capital city was later moved to Jezreel under Ahab (ca. 875–854 B.C.E.).

Other cities formerly dated to Solomon's time, such as Beth Shean (Mazar 1993) and Beth Shemesh (Bunimovitz and Lederman 2001), require redating in line with Jezreel, Megiddo, Hazor and Samaria (so Wightman 1990). Archaeologically speaking, no indication of the trappings of statehood exists prior to the ninth century in any of the major Israelite centres. Any debate about the role of Solomon or David in creating a more stratified society in the tenth century is rendered null and void by the Lower Chronology. The blame should instead be carried by the Omride dynasty and their Judean neighbours.

4.3.3. *Full Statehood Comes to Judah*

Stage three in Finkelstein's process relates to the late eighth century, when full statehood comes to Judah (Finkelstein 1996, 1998a, 2001; Gottwald 2001, 198). Traditionally, the commencement of the Southern Kingdom is dated from the tenth century and associated with Saul, David and Solomon. Following the Lower Chronology, Lemche (1993) posited a date of ca. 850 B.C.E. for the induction of the monarchy for both Judah and Israel. Three years later, Lemche changed his mind with regard to Judah, while retaining the ninth-century date for Israel. He argued that there is simply no archaeological evidence to support the notion of a centralised state organisation for Judah until the eighth century (1996, 106–8). Following suit, Hopkins states that a recognisable Judean culture, in place of the earlier predominant regionalism, comes only in the eighth century with signs of an integrated economy (1996, 121–32). Similarly, Barkay considers that the eighth century is when one can observe "separate and independent material cultures" for Israel and Judah, not least in the ceramic remains (Barkay 1992, 305).

Based on Barkay (1992), Hopkins (1996) and Finkelstein (2001), this mid-eighth-century dating seems agreeable, especially in the light of the archaeological data and the Lower Chronology. Finkelstein suggests that there was an initial period of dominance by Israel over Judah, which is reflected in some architectural modifications in Judahite centres and which preceded the rise of the Judahite state (1998d). We come now to the key sites.

4.3.3.1. *Jerusalem*. Shiloh had originally dated Jerusalem's acropolis, with its famous step-stone structure (the glacis from Area G), to the tenth century—the time of Solomon (1983–84, 26–29; 1985–86, 27–30), correcting the earlier Hellenistic dating of Kenyon (1978). The structure is

now dated to the Late Bronze period (thirteenth to twelfth centuries B.C.E.); it was subsequently modified in the tenth [or eighth] century and again in the seventh century to accommodate a four-roomed house—the house of Ahiel (Cahill 1998). The water system of Jerusalem at Gihon and the associated Warren's shaft appears to have been cut in two stages, namely Middle Bronze II and Iron II (eighth century). It was then abandoned at the end of the eighth century perhaps in favour of Hezekiah's tunnel (Reich and Shukron 2000b, 2004). Hezekiah's tunnel may well be more closely related to the population increases than to the Assyrian invasions. Two stretches of city wall dated tentatively to the eighth century were found east of the old Middle Bronze wall (Reich and Shukron 2000b).

Steiner (2000, 280–85), who has been charged with collating Kenyon's material on Jerusalem, suggests that during the tenth and ninth centuries, Jerusalem was a provincial centre for the immediate region (cf. Thompson 1992) but only of minor importance. Gottwald (2001, 199) argues that the subsequent building and rebuilding that took place in Jerusalem could easily account for the lack of public building for the Iron I. Actually, the critical area, west and above Area G (the so-called Penthouse) has still to be excavated since the land given for the City of David excavations excludes the top of the ridge occupied by residences.

The evidence from Jerusalem has been reinforced by the discovery by Eilat Mazar, granddaughter of Benjamin Mazar, of a four-chambered gateway, which she dates to the ninth century (1987, 63; 1989) in line with the northern kingdom gateways. We suggest that Jerusalem served initially as an outpost of the Omride dynasty in the ninth century until Judean independence sometime in the eighth century. There was a significant growth generally in Jerusalem through the eighth century and by the time of Hezekiah (late eighth, early seventh century B.C.E.), Jerusalem was an urban centre of "exceptional dimensions" (Steiner 2000, 287–88).

4.3.3.2. *Arad.* Arad's casemate fortifications and its temple, previously thought to be ninth century, are now dated to the second half of the eighth century (Herzog 2002, 50). This would mesh with the date for centralised statehood, along with the evidence within the Negev desert. The Negev was occupied in the eighth century by fortress-like structures (Cohen 1985, 67–70) with nearby settlements and terraced fields, presumably forming a part of the defences of the Judean state.

4.3.3.3. *Lachish.* Canaanite Lachish was replaced by a Judean palace-fort dated to the middle eighth century and which apparently formed part of the Judean state defensive plan along with Arad and the desert fortresses of the Negev. A system of fire-signals linked these various fortress towns to Jerusalem as the Lachish Letters indicate.

The rise of the states of Israel and Judah is clearly evidenced in the renewed architecture of the cities of these two lands. Shiloh (1987) traces the evolution from the circular village plan of the Iron I villages into the later city plan with a surrounding casemate wall, which might incorporate houses or be a separate structure. As the states arose, so the city structures changed, reflecting their increased importance as regional and national centres. So much is evident from the archaeological excavations. What the New Chronology has done is to move this urban transition, dated originally to the united monarchy, forward by between one and two centuries, primarily on the basis of better stratigraphy. Israelite and Judean society became increasingly divided between its urban centres and its peasant villages, accelerating through the eighth century until the destruction of Jerusalem in 586 B.C.E. The prophetic period, from Hosea (ca. 750 B.C.E.) to the Exilic prophets (Jeremiah and Ezekiel) coincides well with this dating, which adds credence to the message of the prophets.

4.4. *The Fate of the Common People*

Gottwald sums up the political situation of the divided monarchy: "Structurally, the kingdoms of Israel and Judah were small-scale monarchies, constituted as tributary states that drew on the agrarian and pastoral surplus of subjects to sustain a privileged ways of life for the crown and the bureaucracy that ran domestic and foreign affairs of state" (2001, 153). This pattern then continued for the duration of the monarchies. Holladay concludes, "In short, on good present evidence, it is clear that Israel and Judah remained peasant economies (which characteristically display wealth distinctions) throughout their independent existences" (1998, 392).

I suggest that the Israelites were from their inception an identifiable group of peasants. This was true in the Amarna period, when they farmed in the Coastal Plains before being driven out by the migrating Philistines and other Sea Peoples. It continued in the early stages of the settlement of the Central Highlands as they were obligated to share their surplus with village chiefs and other people of power, including the Philistines, the rulers of the city-states, marauding bands (cf. Judg 6:1–6) and David-like social bandits (Chaney 1986, 53–66). Then, with the rise of urbanisation, a more formal aspect prevailed, but the system of peasantry remained. What changed was the identity of those who laid claim to the surplus generated by the peasant majority.

Urbanisation in Israel and Judah during the ninth through the eighth and seventh centuries B.C.E. (under monarchs like Omri and Hezekiah), created the climate for an increase in peasant exploitation (cf. Herrmann 1981, 236; Dever 2000). While there was probably little alteration in the general structure of peasant society, there seems to have greater opportunity for the system of patronage, offering the peasants both advantages and disadvantages. Correctly, Gottwald points out that "with the change of political and economic forms came the evolving forms of ideology and religion" (1993, 182–85).

From the peasant perspective, little may have changed, but there was another factor which should be considered, namely the impact of Assyria. Not long after the establishment of the Southern Kingdom, Israel was destroyed; Judah was then incorporated into the Assyrian provincial system (Finkelstein 2001, 105–15), an event which had cataclysmic repercussions for the peasants of Judah—far more so than the rise of statehood. The Assyrian invasions at the end of the late eighth century decimated Cisjordan, especially in the north (Gottwald 2001, 135–37). Gal's study of Lower Galilee in the Iron Age concludes that 25 percent of the sites were destroyed in the mid-ninth century (possibly as a result of Shalmaneser III's campaign of 842 B.C.E.). In 733 B.C.E., another wave of destruction occurred, with the campaign of Tiglath Pilaser III. The survey revealed no seventh-century pottery in the region, strongly suggesting "that Lower Galilee was almost totally deserted during the seventh century B.C.E." and remained so until the Persian period (Gal 1988–89, 62).

Jerusalem expanded fourfold in the eighth and seventh centuries, either as a result of refugees pouring in from the conquered northern kingdom (Finkelstein 1994) or the influx of people wishing to escape Philistine controls (Broshi 1974). The estimated population of Jerusalem in Iron II probably reached some ten to twelve thousand people and covered 50–60 hectares (Broshi 1974, 1980; Stager 1982, 121; Shiloh 1980). De Geus (Num 13:28) points to the Assyrian illustrations of Lachish and biblical descriptions to suggest that two-storey houses were not uncommon, including houses erected on top of the actual city walls (1986, 224–27). This allowed for a greater population within a small walled area (1986, 227).

Other signs of a marked increase in population in Judah and Moab appear after the destruction of the northern kingdom of Israel. For example, agricultural terraces appear in the neighbouring valleys (Rephʾaim and Mevasseret Yerushalayim) bordering Jerusalem (Edelstein and Milevski 1994), along with the recurrence of farming in marginal areas to the south and west of the Judahite state (Finkelstein 1994). Iron Age Moab, like neighbouring Judah, experienced a peak in extent and density of human settlement in the late seventh to mid-sixth centuries (Routledge 1997).

Such increases both within and without the borders of Judah must have put pressure on the fragile ecosystem and on its ability to sustain peasant life. For the poor, all this spelled difficult times. To understand why this created such a problem, we need to examine the delicate balance that would have existed between peasant and patrons and in particular the role played by the peasant surplus as part of the survival modes of the Israelite peasant.

Chapter 5

AGRARIAN PRACTICES AMONG THE PEASANTS OF ISRAEL

Peasants, one of the most long-lived forms of human organisation known to recorded history, seemed always to walk a razor-thin line between survival and extinction

—David Arnold.

5.1. *Peasant Poverty*

Peasant economic well-being, speaking generically, is an uneven affair. Not all of the peasants of any given society are poor, nor are they all equally vulnerable to the conditions through which poverty might arise. The economist Nash (1966, 3–12) draws attention to the latent hierarchy to be found in and between peasant communities. In similar vein, De Ste. Croix (1981, 211) posits three categories of peasantry, namely, small, medium and large, depending primarily upon their access and control of land. Gallant, speaking of Mediterranean peasants, observes differences in family size, wealth and standard of living, and divides them into "rich and poor peasants," with only "a fluid line" separating the two (1991, 4). Poverty strikes most ferociously at those occupying the lowest rungs of the ladder.

Poverty comes in different forms. "At its simplest, poverty refers to a basic lack of the means of survival; the poor are those who, even in normal circumstances, are unable to feed and clothe themselves properly and risk death as a consequence" (MacPherson and Silburn 1998, 1). The World Bank defines such poverty as absolute poverty—a condition of life so characterized by malnutrition, illiteracy and disease, squalid surroundings, high infant mortality so as to be beneath any reasonable definition of human decency (World Bank 1978, 111). At the other end of the scale is relative poverty, which is the misdistribution of assets, income and power (Øyen 1997, 127). Peasant poverty might belong to either form.

What, then, are the marks of peasant poverty? Peasants, including those in Iron Age Israel, were caught upon the horns of a dilemma: faced on the one hand with the reality of inadequate means and on the other by the demands of those who preyed upon their surplus. The image of balancing on a precipitous knife-edge is an appropriate metaphor for the lives of these peasants in their struggle for survival. One the one side, the household was an unreliable source of labour—allotments were too small, the soil was often poor, climates were harsh, droughts frequent and farming methods were antiquated and inadequate. Indeed, the whole farming system for Iron Age Israel "was fraught with risks" (Marfoe 1980, 5). Survival depended on centuries-old coping mechanisms and when those failed or were subverted, poverty came knocking, wolf-like, on the door. On the other side, the agrarians of Israel faced those who laid claim to their precious surplus, which should have formed a barrier against bad times. Instead, the surplus was used instead to pay off creditors, landlords and tax-collectors. The combined pressures of these two sides squeezed the peasant poor within their grasp like predatory pincers.

Here is the stark horror of peasant poverty—it was not something that was rare and to be avoided but was instead an all too common occurrence. This is what we often forget—the constant vulnerability of peasant life and the sheer numbers of the poor and needy. Most peasants were only a shadow away from poverty and starvation. The poor, then, were not the isolated few—rather they were the ordinary people next door, the families of the next village. Yet for those who lived secure in the cities, the peasant poor were the faceless crowd, the unnamed multitude. In this chapter, we look at the dimensions of peasant poverty and the way in which the peasants of Israel responded to the challenge for survival in the Central Highlands.

5.2. *Sources*

In comprehending the life of the peasants of biblical Israel, several resources are available. Hopkins' (1985) and Borowski's (1987) work on the villages of Iron Age Israel form the basis for an understanding of agricultural practices of Israel under the monarchy. Also valuable are the studies of Hamel (1989) and Oakman (1986) of Roman Palestine. Added to these are the modern studies of the Middle East, including Israel, at the close of the nineteenth century and into the first half of the twentieth century (Warriner 1957; Granott 1952). More specialist works include the classic work on the plants of the Bible by Zohary (1966, 1972). Complementing these is the ever-increasing volume of information from archaeological excavations from the Negev, through the Central Highlands of Cisjordan, and the valleys of Galilee. Together, they supply a rich resource for accessing the agrarian history of biblical Israel along with ANE texts and technical studies (soil types).

Among the archaeological data there are two important texts. The Tale of Sinuhe (preserved in written form from ca. 1800 B.C.E. in Egypt), connected with the twentieth century B.C.E., describes Cisjordan as "a goodly land named Yaa: figs were in it and grapes. It had more wine than water. Plentiful was its honey, abundant its olives. Every (kind of) fruit was on its trees. Barley was there and emmer. There was no limit to any (kind of) cattle" (*ANET*, 19). The Gezer calendar dated to the tenth century B.C.E. (Davies 2002), with its annual pattern of planting and reaping, is the second text. As interpreted by Borowski, it reads: "Two months of ingathering (olives) / two months of sowing (cereals) / two months of late sowing (legumes and vegetables) / a month of hoeing weeds (for hay) / a month of harvesting barley / a month of harvesting (wheat) and measuring (grain) / two months of grape harvesting / a month of ingathering summer fruit" (1987, 38). Uyal (2003) elaborates: Tishrei—the month for ploughing; Heshvan—the time to sow wheat; Kislev—the olive harvest; Tevet—the time for the lily of the valley; Shvat—when the lambs start to jump on their own; Nissan—red buttercups and songbirds; Iyat—attention to olive branches; Sivan—time to harvest wheat; Tamuz—figs ripen; Av—the time for gathering grapes; Ilul—the sun starts to wane a little and the cycle begins again.

A useful starting point for our purposes are the technical resources, which include studies of the physical geography and soil types. Hopkins (1985) and Goldberg (1998) discuss the five soil types that are the composition of the present-day region. The first of these and the most common is the terra rossa, "the most fertile of the mountain soils" (Karmon 1971, 30, cited in Hopkins 1985, 127–28). The less frequently found Mediterranean brown forest soils are also fertile but tend to be more acidic (Hopkins 1985, 128). The third type is the rendzina soils which, while not unsuitable for agriculture, lack the fertility of the previous two types (1985, 128–29). The basaltic soils are found in eastern Lower Galilee and are well suited to agriculture (1985, 129). Colluvial soils are found in the floors of valleys and "provide productive agricultural environments which are persistently enriched by downwash from adjoining hills" (1985, 129). The chief challenge faced by farmers of the Central Highlands would be to preserve the fertility of the soils and to ensure that especially the terra rossa was not eroded (1985, 133).

In terms of vegetation much has been written. Danin (1998, 24) makes mention of 2,682 species of flora that are found in Israel and the West

Bank today. In historical times, the mountains of Judea, Samaria, Carmel and Galilee and lower elevations of Mount Hermon were covered by forests (Danin 1995, 30). Hopkins (1985, 115–18) draws attention to the process of deforestation especially in the Central Highlands. In the Central Highlands, terrace farming increased the possibility of farming but even so that region was prone to drought and entirely dependent on rainfall. Generally, the soil and topography determined the form of agrarian pursuit varying from the deeper soils used for fruit trees, olives and grapes, to the shallower soils used for cereals and pulses (Danin 1998, 31; cf. Goldberg 1995, 40–54). Thus, even at the outset it is clear that the peasants of Israel faced considerable challenges with marginal land and a lack of good soils to which we should add infrequent and unreliable rain patterns. This was a challenge that had been taken up millennia before by the first inhabitants to practise agriculture in the region.

5.3. *A Marginal Land*

Agriculture in Israel has its roots in the Natufian period, as stone tools such as sickles (for the cutting of natural cereal), mortars and grinding bowls indicate (Negev 1972b, 13). The Neolithic period brought the domestication of animals, as is evident from the figurines found in places like Jericho (1972b, 13). Sedentary habitation begins in the fourth millennium (the Chalcolithic period)—Gonen describes the largest concentration of dwellings for this period as that found in the western Negev (near to the valleys of Beersheba and Arad). Opinion is divided as to whether these settlements were seasonal (Gonen 1992b, 43) or permanent (Avner 1990). Indications of the planting of grains, fruit trees (olive, date and pomegranate) and flax in the cutting and grinding elements were found, suggesting some permanence (Gonen 1992b, 43–45, 61). Alongside cultivated fields, a natural irrigation system of walls and dams allowed run-off into the fields (1992b, 43). Numerous storage jars have been found, along with traces of grain, legumes and olives.

The dating of the bones of the domesticated animals indicates longevity consistent with their use for secondary products such as milk and wool. Remains indicate diversity including sheep, goats, pigs, cattle, horses and donkeys (Gonen 1992b, 61). An interesting case study comes from the work done in the Uvda Valley in the southern Negev. Avner (1990), the excavator of the site, concludes that most of the sites in the Chalcolithic period were permanent settlements, supported by a combined economy of agriculture and animal husbandry. If this was so, then we have the origins of the agrarian practises of the Central Highlands already evident millennia before the Highland Villages of Iron II, and in a closely related region.

The Bronze Age brought with it the bronze ploughshare, as an example from Beth-Shemesh indicates (Negev 1972b, 13–14). The general agricultural pattern continues into the Iron Age and beyond, but with a movement from one geographical region to another. So, in the early Iron Age one witnesses a return to the Central Highlands, and in Iron II, a return to the Negev consequent upon the increasing population—the refugees from the Assyrian invasion of Israel (Negev 1972b, 13–14; Finkelstein 1994). The practice of combining planting of cereals with herds, dating back to Chalcolithic times, was carried through right into modern times and has long served as one of the key survival mechanisms in the face of difficult climatic and geological conditions

Like many parts of the Mediterranean region, Israel/Judah of the Iron Age was a marginal area in terms of agriculture. The Fertile Crescent was only fertile in relation to the surrounding desert. "It is a semi-circle of cultivatable land defined by the 8-inch [200 mm] rainfall line" (Warriner 1957, 57). In Israel, the amount of rain diminishes from the northern parts of Galilee, through Judaea and into the Negev and from west to east (Evenari, Shanan and Tadmor 1971, 30–33). Three areas may be discerned (cf. Deist 2000, 137), ranging from the northern sections of the Coastal Plain (over 350 mm), the Central Highland region (150–350 mm), and the southern regions (25–150 mm). Indeed, the whole region formed a transition zone between the desert areas of the Sahara type in the southern and eastern parts, and the Mediterranean zones in the north (Danin 1998, 24). A lack of reliable water and the encroachment of desert on two sides, south and west, with the sea on another, made farming a risky occupation. In the face of such extremely difficult conditions the resilience and tenacity of these early farmers is much to be admired. A fine line separated survival and famine.

Climatic changes in Israel during human history have included a shift that occurred between the Chalcolithic time and the Early Bronze Age, leading to a drier climate (Grigson 1998, 256; Hopkins 1985, 107). In the Middle Bronze Age, the Negev was believed to be considerably more hospitable than today, based on archaeological finds, so that a process of desertification needs to be understood during the succeeding millennia (Evenari, Shanan and Tadmor 1971, 11–28). Neumann and Parpola (1987) suggest that 1200 to 900 B.C.E. in the ANE was a time of increased temperatures and aridity, leading to the temporary decline of Assyria and Babylonia, although southern Judah seems to have been less adversely affected (Drori and Horowitz 1988–89).

Rainfall in Israel comes in the winter months (mid-October to the beginning of May), in two separate spells, known as the former and the latter rains. Various Hebrew terms were used to describe different types of rain or periods of rainfall (Deist 2000, 106; cf. Ps 65:9–13). The former rains included the peak three months of December, January and February and served to create a climate for ploughing and planting (Hopkins 1985, 84–91). The latter rains fell in the months following until April and coincided with the time of ripening just prior to harvest. Aside from rain, dew may have contributed to the moisture of the subsurface strata but Katsnelson (1971, 5:1601) rules against its value in watering crops.

Any delay in the arrival of the rains was problematic—an occurrence which happened with some regularity. Amiran writes:

> Israel, like all other semi-arid countries, is distinguished by prolonged series of sub-normal rainfall years. These do not always repeat the grim Biblical story of seven lean years, but three consecutive lean years, each with a negative deviation of 30 percent or more from average values are unfortunately part of the experience of every farmer. (1962, 104)

Hopkins (1985, 87) posits an average of six or seven years of reasonable precipitation out of ten, with a reduced spread of rain in the other years. Borowski (1987) takes a more negative view, estimating that bad years outnumbered the good with the latter being as few as two out of seven. Adding to the burden of drought is the hot sirocco, a dry, dust-laden wind, which can drop the relative humidity to below 10 percent, while markedly increasing the summer temperatures throughout Israel (Evenari, Shanan and Tadmor 1971, 37).

Lang calculates on the basis of comparative studies from twentieth-century Iraq that the Near Eastern peasant needed to secure a minimum of three successful harvests in four, in order simply to break even (1985, 86). Yields have increased dramatically in modern times with better fertilisers and modern farming methods. In ancient times there was a wide range of yields, depending on various factors such as the type of soil, the use of fertiliser and the abundance of rain. Warriner, referring to modern peasants in the Near East, writes "Yields vary around the average to a far greater extent than they do in Europe, owing to the irregularity of rainfall. In Syrian Jezira…wheat gives a tenfold return in a good year, sevenfold in a normal year, while in a bad year it will only give back the equivalent of the seed" (1957, 57). This is in line with Oakman's computerised projection for New Testament Palestine of the order of 1:5 (1986, 26, 253–69). The reality is there—peasant farming in Israel was an unequal contest with the elements. No wonder the prophet Joel writes:

Under the clods the seeds have shrivelled, the water-channels are dry, and
the barns lie in ruins; for the harvests have come to naught. How the
cattle moan! The herds of oxen are distraught because they have no
pasture; even the flocks of sheep waste away. To you, Lord, I cry out; for
fire has consumed the open pastures, flames have burnt up every tree in
the countryside. Even the beasts in the field look to you; for the streams
are dried up, the fire has consumed the open pasture. (Joel 1:17–20)

A farmer in Palestine has never had an easy life; its land is stony and
hilly, the sirocco is oppressive, fire is a constant danger and blight, rust
and black rot is devastating. Added to this are the tribulations of sickness
among the cattle and sheep (Hab 3:5; 1 Kgs 8:37), weeds (Borowski,
1987, 153–62; King 1988a, 108) and insects (Nah 3:15–17). Famine,
hunger and thirst are so much part and parcel of life that they become
symbols of the common person's relationship with God (Navone 2001;
cf. Amos 9:11; 1 Kgs 17:11; Jer 2:13).

5.4. *Vulnerable Villages*

I have made mention already of the settlement pattern in Israel. According to Dever (1998b), the settlement pattern in ancient Israel included a
three-tier hierarchy consisting of a few large central places that functioned as administrative and economic centres (level one). Then there
was a much larger number of middle-sized towns (nodes in the network)
relatively evenly distributed across landscape, for the exchange of goods
and services (level two). To this I should add Gottwald's administrative-
military centres, which would have found a place between levels one and
two (2001, 189). Finally, there was a still larger number of small villages,
hamlets and farmsteads (level three) in rural areas (Dever 1998b, 418).
This third level was the most important from a peasant perspective.

Redfield (1956, 4) defines peasant village as "a little community,"
which includes the vital ingredients of "smallness, homogeneity and all
providing self sufficiency." The reality was probably little different
for Israel. Such self-sufficiency must have been often stretched to its
limits—a village could not survive without regular outside intervention,
if only from the next door village. The villages of ancient Israel were the
setting in which the peasantry of Israel found their social context and
identity (Finkelstein and Zilberman 1995). This was also the place of
local politics, which from the peasant perspective often overshadowed
national politics (Knight 1994, 105–9).

I have already mentioned some of the distinguishing marks of the Iron
Age villages, namely underground silos, terraces, cisterns and three- or
four-roomed houses. Other features included cobbled streets (Callaway

1976, 28–30) and the pattern of building the homesteads in a circle which is suggestive from the start of the protection of herds within the village boundaries (Mazar 1992, 288). While none of these elements was unique to these villages, the combination tended, in time, to set them apart from the settlements of Galilee and of the Negev. Notably, each element formed a coherent part of the survival strategy of these Highlanders.

Stager (1976, 13) suggests that the average size of villages in the Highlands of Judah were of the order of about 5 acres, although Hopkins (1985, 140) shows that many of the sites (e.g. Ai, Tell Qiri) were considerably smaller than this. The distance from one village to another varied from 1–2 km to about 5 km (sometimes just far enough to fall into a different precipitation zone). Estimates of population sizes for individual villages, based on people per acre, vary greatly from scholar to scholar (cf. Hopkins 1985; Dar 1986). Excavations of what seem to be Iron Age II farmsteads suggest that up to 30 people might be housed together, with the addition, in later times, of further dwellings along the fringes of the fields (Dar 1986, 7–8).

In twentieth-century Palestine, as throughout the history of Israel, there was a preference for building villages on the hilltops. These hilltops provided security from enemies and avoided the diseases of the lowlands like malaria. Such locations took advantage of the anabatic breezes of the summer evenings, and the warmer thermal layers of the winter times. Watch-towers were built (Isa 5:2) for the protection and early warning of the inhabitants of the village. Religious shrines frequented on the whole by peasant worshippers dotted the hillsides.

The area of a typical Arab village of the early twentieth century (Warriner 1957, 197–201) was divided into three parts. Conjecturally, we may suggest this was true also for the Highland Villages of Israel based on the work of Hopkins (1985) and Borowski (1987). First of all there was the centre in which we find the built-up area of village. Secondly, there was the *hawakir* or garden area—a belt surrounding the village, which was fertilised and watered. These plots were small (about half an acre). Here, fruit trees and vegetables grew, which, on account of their closeness to the village, did not require much guarding against grazing animals. In some instances, however, the area was fenced with cactus plants. Peasant wives and daughters spent much of their time here. This land was highly valued and treated as private property, and not subject to division of land into summer and winter crop zones for purposes of crop rotation (Warriner 1957, 197).

The third area was the fields, which for twentieth-century Palestine averaged about 5 acres and which were subjected to division and crop rotation (Warriner 1957, 198). This figure is in line with the suggested size of plots in biblical Israel of land under plough of about 2–3 acres (discussed below). Given the small size of many of these holdings, one can understand the constant struggle for survival (cf. Broshi and Finkelstein 1992). Most fields were located nearby, either in the low-lying areas or on terraced platforms. Some plots, however, were distant and could take time to reach, thus increasing the burden of farming, and tended to be allocated to the young males who made up about 21 percent of village (Warriner 1957, 200). Marfoe cites Syrian examples from the modern period with a pattern of concentric circles with the innermost plots being irrigated and the furthest plots being the least productive and prone to unpredictable yields (1980, 5). In addition, villages normally owned areas of common land, which included areas of pasture rights and meadows (Stirling 1971, 41), all of which were probably true also for Iron Age Israel and Judah.

Some farming lands in early twentieth-century Palestine were so distant that temporary villages were established in the plains. The peasants took up residence in these villages in ploughing and reaping seasons, so as not to lose time in travelling. These dependent villages, which for the greater part of the year stood empty and desolate, were called *khirbeh*, the usual name also for actual ruins (Warriner 1957, 169). Many of these have preserved their Israelite names, with the presence of artefacts attesting to their antiquity and to the antiquity of the practice (1957, 171). Indeed, much of what is evident for the peasants of Palestine in modern times was probably true also for the peasants of biblical Israel.

5.5. *Vulnerable Households*

Wilk and Netting (1984) define the peasant household as both a productive (in terms of labour and children) and protective (in terms of caring for the extended family) organisation. In terms of the former, the generic peasant depended upon their own immediate household for their supply of labour (Wolf 1966, 2), placing it in an extremely vulnerable position. So much is evident from comparative studies of peasant households across both time and space, but what of the situation in Israel during and after the Iron Age? What do we know from the archaeological and comparative data?

Peasants in Iron Age Cisjordan and Transjordan lived in a three- or four-roomed house (or, better, four-spaced home—Shiloh 1970, 1973) with added side-sheds (Faust and Bunimovitz 2003). Clark puts the mean size of four-roomed village homes at ten to twelve metres long and eight to ten metres wide (2003, 34–36). These homes included place for storage and accommodation of some animals. In view of the weather, the inside–outside flow of the house was critical. The simple view of agrarian tranquillity asserts that "every man [*sic*] will sit under his own vine and fig tree" (1 Kgs 5:5; Mic 4:4; Zech 3:10) indicating the extent to which the forecourt was integrated into the peasant home. An alternate broad house design is common in the villages of the north of Israel, probably intended only for nuclear families (Faust 2000b, 15–22).

Faust's study of the excavations of 28 rural Iron II sites in Cisjordan suggests that the norm in villages, evident from the size of the four-roomed homes, was the extended family (2000a, 30–39), but that in cities it was different. He distinguishes (1999) between the smaller four-roomed homes in cities (for nuclear families) and the larger homes in villages (for extended families). Basing his work on the biblical text, Gottwald (1979, 257–92, 323–28, 697–700) discerned the basic unit available for labour as the extended family (beth-ab), and then distinguished this from the larger association of families (cf. Lemche 1985; Hopkins 1985, 252–61; Blenkinsopp 1997; Meyers 1997). Several such associations made up the tribe (Gottwald 1979, 257–84; cf. Cohen 1965, 4).

Extended families in ancient Greece (Gallant 1991, 24–25, 75–78) were actually fairly small, consisting of one or more grandparents and unmarried siblings but rarely more than ten persons (*pace* Pilch 2002b who thinks in terms of 50 to 100 persons). Childhood diseases and the very trauma of the birth process worked together to keep the size of families down. This agrees with estimates for Iron Age Israel (Shaw 1987) so that we may understand a similar size and vulnerability about the households there.

Life expectancy rates generally in the Mediterranean world of antiquity were about 42–45 years for men and 36 years for women (Goubert 1987, 47–90), although some contemporary examples suggest a lower figure for both might be in order. For example, the National Center for Health Statistics (USA) for the year 1900 gives Black expectancy as 33 years of age (averaged between men and women). Disease, war, starvation, oppression, injustice and not least poverty were major factors in the life-expectancy of the peasants and Israel would have been no exception to the rule (cf. Isa 35:4–6; Stuhlmueller 1989). Moreover, modern studies indicate that "minor ailments in well-nourished individuals are devastating to the malnourished" (Wilson and Ramphele 1989, 106). Burial statistics indicate a high infant mortality rate throughout the ANE (Willett 2002, 27–30). Labour was thus always at a premium (Hopkins 1987, 188–90) especially with mother and child deaths.

The life cycle from one new family group to the next, based on classical Greek and Roman data, was about 24 years (Hopkins 1965; Gallant 1991, 27). The new group begins when the oldest son is married and his

bride brought into the natal home (Gallant 1991, 27). Comparative studies from the Greco-Roman world suggest that men married on average in
their late twenties to early thirties (Saller 1987, 25–30), and women in
their late teens. The eldest son often married following the death of his
father or his own taking over of the main household. Legal maturity in
biblical law was probably the age of twenty, based on analogies from
ANE and later rabbinic materials (Fleishman 1992).

Hebrew has no word for marriage. Instead the understanding of the
process is subsumed within a patriarchal context with the father giving a
woman, and a husband taking a woman or giving a dwelling to the
woman (Pilch 2002a). Male heads of households are the norm, and the
submission of women to men is assumed, as is patriarchy for all the biblical periods. Meyers' studies of women's culture in Iron Age Israel
(1978, 1988; cf. Hopkins 1985, 168) detail the role played by women in
the Highland villages, especially within the context of the family, reminiscent of peasant women in third-world situations today. These included
specific religious roles, and involved networking systems and complex
hierarchies, which operated quite separately from the male structures
(Myers 2002, 277–303). Women would always have been among the
most vulnerable members of the society, with values such as shame and
honour joining forces to keep them under patriarchal subjection (Bechtel
1991). If this is still true of third-world situations today, it undoubtedly
would have applied to ancient Israel at all times and not just to the later
periods. The poorest of the poor in Israel would have been peasant
women and children.

As the generic peasant household evolved through its various cycles
(cf. Chayanov 1986, 5–6; Gallant 1991, 27–30, 75–78), the labour supply
itself varied greatly. When the children were old enough to supplement
the work of the parents, the demands of labour to feed the household and
the labour available might match. At other times, as when the demands
of motherhood were paramount, or an elderly parent was present, the
labour available might be insufficient to produce sufficient food. Shock-
ingly, Gallant concludes that "both historical and computer simulations
have shown that with the type of demographic constraints outlined
above, even if every family was consciously seeking to produce an
extended or multiple household, only about 30 percent would ever be able
to do it" (1991, 25). "With alarming regularity they would have found
themselves running short of food in the face of climatically induced
shortfalls in production" (1991, 110).

In Iron Age Israel, and in the centuries immediately following, a similar situation undoubtedly prevailed (cf. Marfoe 1980, 5; Dar 1986, 4–6).

The extended family was a buffer for peasant survival. However, Bendor (1996) demonstrates that the lack of social solidarity (within the beth-ab, with its discreet familial units) contributed directly to the impoverishment or debt-bondage of its weakest and most vulnerable members. For even when a family reached maximum size with three generations present, the average farm would have been able to supply only a portion of the household's needs (cf. Broshi and Finkelstein 1992). Here in a nutshell is the reason why the peasants of Israel (both before and after the Exile) were intrinsically susceptible to the onset of extremes of poverty. In good years, and when the family cycle is most efficient, the food supply would be only barely sufficient. In bad years the vulnerable members would starve. If the primary unit was not the extended family but the nuclear family as some scholars maintain (Lang 1985, 85–86; Stager 1985, 18–23) or a combination of the two (Faust 1999, 2000a, 2000b) the situation may well have been even worse. What survival mechanisms there were would have been put under tremendous strain even without human interference.

One of the major factors, referred to above, in changing the lives of the peasants of Judah, was the invasion of the northern kingdom of Israel and Judah herself by the Assyrians. This period was a time of great upheaval. Finkelstein (1994) suggests that following the devastation by Sennacherib, the Shephelah lost up to seventy percent of its population. The Judahite state and Jerusalem grew significantly in size as refugees from the Assyrian incursions arrived (Gibson 1983–84). Even the arid zones to the south and east of the Judean hills, including the valley of Beersheba, were settled. Such demographic pressures and economic necessity due to the loss of the rich cereal-producing lands of the Shephelah led to the farming of marginal lands (Finkelstein 1994, 175–87). The lives of the Judean peasants, never easy at any time, would have become more difficult in such lands and poverty must have increased.

5.6. *Peasant Survival Mechanisms*

Survival was the primary goal of the occupants of the Highland villages. Intemperate weather (droughts and floods), natural disasters (locusts, blight and mildew), diseases (of people and of cattle), predators (both human and animal or reptile) and the incursion of bandits and robbers or wars were just some of the challenges these peasants faced. Garnsey (1988) and Gallant (1991) have shown how Mediterranean peasants, over the centuries, depended on various mechanisms for their survival. Apart from pure survival, "peasants are averse to undertakings which put their subsistence at risk, or to phrase it another way, they would actively seek to minimise subsistence risk and so avoid activities which would increase the level of risk" (Gallant 1991, 7; cf. Popkin 1979, 18). The peasant poor of Israel did not slide into poverty and starvation without fighting for their survival.

For Gallant, knowledge of the system of "culturally constructed coping mechanisms" is critical for establishing the level of risk or vulnerability of a given society (1991, 5; see Timmerman 1981, 17–36). Gallant lists and discusses several of these coping mechanisms (1991, 113–96) as they were applied in classical Greece. These included watching the weather and adapting one's farm management in response, crop diversification, storage against bad years and various crisis interventions, including selling one's land or one's family, and even abandoning one's land (cf. Garnsey 1988); "Since most peasants exist much of the time on the very margin of viability anyway, they consistently and predictably select production strategies which enable them to lessen the risk of production failures" (Gallant 1991, 7; cf. Popkin 1979, 18).

Hopkins (1985, 211–62), with specific concern for the Highland villages of Iron Age Israel, specifies a number of other strategies, which he calls "risk spreading," ranging from choice of crops, timing of planting and harvesting, to livestock husbandry, social structures and institutions. The norm was a multi-crop risk-spreading strategy, which involved herds and flocks, cereals and gardens, vines and fruit trees to ensure the survival of peasant families (1985, 250–54). The key to peasant life in Israel similarly was adaptability, with strategies such as staggered sowing and other techniques of coping being implemented, in a climate where as many as three years out of ten might end in crop failure (Matthews and Benjamin 1993, 38). So the peasants attempted to store a portion of their crops each year, to extend their allotments as far as labour permitted, and to use different farming techniques to achieve a reasonable return for their efforts and expenses (Hopkins 1985; Borowski 1987).

5.6.1. *The Supply of Food and Other Resources*

Ensuring adequate food supplies was the first priority for peasants. Without such resources, they would have been unable to work their lands. The effectiveness of their labour was related to the amount of calories consumed by the individual workers, although estimates of the quantities required vary (Dewalt and Pelto 1977). Peasant diet in the Mediterranean region (see Foxhall and Forbes 1982; Gallant 1991, 62–78; Angel 1975; Bisel 1980) has changed very little over the centuries. Traditionally, it has included cereals (wheat and barley, and less often maize and millet), pulses (chickpeas, broad or kidney beans, lentils and peas) and various fruits including vines and finally olives (Foxhall and Forbes 1982). Approximately 65–70 percent of the diet of Mediterranean peasants was cereal products, 20–25 percent fruits, pulses or vegetables, and 5–15 percent oils, meats and wine (Gallant 1991, 68). Osteology and paleo-pathology suggest both the sufficiency of the ancient diet compared to modern diets, and a probable higher intake of pulses than today, which is not always reflected in the written sources (Angel 1975). This diet is consistent with the pattern observable for biblical Israel (Hamel 1989, 9–10) in the choice of crops, with only minor variations (cf. Sir 29:21; 39:26; Pilch 1993).

During the Early Iron Age, as the plant finds from Lachish indicate, crops of wheat, barley and other cereals and pulses were grown (Negev 1972b, 16). The most important cereal for the Iron Age right through to New Testament times was barley (Hamel 1989, 30, 34) because of its hardiness and tolerance of harsh conditions—producing rough peasant bread (Borowski 1987, 7). Wheat was rarer, being less hardy than barley, but producing superior flour and so was the preferred choice for bread where climate and wealth allowed (Turkowski 1969, 110). Bread formed the principle focus of diet, as is evident from the biblical texts on rations and foodstuffs (Deut 8:8; 2 Sam 17:28; 2 Chr 2:10; Ezek 4:9). Added to bread was a kind of gruel (vegetable based) while dishes of vegetables, salads, olives and fresh or dried fruit extended the meal.

Peasant agriculture in Israel also included plantations of olive trees, carobs, figs, dates, grapes, ethrogs (citrus), apples, pomegranates, apricots and other fruit (eaten fresh or dried) and a variety of vegetables including leeks, onions, lentils, broad beans, bitter vetch, chick-peas and garlic (Borowski 1987, 7). Fish, salted or fresh, shell fish and other edible sea or river creatures complemented poultry, eggs, cheese (or curds), sour milk, game or other meat and nuts, and yoghurt used to make cheese (Grigson 1998, 265). Rations, whether for soldiers or widows, were calculated in terms of bread and wine. Implicitly vegetables were included, especially legumes, and these would have supplied some of the necessary vitamins, minerals and trace elements (cf. Deut 11:10; 1 Kgs 21:2; Num 11:5; GiPad 1990–91). Olives, wine and beer (Judg 13:7), various herbs and spices (cumin and coriander) and other local edibles completed the menu, and flax, linseed and sesame completed the types of crop (Grigson 1998, 249–50). The summer crops of cumin and flax were sown first and then the wheat and barley. The timing of the sowing was critical and the observant farmer watched the weather very carefully (Deist 2000, 150–51).

Olive production for both oil (Mic 6:15) and fruit (Num 18:12; Deut 28:51) is known from Natufian times (Jericho) and was in regular use in the Iron Age (Patella 1988; Frick 1999, 3). Olives were used for food, cooking, treating leather, lamp fuel, cosmetics, offerings and medicines (Frick 1999, 5). Olive oil also served in social situations (the finest forms of olive oil are mentioned in the Samarian texts of the eighth century; cf. Stager 1983; Amos 6:6) and for religious purposes (cf. Ps 133:2). Archaeology also testifies to the early use of viticulture for wine, vinegar and grapes (Ruth 2:14; Hos 2:7; Dan 10:3; Amos 2:8). Wine formed a critical part of Israel's social and religious life (Matthews 1999b). Isaiah 5:1–7 details the various practices that attended the planting of a vineyard and may be considered relevant for the Iron Age periods.

Flocks provided milk, clothing and meat. Proverbs instructs:

> Be careful to know the state of your flock and take care of your herds; for possessions do not last for ever, nor will a crown endure to endless generations. The grass is cropped, new shoots are seen, and the green growth on the hills is gathered in; for the lambs provide you with clothing, and the he-goats with the price of a field, while the goat's milk is food enough for your household and sustenance for your servant-girls (Prov 27:23–27)

Aside from slaughter of live-stock, hunting and trapping and fishing provided additional sources of protein (Bratton 1987, 225). One of the gates of Jerusalem was designated as the Fish Gate (2 Chr 33:14; Jer 16:16), signifying the importance of fish during the later Iron Age (cf. Deist 2000, 136). Meat rarely occurred in the diet of the peasants of Israel (Hamel 1989, 19) except for festal occasions when it was a part of the celebration. Faunal remains from the Iron Age site at Mount Ebal included four species of large mammals, making up 96 percent of the bones found, namely, sheep and goats (65%), cattle (21%) and fallow deer (10%). Other bones included those of small animals, birds and fish (Horwitz 1986–87). The constraints of a community without refrigeration usually meant that meat, unless dried, needed to be consumed within hours of slaughtering, which led to the sharing among the community of anything larger than poultry and birds.

All sources of food came at a price, either in terms of exchange value or in terms of time and expended labour, especially for rural women. In the contemporary South African situation, a rural woman might spend more than four hours per day or more collecting firewood and water for the household (Key Indicators 1995, 18). Peasant women in Israel would also have spent time grinding wheat or maize, baking bread or porridge and taking care of the vegetable garden, aside from the routine of helping in the fields, together with caring for the young children and infants (little happens outside of daylight hours). In times of famine, in addition to these tasks, the woman must venture into the hills and surrounding valleys in search of edible roots, fruits and herbs (cf. Rackham 1983, 347–49; Hamel 1989, 18). Food was a constant time-consuming reality and we have seen that only a small group of peasants ever had more than the bare minimum.

The size of land allocations varied more between rich and poor than from one peasant community to another, and this is true both for the ANE and for modern times. Gallant cites ancient and modern sources which show that peasants considered 3–6 hectares to be a desirable subsistence farm in the Mediterranean region (1991, 84). Modern peasant studies, from Greece (Gallant 1991), Portugal (Cutleiro 1971), Russia (Chayanov 1986, 174–79) and Palestine (Warriner 1957), show that 50 percent of the peasant farms are on average smaller than 3 hectares and about 66–75 percent are smaller than 5 hectares (Gallant 1991, 85 fig 4.7). In ancient Ur, where land formed a substitute for food rations, the size of an allotment varied from 2.25 acres for a common labourer (0.9 hectares) to 96 acres (38.88 hectares) for a priest (Waetzoldt 1987, 129). This means that most of the peasants of Ur farmed areas of land which were barely adequate for subsistence. Speaking of modern Syria, Marfoe (1980, 6) notes that 7 percent of the owners of land held almost two-thirds of the cultivated lands, meaning that most farmers were actually share-croppers, tenants or wage labourers. Their average farms were barely half a hectare, and yields were of the order of 300 kg per hectare in some places, meaning that the peasants were operating under the subsistence level in some years (1980, 6).

The pattern for biblical Israel evidenced from Dar's analysis of the archaeological data (1986, 4–6) is similar. Dar's studies of farms in Israel in the Late Iron Age (IIA and B) puts the average size of such farms at between 10 and 16 hectares of which only 10–20 percent was under agriculture (1986, 4–6). Even in good years and with reasonable soils and rainfall, this would barely suffice for an average nuclear family and their needs, especially if rents and taxes are added into the equation (cf. Marfoe 1980, 5). The allotments were simply too small to sustain life other than in the most marginal of fashions and yet the peasants survived. In this unequal struggle, new tools, like the iron plough, would play a major role.

5.6.2. *The Iron Plough*

The early history of agrarian Israel comes with the start of the Iron Age and the gradual transition from the bronze to the iron plough, with the introduction also of other iron tools. The assumption that the iron tools were a critical factor in the settlement within the Central Highlands (Gottwald 1979, 655; Borowski 1979, 10; Chaney 1983, 50) is probably correct, but that such tools provided the technological basis for the settling of the Highlands (Chaney 1983, 50) may be challenged. The transition from iron to bronze was a gradual one, and throughout Iron Age I, bronze continued to be "the chief metal, used for most of the tools, weapons, vessels, and art objects" (Mazar 1992, 298). Limited numbers of iron tools appeared for the first time in the eleventh century B.C.E. (1992, 298). Until the discovery of carburization and quenching sometime in the tenth century, bronze remained superior.

Indeed, it was not until the beginning of Iron Age II that iron overtook bronze as the dominant metal used, perhaps as a result of a shortage of tin (Waldbaum 1978). The nearest known region for mining tin was present-day Afghanistan (Mazar 1992, 298). The original source of the iron technology found in early Israel is still unclear, but the indications point to Greek origins. At present, the oldest iron implements are those found in Philistine contexts (Tell Qasile; cf. Mazar 1992, 298). In the light of these finds, 1 Sam 13:19–22 might refer to a Philistine monopoly of iron-working (Bright 1974, 169, 181), but, as Mazar points out, the type of metal envisaged is not actually mentioned (1992, 298). Presumably, as the Proto-Israelites migrated ahead of the Philistine expansion, they carried the new iron technology with them.

From the tenth century onwards, the new iron technology clearly dominates, and iron tools abound in the Highlands and elsewhere in Cisjordan (Mazar 1992, 298). Among these tools are the iron sheaths that were part of the plough, an example of which was found in Beersheba and dated to Iron II (Thompson 1984). The so-called scratch-plough, the oldest form of plough known, was a bent wooden pole, one end held by the operator and the other sheathed in iron, forced into the earth (Wolf 1966, 32). "The plow-point was an elongated tool, 20–30 cm long, with a pointed tip for soil penetration. The other end was shaped like a pipe ca. 8–10 cm wide. A wooden shaft, which was part of the plow-handle, was inserted into this end" (Borowski 1987, 51). Examples have been found at various archaeological sites, including Beersheba and Beth-Shemesh (1987, 49–50).

Unlike the heavier European version, the Mediterranean plough cut less deeply, but, at the same time, prevented loss of moisture from beneath the ground.

> The ard [plough] is especially adapted to light and friable soils where the chief problem is to prevent moisture from rising to the surface by capillary attraction. Where a heavier plough would damage the capillaries and cause the water to evaporate during the summer drought, the ard merely scratches the soil, thus keeping the capillary system intact. (Wolf 1966, 32)

This plough was still used in northern Jordan when Palmer conducted her research there in 1989–92, indicative of the intense conservatism of peasant life as well as the usefulness of the value of such modern parallels for biblical times (Palmer 1998).

The iron-cased plough had several advantages over the hoe, especially in the rocky areas of the Central Highlands of Israel (Hopkins 1985). The plough was drawn by oxen or cattle and was able to turn the ground more effectively than hoes (cf. Prov 14:4), cutting more deeply into the soil and at a faster rate. Both in antiquity and today, the plough and the hoe are used side by side (Gallant 1991, 50). Isaiah refers to both the hoe (7:25) and the plough (28:23–25). Deist, following contemporary examples, writes, "the custom in these regions is first to dig up the virgin soil by hoe and then to plough it" (2000, 149).

The economic aspects of the use of the plough are not difficult to uncover. Both plough and oxen were expensive commodities to acquire, and the oxen had also to be fed (cf. Isa 30:24) even when they were not being used for ploughing, which was most of the time (Wagstaff and Gamble 1982, 100). Some farmers, like their Greek counterparts, may have preferred to share or borrow oxen, or used donkeys and mules (Gallant 1991, 51). If villages were unable to supply such animals, the way was opened for forms of share-cropping. Already the seeds of inequality are present. In spite of the costs involved in the use of the plough, the alternative forms of working a field, such as by hand or by hoe, were time consuming, especially given limited labour supplies.

Where possible, peasants over the ages preferred to conserve their labour for other labour intensive activities like weeding (Jordan and Shaner 1979, 267). For example, Basler estimates that weeding fields of lentils would have required about 56 days labour per hectare (1982, 147). In times of drought, effective weeding would greatly increase the final yield so there was a powerful motive. Weeding was done using hoes, and some weeds might be used as feed for the animals, along with legumes, barley and chopped straw and hay (Negev 1972b, 16).

Harvesting from earliest times was done by sickle, with the stalks being cut high to supply stubble for grazing, which in turn offered a chance for the fertilisation of the field by the cattle (Negev 1972b, 16; Deist 2000, 149). Deist comments upon the various stages of harvesting and shows how these provided a rich metaphorical source for many biblical passages (2000, 153–55), extending from celebration to judgment. Flint sickles continued in use throughout much of the Iron Age in Cisjordan, and were only gradually replaced by iron equivalents. Peasant societies are exceedingly conservative and inimical to change.

The labour intensity of peasant agrarian pursuits is evident in the HB. "Dill must not be threshed with a threshing-sledge, nor the cartwheel rolled over the cumin; but dill is beaten with a rod and cumin with a flail. Grain is crushed, but not too long or too finely; cartwheels rumble over it and thresh it, but they do not grind it fine" (Isa 28:27–28). The reference is to oxen pulling a threshing sled or stone-threshing roller over the grain (Negev 1972b, 16). Borowski amply illustrates both the processes and the tools employed (1987, 57–69). Straw was used for kindling (Isa 5:24) or in small pieces as a binder for brick making (Exod 5:7, 12) or as animal fodder (Isa 11:7), while the chaff was either thrown away (or blown away; cf. Ps 1:4) or used as cushioning between the storage jars. Little was wasted in this economy of thrift. Lives depended on eking out every advantage for survival.

5.6.3. *Irrigation*

The most critical survival mechanism for the peasants of the Central Highlands and the Negev of Iron II related to the supply of water. The agrarians of Israel throughout the millennia have practiced two forms of farming, namely, what is called dry or dry-land farming (Oakman 1986, 20) and run-off farming (Evenari, Shanan and Tadmor 1971). Run-off farming involved some form of primitive irrigation, usually involving cisterns or rainwater channels. Dry farming had no irrigation at all, relying instead strictly on the normal rainfall. In the case of dry farming, terraces served to maximise the rainfall.

In the Negev, natural wadis and artificial conduits channelled rainwater into the fields (terraced or otherwise). "Each farm had its own well-defined catchment area, which constituted its water right. Since every square metre of every hillside was allotted to specific water rights, an intricate pattern of catchment boundaries arose" (Evenari, Shanan and Tadmor 1971, 109; see further 95–147). Once again, in these restricted water rights, we see the seeds of inequality. While many of the Negev features surveyed belong to the Nabateans, earlier remains have been found that may be dated to the beginning of Iron II, with subsequent settlements in the eighth and seventh centuries respectively (Stager 1976; Borowski 1987, 18–20). These are the indications, most likely, of the increased pressure on agricultural land by population spread following the fall of the Kingdom of Israel.

For Iron Age Cisjordan, only limited use was made of water from rock-hewn cisterns, or from wells (e.g. Beersheba). Some hand watering took place in the small plots used for vegetables or spices, but it was not practical, of course, for the fields or vineyards (Evenari, Shanan and Tadmor 1971, 132). Dry farming, the norm for the Central Highlands, is a practice typical of countries in which figures for rainfall average less than 250–500 mm (20 inches) and operates without any form of irrigation, relying purely on natural precipitation (Hopkins 1985, 91–94). The Gezer calendar (see above) speaks of ploughing after first rains and planting barley and wheat (late October/November). Barley was harvested just after the second rains, in April/May, and the wheat one month later. Grapes were gathered in August/September (King 1988a, 108–9).

The nature of the terrain has meant that the agrarians of Israel outside of the Coastal Plain have little opportunity to use rivers, like the Jordan or the Yarmusk, to water their crops. The primary reason was the abrupt changes in height from one part of the country to the other—Hebrew lacks even a term for irrigated land (Hopkins 1985, 186–87). The Jordan Valley lay deep inside the extension of the Great Rift Valley, meaning that its water (including the Huleh Lake and Galilee) could only be transported into a very limited area for irrigation (Negev 1972b, 16). Only the Coastal Plains and the plain of Megiddo were suitable for irrigation, and much of those areas were controlled in the early Iron Age by first the Philistines and then the Phoenicians. Rainfall, therefore, played a key role as the list of terms for rain suggests (Deist 2000, 125) and the various symbolic allusions and narratives indicate (2000, 124–28). Rain meant life for Israelite peasants, but it had to come at the right time and in the right quantities.

Major centres like Hazor, Megiddo, Beersheba and Jerusalem all had elaborate water systems (Barkay 1992, 332–33). For example, Jerusalem's water supply centred on the Gihon spring (Reich and Shukron 2000a) and use was made of the so-called Sheloach tunnel, which carried water from the spring to the nearby fields by means of a series of openings and a system of gates (Shiloh 1984, 22–23). While some of these systems may be dated to the Middle Bronze Age, most belong to the later Iron Age—the time of Hezekiah (Barkay 1992, 333; Reich and Shukron 2000a). Their very nature suggests they served the interests primarily of the urban elite. In times of war, even water and firewood became commodities for sale as underlined by at least one text. "We must buy the water that we drink; our wood can be had only at a price" (Lam 5:4). Worldwide, and throughout time, peasants have struggled daily with these two necessities of life, water and wood.

5.6.4. *Terraces*

More efficacious than irrigation for the Central Highlands was the use of terracing, still widely practiced today. Modern Israel is a patchwork of terraces, particularly across the Central Highlands and large areas of the West Bank. The dating of the terraces is a complex issue (Hopkins 1985,

183). Gibson (2001) finds their origins as far back as the Early Bronze period, although he notes that widespread terracing did not occur until the Iron Age II period. Borowski believes that terrace farming was a prerequisite for settlement within the Highlands (1979, 29). Hopkins argues that terracing was a delayed response to the exigencies of settlement, particularly the issue of increased population (1985, 179–86). Whatever the date of the earliest terraces, it is clear that they were part and parcel of Iron Age agriculture in the Central Highlands (Stager 1976, 13). They would have been found initially only on the northern warmer and drier slopes of the Judaean hills, with later terraces occurring also on the cooler southern slopes (Ron 1966, 38).

Cities of the Central Highlands, like Jerusalem, were surrounded by terraced fields. For example, the City of David excavations (1978–84 in Jerusalem) revealed agricultural terrace walls along the eastern bank of the Kidron Valley. These walls date back to the Bronze Ages, and were prominent in the Iron Age II from the eighth century onwards and again in the Hellenistic period (De Geus 1975, 68–69; Shiloh 1984, 2). Agricultural terraces first appear in the neighbouring valleys (Reph'aim and Mevasseret Yerushalayim) bordering Jerusalem in the Iron II period (Edelstein and Milevski 1994), indicative of the growing urban needs and the pressures of population.

Terracing throughout the Central Highland region offered a way of capitalising on the limited rainfall, by allowing water to seep from one terrace to another and so favouring the lower terraces over the upper ones (Turkowski 1969). The predominant type of terrace used in the region may be described as a linear sloping, dry field terrace (cf. Spencer and Hale 1961, 4–15), which is essentially the "creation of arable land behind a stone wall built laterally across a hillside" (Hopkins 1985, 174). Edelstein and Gibson (1982, 52) draw attention to no less than five types of walls used in the Highlands.

Depending on the terrain and the soil profile, there were occasions when soil was transplanted from the valley floor to form the fill (Edelstein and Gat 1980–81, 73). Clearly in most instances, the building of terraces required considerable human labour (Edelstein and Gat 1980–81, 73), not forgetting maintenance (Turkowski 1969, 24). "The purpose of the terrace walls was to stabilise the terraces and also to allow flood water to be ponded in the terraced field where it could soak into the soil and be stored for subsequent use by the crops" (Evenari, Shanan and Tadmor 1971, 110). Terracing hillsides increased the available area of land for planting, while preventing loss of top soil through erosion (Dar 1986, 6). The upper levels of the terraces would be kept for the planting of olive trees requiring the average rainfall or less. In the lower levels, where the water from above joined with the natural precipitation, more thirsty crops were found (cereals or legumes). Cattle grazing the stubble of the fields served to fertilize the various levels.

Vines, olive and nut trees were the primary crops to benefit from the use of terraces. However, the early Iron Age farmers of Ai and Khirbet Raddana grew cereals, and so established a pattern that was to become common for the villages of the Central Highlands (Stager 1976, 13). In this way, these villagers were able to exist in independence from the main wheat- and barley-growing areas of the Coastal Plain and the valley of Megiddo (Chaney 1983, 50). This is consistent with the idea that these settlers were escaping from the pressures of the coastal dwellers, particularly the invading Sea Peoples. In the later Iron Age, Israelite control of substantial parts of both of these areas led to a specialisation within the Highlands, and a form of exchange with the low-lying areas. The difficulty of moving large quantities of cereals, in particular, probably militated against the complete abandonment of the growing of cereals in the Highlands.

5.6.5. *Storage*

Scott speaks in terms of "the need for…reliable subsistence [as] the primordial goal of the peasant cultivator" (1976, 5). One significant coping mechanism is the reservation, in good years, of a percentage of the crop against future bad years. Hopkins stresses the value of storage as a "buffer against the greatly variable yields of Highland agriculture" (1985, 169). This is often done as a community, and under the guidance (or authority) of the head of the village. According to Gallant, peasant communities in classical Greece, left on their own, will aim to have a year to eighteen months supply of food set aside (1991, 94). Naturally, storage brings its own risks like damp, insect infestation or rodents. Part of each year's crop will be lost and this needs to be factored into the equation. While storage is equipped to deal with the periodic droughts, famine would pose a severe problem.

5.6.5.1. *Large Scale Storage Facilities*. As the demand of the royal court (cf. 2 Chr 8:4–6) and the Jerusalem temple grew, so the peasant surplus became a critical part of the economy. Public grain storages are found at Samaria, Megiddo, Hazor and Beth Shemesh, including the so-called pillared storehouses labelled initially as Solomon's stables, but now seen to belong to the Omride dynasty (Borowski 1987, 8; cf. 2 Chr 32:28). Herzog links these storehouses with tax collection and distribution

(1992a, 225–28). The stamped jar handles found in Iron II Judah appear to testify to a similar administration system imposed by Hezekiah (Barkay 1992, 346). The excavations of Megiddo and other sites have produced some very large silos (Silo 1414 from Megiddo had a capacity of 450 cubic metres), which Borowski believes were for communal storage purposes (1987, 74–75).

Holladay (1998) disagrees. Certainly palaces, military sites and religious centres would have had their own storage facilities and their "own dependency networks, presumably based on localised patterns of taxation, purchase and tithing" (1998, 393), but the norm remained for individual family units to create their own storage facilities. He cites examples drawn from Lachish, Khirbet Radana, Beth Shemesh, Tell Beit Mirsim and Beersheba. Based on a calculation of 15 cubic metres per household with average of 100 houses per village, Holladay shows that this is nearly four times the capacity of the silo at Hazor (Area G) or that of Megiddo (mentioned above)— two of the largest silos in ancient Israel (1998, 393). In fact, it is only in post-exilic Judah, with a changing economic climate, that one finds indications of large-scale storage facilities that would have served communal purposes (Dar 1986). This meant that for the peasants of monarchic Israel, storage was their concern, with both the advantages and disadvantages of such a system.

5.6.5.2. *Small Scale Storage Facilities.* In the Early Iron Age villages of Ai, storage was affected through the use of underground silos or grain-pits, carved out of the limestone rock and accessed from above (Callaway 1976). The silos were bell-shaped and very similar in shape and design to the underground cisterns. Most of the grain silos, from their frequency and association with particular houses, appear to have served one or two households only (Borowski 1987, 72–73; Holladay 1998, 389). These underground silos, often lined with plaster, occur across both the Central Highlands, as far north as Dan and as far south as Beersheba. Such pits are, indeed, a characteristic feature of the Iron Age (Mazar 1992, 289). In the mid-1980s, the Lahav Grain Storage Project constructed four replicas and found them to be effective in storing grain with the benefit of retarding rodent activity, moisture build-up and bacterial formation, but not insect intrusion (Currid and Navon 1989).

Home storage continued as the norm for the divided monarchy until the Exile and even beyond (Holladay 1998, 389). Holladay concludes "In ancient Israel, debts, rents, tithes, and taxation exempted, the harvests of field, vine, orchard, flocks and herds were gathered into individual houses.... In economic and logistical terms, these houses were 'the storehouses of Israel'" (1998, 393).

In individual homes, heavy storage took place on the ground floor and lighter materials were stored on the roof. Mazar draws attention also to the various storage vessels (*pithoi*), including the collared rim jar (about 1.2 m in height) used for the preservation of liquids, and characteristic of the settlement period (1992, 290). Sometimes called the "settlement jar," the container (*pithos*) in fact appeared in the Late Bronze Age (Aphek) and was common to both Israelite Highland villages and to Transjordan sites (Sahab, Tell Qasile and Megiddo stratum 6) which belonged to non-Israelite communities (Mazar 1992, 290). In Galilee, a different shaped storage jar appeared in Hazor during the Late Bronze Age (Mazar 1992, 291). The function of such jars was primarily storage, with smaller *pithoi* being used for trade. Canaanite jars from the Late Bronze Age have appeared throughout the Mediterranean region indicating extensive trade links (Holladay 1998, 389).

Albright (1960, 113) speaks of the art of lining water cisterns (in the early Iron Age) with waterproof lime plaster, a great improvement over the unlined cisterns, and a means to settlement in areas deemed previously to be uninhabitable. In this connection, the Moabite stone carries an instruction from Mesha (king of the Moabites) to a captured Israelite city, to the effect that there was inadequate provision for the storage of water. Mesha then instructed the people "Make yourselves each one a cistern in his house" (Cogan and Tadmor 1988, 333–34). Self-reliance for storage either of grain or water seems to have been the norm for the region. By placing the onus of the individual families, the peasants of Israel enjoyed a particular level of independence. There was, however, also a marked increase in the level of risk. If drought struck their area, they would need to find help in other areas not so badly affected—a difficult thing for ordinary peasants to do.

5.6.6. *The Fallow Year*
Fallowing was another strategy used throughout the Mediterranean (Boserup 1965; Gallant 1991, 52–56). Different soil types required different responses. Allan (1965, 30–35) suggests that at one end of the spectrum was the soil of land that could sustain alternate years of cropping, over against soils that demanded much longer periods of fallow after just a few years of cropping, due to the depletion of the soil. Nevertheless, it was widely practised in the ANE.

Writing about peasants in the early part of the twentieth century in Iraq and Syria (including parts of the West Bank), Warriner comments that "For wheat and barley the fallow system, with fallow every second year or even two years out of three, is the general rotation" (Warriner 1957, 57). She goes on to write that in the Central Range the abundant rainfall and fertile soil allowed for a form of semi-intensive agriculture, based on the continuous cultivation of the soil. Winter and summer crops might be produced on the same fields, and there would be a two- or three-yearly rotation of crops. Large-sized villages were found in the dry zones of the country where the land worked in alternate years and only for the production of winter crops (1957, 166).

Stirling, speaking of Turkish peasants, makes mention of alternate years of fallow, with a switch from one side of the village to the other, including switching pasture (1971, 45). Taking the various studies into account, one might argue that the norm for Israel over the centuries would probably have been a bi-annual fallow with crop rotation (see below). Peasant practices over the centuries rarely change without the introduction of some new technology. Each field would be worked once out of every two years, leaving the ground fallow in the intervening years, to be used as grazing lands, and so fertilised. Such fallowing excluded distant grazing land and land reserved for orchards, for vines or for vegetables.

For the Highland villages of Iron Age Israel, Turkowski (1969) pre-supposes a biennial fallow. He describes the process as follows: Virgin land was cleared of bushes and stones. The soil was dug by hoe, and ploughed several times in succession. Then the land was divided in two. Half of the land was planted and the rest left fallow, for the pasture of herds, whose droppings in turn fertilised the soil. The following year, the fallow land is ploughed and the process reversed. The breaking of the soil is timed with the first winter rains (December to January), without which the ploughing would be too difficult. The ploughed field in turn is able to absorb more moisture, as the rains continued (Turkowski 1969, 25–33).

The provisions of a seven-year Sabbath for the land (Exod 23:10–11) is held by Borowski (1987, 144) to signify that each farmer left fallow one seventh of his land each year, while recognising that modern prac-tices in Israel employ a two- or three-year cycle (1987, 145 n. 2). Hopkins (1985, 192–95) concludes his discussion by opting for a combination of biennial fallow together with the seven-year law (so too Negev 1972b, 16; Turkowski 1969, 25–33; Deist 2000, 145). More fallow rather than less appeared to be the guiding principle, so long as sufficient land was available (Kaufman 1984, 280). Modern parallels concur (cf. Turkowski 1969; Stirling 1971). Halstead (1987) reasons that more productive than fallowing was the use of manured annual cropping and some form of legume–cereal rotation. The peasants of Israel with their herds would have been able to make some use of both manure and legumes, without excluding the use of fallowing.

5.6.7. *Herds*

Archaeological data over the millennia in Israel testifies to the practice of combining flocks and fields (Ben-Tor 1992a). The remains of domesticated animals date back to Neolithic times (Bar-Yosef 1992, 27–28). Sheep, cattle and goats formed the major herds in Iron Age Israel (Callaway 1976; Deist 2000, 159–65) and the shape of the village formed a natural protective environment. Aside from using cattle and flocks as forms of investment and as sources of food and clothing, grazing herds in harvested fields, orchards and fallow land contributed, through manuring, to the fertility of the land (Hopkins 1985, 247). In turn the remains of the harvested crops supplied food for the animals. This pattern of symbiosis has a lengthy history within Israel (Ben-Tor 1992a), appearing long before the Iron Age settlers of the Central Highlands.

In what has all the markings of a genuine historical reflection, the HB testifies to the keeping of royal herds. Under the divided monarchy, Uzziah is said to have erected towers (fortresses) in the wilderness and dug many cisterns, in order to provide both protection and water for his herds of cattle located both in the Shephelah and the plain (2 Chr 26:10a).

5.7. *Conclusion*

Gallant (1991, 5) in reference to classical Greece, argues "that drought, floods and warfare are not on their own sufficient cause for famine." He concludes that the occurrence of famines is related to multiple interactive causes (1991, 4–7). Drought is more than an issue about weather, and has much to do with human interaction. Cipolla (1976, 129–35, 151) cites ancient Greek sources, which speak of passing enemy armies burning barns, confiscating livestock and spreading plagues across the land. When the Romans besieged Jerusalem in 70 CE, they cut and burned every olive tree in the vicinity and so crippled the economy for many decades (Patella 1988). Invariably, peasants suffered from such actions as they did from drought and famine and yet where else might help be found except through some form of human intervention?

What the study of the agrarian methods, which obtained in the Highland villages, is unable to portray is this human factor. The peasants of Israel succeeded in carving a life out of the Highlands of Israel. That they did this in spite of the troubled climate, the difficult terrain and the poor soils is certain and that they did this with simple but effective technology is beyond doubt. Certain also would have been the slow drift into some form of patronage. This is the focus of the next chapter, as I move toward understanding the impact of human intervention, rather than natural challenges, on the peasants of Israel.

Chapter 6

PATRONAGE IN ANCIENT ISRAEL

6.1. *In Times of Need*

The extended household, when other forms of survival failed, served the peasants of Israel and Judah as their first line of defence (cf. Eisenstadt and Roniger 1984). Such needs might be anything from temporary food supplies to tide one over, to more lengthy assistance in times of drought or war. The next option was for these peasants to locate someone or some community with food reserves, and barter for such supplies. So much may be deduced from parallels with other peasant communities in the ancient Mediterranean world (cf. Gallant 1991, 143–69; Eisenstadt and Roniger 1984).

Given the fact that, in most of the Mediterranean region (as in the ANE), drought or floods or other natural disasters tended to be localised, help might be found in a neighbouring province, or even in a neighbouring village (Gallant 1991, 158). In Nuzi (early second millennium B.C.E.), for example, texts speak of peasants coming into alliance with one another (Dosch 1987, 224). Indeed, such an arrangement (a bilateral exchange agreement between two communities) was on occasion set up in advance, so anticipating a future crisis (see Gallant 1991, 181, for examples from classical Greece). The third option was to appeal to the state or the temple for assistance. Only if all these systems failed was the answer to be found in some form of patronage, simply because of the long-term implications of such an alliance, particularly the loss of personal freedom.

6.2. *Temples and the State*

In some ANE societies, the state or temple might intervene utilising their own reserves in times of drought or famine (see Lipinski 1979a; Gelb 1979). So, for example, at various times in ancient Egypt, the temples could be counted on to take care of thousands of poor peasants, from the resources built up over the years (Janssen 1979; Goedicke 1979).

Similarly, for Babylonia of the first millennium B.C.E., a key function of both the temple and palace was to store provisions from which communities might benefit in times of crises such as famine or war (Dandamayev 1979). Large-scale projects, like building or repairing canals and dykes, might also be funded from these reserves (Chirichigno 1993, 36; Oppenheim 1977, 84–85). Redman suggests that the temples, like those of Egypt in the second millennium B.C.E., were the first sector of the state to develop as a large-scale agricultural project with an extended labour force (Redman 1978, 256–57).

To what extent the Jerusalem temple was seen as provider for the people during the biblical period is uncertain. Appeals to the generosity and care of Yahweh found in the HB, however, may well have been intended for the ears of the priesthood. The tithe and various sacrifices demanded of the populace, apart from supplying the needs of the priesthood, probably were designed to be a buffer against difficult times for the peasants. Similarly, one might presume that the temples of Israel and Judah would have been expected to look out for the interests of the peasant majority in times of need, but actual texts related to this action are scant.

Temple-owned land in ancient Israel is attested to in the use of the term "migras," which implies the common land of the temple (Borowski 1987, 30), and which may well have been quite extensive especially around temples of the size and import of Jerusalem (Neufeld 1960, 50). Temples also performed storage functions, a necessary protection against bad years, and in some instances even functioned as banks (cf. Zech 14:21).

General references to state land occur in the various biblical sources, although their historical accuracy is open to debate. Land might be confiscated by the different authorities (1 Sam 8:14; 1 Kgs 21) or left vacant (2 Kgs 8:1–6); designated as royal estates (in reference to David— 1 Chr 27:25–31); the king might even free certain estates from tax (Weinfeld 1995, 138, on 1 Sam 17:25). From the period of the divided monarchy, one reads that Uzziah's (Azariah's) royal lands included "farmers and vinedressers in the hill-country and in the fertile lands, for he loved the soil" (2 Chr 26:10b NRSV; cf. Gottwald 2001, 66). Hezekiah, who succeeded Uzziah, is said to have had great wealth, with treasuries for spices and precious stones, barns for the harvest of grain, new wine and oil and stalls for various kinds of cattle and sheep all apparently in great quantities (2 Chr 26:10; 32:27–29; cf. Rainey 1982; Hopkins 1985, 20; Dar 1986, 12–16).

Within the Israelite and Judean states, governments most likely played a role for good or ill—especially in times of drought and war. Once again, the details are sketchy, since the HB is largely silent on these mat-ters. The only positive reference is one that included a foreign govern-ment. Nehemiah, the representative of the Persian state, was expected to provide sustenance in times of need (Neh 5:1–12). Conversely, tax and tributes might have formed some buffer against the bad times, but at some cost to the average peasant.

When state and temple failed, the option was to turn to the members of the ruling elite. The situation in Iron Age Israel may be likened to what happened in ancient Greece through the fourth century B.C.E. Where temple and state or even local government (the village) should have come forward to offer relief, the "community effectively abrogated its role as an agent of subsistence relief to private, wealthy individuals" (Gallant 1991, xii) and patronage on a large scale was the result. The way was opened for private individuals to achieve both power and prestige and to join the ruling elite.

6.3. *The Ruling Elite*

I have chosen to use ruling elite in this book to refer to those people who are seen to possess power, prestige or honour and wealth. They demon-strate their power through the exercise of specific rights of control over land, rights to freedom from taxation, and take their place within a hier-archy of honour (Bendix 1978, 106). Lenski offers the parallel term "power class" as "an aggregation of persons in a society who stand in a similar position with respect to force or some specific form of institu-tionalised power" (Lenski 1984, 74–75). The elite may be more or less than a class, in Lenski's view, and may refer simply to "the highest rank-ing segment of any given social unit, whether a class or a total society, ranked by whatever criterion one chooses" (1984, 78–79).

In the time of the Israelite and Judean monarchy, the ruling elite ful-filled the role of the aristocracy (cf. Kautsky 1982). Lenski (1984, 219, 228) defines the aristocracy generally as "those within an agrarian eco-nomy who, without themselves engaging in agricultural labor, live off the land by controlling the peasants so as to be able to take from them part of their product." In terms of the total population, the aristocracy and their retainer class would make up less than 5 percent, "since the peasant surplus was relatively small and the average aristocrat displayed an excessive appetite for consumption" (Kautsky 1982, 119).

The city life of the aristocracy and the peasant world were light years apart (Eisenstadt 1963, 388–93). Aristocrats derived income from a vari-ety of sources but the chief source was peasant surplus. Duby (1974, 49) also lists taxing or robbing merchants, trade, mining, spoils of war and revenue from other aristocrats. "They may be described as a class, whether so defined by wealth, power, status or economic roles, or in the Marxian sense as those who controlled the means of production" (Kautsky 1982, 119). Moreover "aristocrats always control both the land and the peasants whether under the prevailing property system, they are landowners or not" (1982, 72–75).

In Iron Age Israel, the ruling elite or aristocracy arose with the flourishing of the divided monarchy in the ninth and eighth centuries, aided by the elaborate state apparatus (civil and religious) within the urban centres that accompanied that historical process. Dever lists the possible sub-divisions within the population in Iron Age Israel, ranging from the royal family to the poorest of the poor, which he believes were symptomatic of Israel's burgeoning bureaucracy (1998b, 427–28) and which created the opportunity for forms of inequality. The ruling elite succeeded the informal structures in which various groups, including social bandits and chieftains like David and Solomon, pillaged the surpluses of the peasants in exchange for some form of protection. From the peasant perspective, probably little changed in their continuous struggle for survival.

Finkelstein (1998a, 362) proposes that it was the demand for highland horticultural products by lowland communities that led to rise of stratified complex societies in Iron Age II. Dever blames the actual process of urbanisation: "This transformation under the onslaught of urbanisation and nationalisation resulted in an Israelite and Judaean society that, above all, must have been highly stratified" (1998b, 418). I would add the pressures of foreign tribute and erratic climates, all of which meant that some families became very rich while others fell deeper into poverty (Gossai 1993, 277; cf. Mosala 1989, 101–22). I have shown also how the seeds of division are inherent to peasantry.

The pressure of the powerful Assyrian Empire and later the Babylonian Empire made itself felt across the ANE, not least for the vulnerable countries of Israel and Judah, both in terms of political and economic structures (Carney 1975, 207). The technology of the empire, its professional bureaucracy and army along with the transportation of large numbers of the population, taxation and looting, brought in its train both positive and negative consequences for the people of the Bible. Such pressures must have impacted the Divided Kingdoms and created additional burdens on the peasant population, as we have seen and to which I believe the prophets alluded.

Wealth and power are attracted to the urban areas with an increasing strain on peasant supplies. As the people of the cities grow wealthy, the peasants grow poorer. Estimates are that for every one person in a city, there needed to be fourteen peasants on the fields (Sjoberg 1960).

6.4. *The Signs of Wealth*

Where peasants populated the Highland villages, the wealthy among them chose to move into the urban areas. Based on six archaeological sites in Israel and Philistine, from Iron II (Jerusalem, Dan, Hazor, Gezer, Lachish and Ekron), Dever ventures to postulate a threshold for classification of cities in Palestine of 20 acres or 2,000 people, rather than the traditional figure of 5,000 (1998b, 418; cf. Daviau 1997). Along with Beersheba, these seven sites probably represented the regional administrative centres for Iron II (Dever 1998b, 419). The ground plans of these sites indicate a highly centralised layout, government storehouses, and other signs of centralisation whether political, economic or religious (Herzog 1992; 1992b, 250–61). Thus, these centres formed the natural gathering point for those involved in government and civil administration and their staff. Offering multiple advantages, not least that of safety, cities were attractive places to be and signs of wealth soon became obvious in the size and nature of the dwellings (see below).

Outside of the urban areas, a different picture prevailed. Holladay argues that there was a "remarkably limited range of household sizes... aside from rulers' palaces and associated elite structures in cities" (1998, 395). While there may be a few large four-roomed houses at Tell en-Nasbeh, he interprets these, along with Stager (1990, 94), as an extended family home and so quite different to the large estates of post-exilic times (Holladay 1998, 391). Faust's survey of Highland villages notes the same uniformity of house sizes throughout Iron II (2000a). This sharp contrast between villages and urban areas is consistent with a peasant economy such as that of Israel and Judah until the Hellenistic age with the rise of large estates with their attendant dwellings (Holladay 1998, 391). We come now to examine the evidence for people of wealth in the ethnography of the HB and the archaeology of Israel.

6.4.1. *The Ethnography*

The HB regularly contrasts the peasant poor with a group of people, to whom we might refer as the wealthy or the ruling elite. In his description of the elite in Iron Age Israel and Judah, Dever (1998b, 418–26) mentions royalty, courtly circles, military, aristocracy (nobles and landed gentry), professionals (judges, governors) and religious leaders, particularly those in urban areas. Based on the texts of the HB, Neufeld writes of the social contrast in Iron II Samaria:

Houses of wealthy townsmen had carved wooden ornaments representing human figures, there were winter houses and large summer houses made of ashlar or cedar or panelled in cedar wood, decorated with artistic panels made of ivory and painted with vermillion. This growing love of luxury, pretentiousness and ostentatiousness was in striking contrast to the spirit of unsophisticated and natural life traditional to the old pre-monarchical Israel and still maintained in the villages. (1960, 44; see also King 1988b)

Who were the inhabitants of these wealthy urban houses? I begin with the Hebrew roots. In comparison to the many roots for the poor or oppressed, the HB has fewer terms for the rich and powerful. These include the following four terms which I discuss below. The numbers (#) refer to the *NIDOTTE* listing.

6.4.1.1. Hwn *(#2103): Having Great Possessions*. The majority of instances of the noun form *hôn* (#2104) from the root *hwn* are to be found in the book of Proverbs (e.g. 3:9; 8:18; 24:3–4). Twice *hôn* is used in opposition to the poor (19:4; 28:8). The basic sense of the noun is material possessions including riches and wealth (Domeris 1997g). Proverbs at times depicts such wealth positively (24:3–4) and at other times negatively (13:11). This is in keeping with the sages using both wealth and poverty as heuristic devices (Pleins 1987, 67–72).

6.4.1.2. Ḥayil *(#2657): The Powerful*. *Ḥayil* belongs essentially to the domain of power, occurring 246 times in the HB with the general notion of strength (Wakely 1997). On occasions it is juxtaposed with the poor and weak (e.g. 1 Sam 2:4). Wakely writes, "Because of his concern for the downtrodden and the oppressed, Yahweh intervenes to alter the disproportion of power in human relationships…by ensuring that the bows of the mighty are broken whereas the stumbling (i.e. the weak) gird on strength" (1997, 117; cf. Brueggemann 1990, 18). Twenty-five times *hayil* may be rendered as "wealth" or "riches" but understood with reference to these as the resources of the powerful (Domeris 1997h, 3:560).

6.4.1.3. Nekasîm *(#5794): Wealthy Stock-Owners*. The term *nekasîm* belongs to the domain of wealth, and in its five instances in the HB carries the sense of possessions including livestock (Domeris 1997e, 3:107). Examples include Josh 22:8 and Eccl 6:2. One could think of wealthy peasants or other people with extensive possessions, herds and flocks like the biblical Job.

6.4.1.4. ʿšr *(#6947): Wealth and Riches*. The root ʿsr and its cognates (ʿāšîr #6938 and ʿōšer #6948) carry the general sense of being or becoming wealthy (Domeris 1997h). Examples of the use of the term are Mic

6:12, 2 Sam 12:1–4 and Prov 10:15. This is the most common term for wealth and is frequently juxtaposed with a lack of wealth (e.g. Job 27:19). Wealth in this context does not mean coins and riches, but rather is wealth in herds, fertile fields and power—especially as these are found within the urban elite.

These four Hebrew terms form part of the varied semantic body of the wealthy, who together with the strong and powerful, were ranged in opposition to the poor in the pages of the HB as the non-poor. The following examples from Proverbs illustrate something of this reality. Friends, allies and patrons are valuable resources in the face of adversity, yet these are precisely the resources lacking by many of the poor. In Prov 14:20, we read that, "the poor are shunned even by their neighbours [Scott 1965, 97 has "companion"; McKane 1970, 232 has "friend"] but the rich have many friends."

In the context of power and coalitions, the web created by one's friends is essential. But the poor find that such people are ashamed of them, and neither help them nor honour them (McKane 1970, 471). Stripped of the protection of reciprocity and social coalitions, the poor are all the more vulnerable to abuse. While wealth brings friends (Prov 19:4), the friends of the poor desert them. Even his or her relatives (literally, brothers) shun them (19:7). When the poor approach the rich patrons, the rich answer harshly the requests of the poor (18:23). The tendency was for the elite to take as much as possible of the peasant surplus, leaving the peasants just enough to survive (Moore 1966, 470–71).

These elite (the non-poor) are the people who live in cities, own large herds and flocks, wield considerable power, including military and religious power, and benefit directly and indirectly from the peasant surplus. So much is clear from the text of the HB. Moreover, these people leave their signs in the dust of the land.

6.4.2. *Indicators of Wealth in the Archaeological Data*

The evidence of wealth in the archaeological excavations in Israel and Judah is abundant. Barkay writes, "The most prominent feature of the Iron Age IIa is the royal architecture" (1992, 305). Urban design included fortifications, city walls, and towers while elaborate gateways served as a political statement of the power and influence of the rulers (Beaudry 1994). These features are the key indicators of central administrative centres and so serve to determine the degree of urbanisation (Daviau 1997). De Geus (1993) demonstrates there were two types of urban planning evident in Israel, namely, cities with and without an acropolis. He suggests that political and economic factors were involved. The appearance of an acropolis, in his view, is commensurate with a growing divide between rich and poor which emerged, and this appears in Iron II throughout the region of the divided monarchy, most notably in Jerusalem (De Geus 1993; cf. Dever 1997, 185–93).

Referring to the middle and later periods of the monarchy, Dever speaks of signs of increased wealth in the elaborate tombs found in the region of Jerusalem (cf. Isa 22:15–16), and dated to the eighth and seventh centuries B.C.E. (1998b, 420; cf. De Vaux 1973, 72–73). Another indication of wealth is the use of ashlar masonry (fine cut stones) in the public and domestic architecture of the late Iron Age in cities like Jerusalem (Mazar 1990, 478–85; Barkay 1992, 332; Netzer 1992; Dever 1998b, 423). The well-known house of Ahiel (named on the basis of ostraca found in situ) in Area G of the City of David excavations, dated to the seventh century, is a classic example (Shiloh 1984). From the previous century, we have a tomb from the village of Silwan (south of the Mount of Olives), which may have belonged to Shebna, a royal steward, who was castigated by Isaiah for his elaborate tomb (Isa 22:15–19; so Avigad 1953).

One of the key signs of the Jerusalem aristocracy occurs in the many inscribed Hebrew bullae from Iron II found in various sites. Avigad's find of 450 bullae include a scribe (Baruch, son of Neriah), the servant of the king, the governor of the city and the son of a king (1986). There are also another 51 bullae found by Shiloh and dated to between 650 B.C.E. and the destruction of Jerusalem, which refer to the scribe Gemariah ben Shaphan and to Zephaniah (Shiloh 1986). Around Bethlehem and Benjamin, burial finds indicate a continued level of prosperity throughout the seventh century (Barkay 1992, 372), thus the "poor of the land" were clearly not the only occupants in the time of the Exile (Gottwald 2001, 236). Patronage clearly continued since we may safely assume that these burial finds indicate the wealth that came originally from the peasant surplus. Finally, Gottwald remarks on the presence of luxury items among the archaeological finds for Iron II and III—the Persian period (2001, 188)—which suggests to me that the problem of rich and poor continued beyond the Exile. Indeed, I shall suggest that the problem became worse.

6.5. *Patronage in Ancient Israel*

Like other peasants over the centuries the agrarians of Israel found themselves forced into contractual arrangements, which carried severe implications for the freedom of themselves and their families and for their ability to make use of their resources (Eisenstadt and Roniger 1984;

Stansell 1999). When all that you had to offer was your surplus and the labour of yourself and your family, forced labour became the unfortunate solution to poverty and famine, or one entered the service of a patron more powerful than oneself. For the peasant, these alliances represented hope for the future; for the elite, they provided further means for exploitation.

Clearly, by New Testament times, the practise of patronage was well established in Palestine (Oakman 1986). Matthews (1999a), Stansell (1999) and Simkins (1999) offer solid reasons for believing that like their fellow peasants worldwide, the peasants of Israel chose the option of patronage—to turn to a more powerful person, with access to greater resources, usually resident in an urban environment. In exchange for the surplus (in kind, in money or in labour), people with power, who might be legitimate rulers, the ruling elite or illegitimate bandits, offered a measure of protection from other possible competitors—rivals for the extraction of the surplus. The patron stood to benefit, not only by the honour gained, but also in real economic and political terms. The elite of the city drew their share of the peasant surplus in various ways, including rents, taxes and interest on loans and implicitly "a morality of violence was regarded as valid" (Neufeld 1960, 50).

Patrons, in the classical world, might be wealthy peasants, members of royalty, merchants, military officers, priests or other members of the ruling elite. "Patronage provided the critical cog in a peasant's risk-management system. Effective subsistence insurance could only be obtained by becoming attached to men of wealth and power because they were the only ones who would have had large, predictable sources outside the community" (Gallant 1991, 169). Such patrons agreed to provide the necessities of life in exchange for the right to take a portion of the surplus production and to be honoured by the peasants (Eisenstadt and Roniger 1984). Moxnes (1988), referring to Iron Age Israel, speaks of "the simultaneous exchange of different types of resources," with the patron offering support and protection based on their access to economic and political resources, and the client responding with loyalty and solidarity (and I would add tax and rent).

Moxnes speaks of a "strong element of inequality and difference in power" with Israelite patrons holding the "monopoly on certain positions and resources" (1988, 42). The extracted surplus might be set aside against the eventuality of a drought or famine, or some other disaster, and then handed out or bartered back to the peasants. In other instances, the surplus was bartered to the urban communities, and the profits might or might not be utilised in the long-term interests of the peasants. In the worst case scenario, the peasants would be stripped of their most important buffer against famine. Such a strategy, in Israel as throughout the ancient world, had implications for population growth, with a proportional increase in the death-rate of the weak and infirm (cf. Kautsky 1982, 106).

The Israelite peasant paid tribute (rent or tax) and gave gifts and honours to his or her patron and hopefully received in return provision for clothing, housing and protection in times of famine (Moxnes 1988)—presuming that the patron agreed. The reality was often very different given the power-inequality in the arrangement. Popkin (1979), speaking generally, saw the pre-industrial village as rife with tensions. Families (both household and kin groups) competed for access to scarce resources, including such intangibles as honour and status, and the vital aspects governing subsistence (1979, 22). The world of the peasant and that of the landlord was separated by a great gulf. Lambton speaks of a lack of a sense of co-operation, "mutual suspicion," and on the part of the landowner, the "barest consideration of the well-being of the peasant" (1953, 263). Nevertheless, there prevailed a sense of rightness, to which the prophets of Israel would appeal—the term for this was positive reciprocity, or, in Sen's language, exchange entitlement (1977, 1981).

6.5.1. *Reciprocity*
There evolved, in ancient Israel, a complex relationship of exploitation and self-protection. In modern times, certain expectations of the role of the patron or landlord of the Middle East were still in place as the work of Bill on Iran shows. The landlord is

> expected to keep the peasants alive and this meant food, clothing, shelter and medicine. During periods of famine, earthquake, pestilence and war, the peasant expected and received help.... The landlord often intervened to help the peasants escape crushing tax exaction and to rescue the peasant's sons from military conscription. (Bill 1972, 19)

If these obligations were not met, the peasant would be left high and dry. This brings us to one of the most important aspects of peasant life for understanding peasant poverty in Iron Age Israel, namely the issue of reciprocity. I touch here on issues that stirred the ire of the Israelite prophets.

A typical peasant economy of the ancient world (like Israel or classical Greece) worked on a complex balance of power and reciprocity (Carney 1975, 138–41; Gallant 1991, 143–69). Each level had its own system of controls (Knight 1994). "Peasants do contend that patrons and communal leaders are obligated to assist them in crisis and to prevent food shortages from degenerating into famine" (Gallant 1991, 9). Conversely,

"Peasants do accept a certain amount of exploitation as legitimate so long as those exploiting them reciprocate by providing subsistence insurance" (1991, 9–10). Nevertheless, things can go seriously wrong for the peasant, especially those on the bottom rungs of the ladder.

Reallocation and reciprocity are the terms used to order the relationship of power, within the dialectical aspect of a patron–client relationship. Matthews, with special reference to Iron Age Israel and Judah, spells out the distinctions between reallocation, which involves "obligation to redistribute goods for religious or political purposes," and reciprocity, which "requires that goods be transferred based on kinship or client relationships on the basis of personal status within the community" (1999a, 93).

Reciprocity is the key for understanding patron–client relationships in peasant Israel (Matthews 1999a). Such reciprocity might take different forms, as the analysis by Sahlins (1972) indicates. He delineates three types of reciprocity, all applicable to ancient Israel. The first of these is Generalised reciprocity, of which the pure gift motivated by altruism, is an example. This might operate between peasants or landlords of equal status or among family members. The second form is Balanced reciprocity, where both parties attempt to find exchange of goods and services. This was the model for the peasant–patron system to operate most effectively even if the "balance" was not one of equal power and status. Finally, there is Negative reciprocity, where the exchange breaks down, and violence becomes a substitute for obligation—the whole idea being "to get something for nothing" (Sahlins 1972, 270).

Kautsky (1982, 113–14) suggests that there was rarely real reciprocity and little freedom for the peasants anywhere in the ancient or modern world. Moore (1966, 204) concludes that the aristocracy often did very little, in spite of their claims to the contrary. Certainly, this is consistent with the impression gained from reading the Prophetic writings where the issues of reciprocity occur implicitly time and again. Underlying the message of the prophets of Israel was an expectation levelled at the ruling elite with regard to their role vis-à-vis the peasants—an expectation at which they were failing.

6.5.2. *The Collapse of Reciprocity*
The tone and character of the Prophetic texts (see below) indicates that sometime in the Iron Age, probably as a result of the pressures of foreign tribute to the Assyrians, positive reciprocity collapsed in Israel and Judah. The prophets do not suggest a change in the economic system had taken place, that debt had suddenly escalate, or that peasants were losing their land. Instead, they seize upon normal aspects of the patron–client relationship, which have become distorted leading to the abuse of the client.

In Greece, following on the growth of urbanisation, there was "a re-evaluation and a redefinition of the moral obligation of the elite to provide subsistence support" (Gallant 1991, xii)—the end of positive reciprocity. The peasants of Israel during the latter years of the Iron Age undoubtedly experienced the same process, hence the prophetic response (Deist 2000, 166–68). In the next chapter, I shall consider some of the ways in which the elite failed the poor. Yet, it was not only the elite who failed the peasants; sometimes, it was other peasants who chose to break the rules.

Wolf describes the rise of powerful peasants who chose to set communal standards aside. He writes:

> As the overarching power structure weakens, many traditional social ties also lose their particular sanctions. The peasant community, under such circumstances, may see the rise of wealthy peasants who shoulder aside their less fortunate fellows and move into the power vacuum left by the retreating superior holders of power. In the course of their rise, they frequently violate traditional expectations of how social relations are to be conducted and symbolized—frequently they utilize their newly won power to enrich themselves at the cost of their neighbors. (Wolf 1966, 16)

Gottwald describes this process being carried out in early Israel:

> The village system of justice administered by elders may not have been equal to checking aggressive violators of this ethic. Even though the communal ethic espoused by the cult of Yahweh was premised on a just order to protect the integrity of all family units, the upholding of this ethic may have depended on moral suasion and religious sanctions that lacked means of assured enforcement. (Gottwald 2001, 174)

The collapse of such reciprocity is particularly significant in the light of the ancient notion of "limited good." Anthropologists use the notion of limited good to describe a society in which good things (honour, blessings and physical well-being) were deemed to be in limited supply (Gregory 1975, 73–75). Peasant society was particularly prone to this pattern of thinking. So Carney speaks of "primitive wantlessness" which holds "that all good things—food, land, honour, and standing—are in fixed quantities and short supply." Where one person receives an undue amount of any of these commodities, he or she is deemed to have gained it at the cost of his neighbours and so is subject to suspicion (1975, 198–99). This is the very thinking which forms the basis for the prophetic invective (see above).

The impact of living in a society of limited good was that visible excesses on the part of the dominant groups in a society was seen to be normal, whereas excess by someone in the same village was not. Since the elite of Israel were expected to sustain a certain level of generosity (Moxnes 1988, 35; Deist 2000, 166–68), the failure to live up to these expectations carried both a real loss of good and a perceived loss—the potential distortion of the proper spread of good through the society. These insights explain much of the ethic that informs the HB's particular presentation of poverty and wealth.

6.6. *Peasant Reactions*

Peasant wisdom and shrewdness (Scott 1976, 1985) militated against extreme forms of abuse, and there were limitations beyond which they could not be pressured (Chayanov 1986). In a fragile world, where subsistence hung in the balance, peasants found the ways and means to survive. In the absence of detail, in the HB, one can only speculate about the reactions of the peasantry in Israel.

Peasants tend to be very protective of their free time and of the extent of their labour, especially with regard to routine activities like weeding. Different geographical locations required different labour strategies. So, for example, the peasants of northern Mesopotamia worked very long hours during harvest and planting seasons, followed by long periods of inactivity. By contrast, agriculture in southern Mesopotamia made yearlong demands on the peasants, including demands on their labour for purposes of the development and maintenance of irrigation systems, such as canal maintenance (Postgate 1987, 264). The peasants of Israel would have stood closer to their cousins in northern Mesopotamia,

For one to separate peasant and surplus, Lenski argues, coercion of the ruling elite is an essential ploy (1984, 64–65). Not only does the process have implications for the peasantry in terms of subsistence risk, there are also implications in terms of peasant labour and free time. The peasants are naturally reluctant to give up their free time, of which they may have a substantial amount. The Mayan peasant, for example, could grow enough corn to survive by working only about 48 days a year (Morley and Brainert 1956, 140). The process of extraction of surplus had labour implications, and therefore required a certain finesse or alternatively simply brute force on the part of the ruling elite.

According to Chayanov (1986, 53–69), the Russian economist, peasants would increase their labour on demand but only up to a certain point. Beyond that point, at which the sheer drudgery of the work obliterated the immediate and obvious benefits for the peasant, the peasants would lose interest and motivation. If too high a demand was made, the peasants would exhaust their reserves. If they did not have enough food for themselves, they would become weak and unable to work properly. Should the demand continue, the peasants would be overwhelmed by a sense of helplessness, and refuse to work or might even abandon their lands. The whole exploitation system, therefore, was fraught with problems. Moreover, some of these problems actually favoured the peasantry.

Kautsky points out that the aristocracy tended to be lazy and the peasants shrewd (1982, 107). The result was a pattern of gross inefficiency, with often only a veneer of supervision (Kautsky 1982, 109, 128–31). Scott (1985) details some of the imaginative ways in which the peasants used this inefficiency to their own advantage in a form of peasant resistance. Peasants deliberately hide the goodness of their fields (Brand 1987, 144), and withhold their products from the aristocracy. They pay their dues, whether rents or taxes, reluctantly and they pay as little as possible. Under some circumstances, the peasant might work as little as possible or as slowly as possible especially when under obligation as with forced labour (Scott 1985; cf. Kautsky 1982, 275). One resort was humour (Scott 1985, 1–2). The Bible certainly bears testimony to the use of insider-humour especially with regard to foreign rulers (Brenner 1994).

The Old Babylonian correspondence reveals some interesting concerns with regard to managing workers, ranging from the necessity of timely payments (to avoid strikes) to ingenious ploys by slaves to avoid work, especially manual labour (Dandamayev 1987, 278). Records of strikes for better rations are also found, which suggests that when all else failed, workers were prepared to risk all for the sake of their survival (1987, 278). Ultimately, a peasant revolt was always a possibility as the Amarna correspondence indicates. The Jewish revolt against Rome in 66 C.E. carries many of the marks of a peasant revolution, including the assassination of key figures, the disruption of tax collection and the burning of debt records (Domeris 1993).

When power is part and parcel of the laws and norms of the land, a relatively small minority can exert a high level of control over a large majority. Mann stresses that the majority do not revolt since "they lack the collective organisation to do otherwise, because they are embedded within the collective and distributive power organisation controlled by others" (1986, 7). In Kautsky's view (1982, 288), revolutions are more likely to occur when elite who are not aristocrats by birth (the new rich) are present in society. Without a champion or the power of the state at their behest, peasants were the defenceless producers (Kautsky 1982, 293–319; Lenski 1984, 274).

Denied the option of revolution, peasants found other ways of resisting. Wittfogel adds, "When taxation becomes unusually burdensome, the peasant may reduce his cultivated acreage, and when the heavy demands continue, he may become a fiscal fugitive, abandoning his fields altogether. He may wander in despair, look for work elsewhere, or turn bandit or rebel" (1957, 331–32). How the peasants of Israel reacted over the centuries we have no way of knowing. That they found ways of fighting back is likely but it is also likely that as oppression mounted their options became fewer. The final resort was fleeing to the cities or into forms of social banditry.

Granott offers an interesting parallel insight from nineteenth- and early twentieth-century Syria:

> Consequently, in spite of intolerable conditions, the *fellaheen* [peasants] were compelled to remain on the soil and submit to the heavy burden imposed on them both by the system of tax-collection in the country and by the conditions of land ownership which placed them at the mercy of the landowners. In those days there was only one way of deliverance for the villagers—to abandon a settled life and to become nomads [better social bandits], a course which had from old been easy in a land bordering on the wilderness. (Granott 1952, 34)

6.7. *Conclusion*

The peasant history of Israel and Judah during the Iron Age is marked by two consecutive movements. The first was movement towards a ranked society in Israel and Judah, which went hand in hand with urbanisation (although the nature of relationship is difficult now to ascertain) and which would have opened the way for the adoption of a system of patronage. The second was the subsequent change in the nature of patronage and a change in the form of reciprocity, which would have had catastrophic effects on the peasants of Israel and Judah. I have suggested that contributing factors were the burden of Assyrian tribute and the flood of refugees that poured into embattled Judah.

Natural environmental challenges were one thing, human intervention was another. Very important in this regard is Sen's theory of exchange entitlement (1977, 1981), which argues in essence that the cause of many famines is not a shortfall in production but the maldistribution of foodstuffs—the human factor in the form of the intervention of the non-poor. Peasants were vulnerable members of a complex society. This is why I have chosen a model of poverty as a social construction—it allows for this human contribution, especially on the part of the non-poor, to be spelled out. I come now to a discussion of the forms of oppression, which impacted the lives of the peasants of Israel, as reflected in the HB. Poverty and oppression are tightly bound together in the history of Israel.

Chapter 7

OPPRESSION UNLEASHED

7.1. *Oppression Described*

In any relationship between patron and client, where positive reciprocity operates, there is some measure of balance governing obligations and benefits. When such reciprocity collapses, the way is open for oppression to enter in. By oppression, I mean the abuse of power in line with the biblical text that explicitly connects the two. The well-known speech of Samuel (1 Sam 8) is a pivotal chapter in this regard (Gottwald 1986, 97–98; Halpern 1988, 217–35), because it verbalises particular instances of the use and abuse of royal power over the ordinary people (cf. 1 Sam 17:14–20). It is but one of many passages which deal with the possibility and practise of the abuse of power. While the dating of these texts remains an open question, my main concern is to demonstrate the way in which poverty, injustice and oppression were interlinked in the thinking of the biblical writers.

The plight of the poor was at the mercy of the non-poor. Such is one of the basic premises of the social construction of poverty utilised in this work and such appears to be a part also of the ideology of the HB as reflected within its manifold texts. Job's eloquent statement about the poor, with which I began this work, is a clear example of this form of thinking (Job 24:5–12). When accord vanishes, violence becomes endemic. For the prophets, oppressors wield power and use violence and injustice to win their cause. Micah 2:1 reads, "Woe to those who plan iniquity, to those who plot violence on their beds. At morning's light they carry it out because it is in their power to do it." Literally, the Hebrew in Mic 2:1 reads "because it is within the power of their hand" (cf. Wolff 1990, 77).

Power, rather than wealth, is the major distinction between the oppressors and the oppressed, between the rich (strong) and the poor. In moving towards a model of poverty, in which power vs. powerlessness and honour vs. shame play a major role, this chapter discerns some of the tools that gave the ruling elite, and their supporters, power and honour over the peasant majority in Israel. These tools should also be seen in the light of the delicate balancing act of the peasant struggle for survival.

7.2. *The Semantic Domain of Oppression*

The HB itself has a rich and varied language to describe oppression, and some of the most memorable descriptions of the injustices of oppression are found there. Therefore it forms a good source for understanding the nature of oppression, and its link with poverty (cf. Shaw 1993, 79–84). In what remains the most significant book on oppression in the HB, Hanks (1983) gathers together ten common and ten less common Hebrew roots. As we read through the ten most common roots, we might easily substitute the term poverty for oppression. The numbers in brackets refer to the entries in *NIDOTTE* (1997) and I offer a brief overview of the terms as a basis for the more detailed study of oppression and poverty that follows.

The term *ʿōšēq* (#6945) carries the notion of "oppress" or to "take by extortion," being summed up by Hanks (1983, 5–8) as carrying forward the idea that oppression involves injustice. The root *ʿšq* I (#6943) is found in its different forms some 59 times in the HB (e.g. Eccl 4:1; Ps 103:6, 7). The forms of the root *ynh* (#3561) are found 19 or 20 times (with Ps 123:4) in the HB (e.g. Ezek 18:7, 12, 16). Von Rad suggested that the literal meaning of the word was "to reduce to slavery; to enslave" (1966, 147). This leads Hanks to speak about the notion of oppression as enslaving people (1983, 8–9). Terms based on the root *ngś* (#5601) are found 23 times in the HB (e.g. Isa 9:3 [4]; Exod 3:7) overwhelmingly in contexts involving poverty and indicating a form of dehumanisation. Citing Job 39:7, Hanks writes, "such texts suggest that when persons suffer oppression, they lose their human dignity and are degraded to animal-like existence" (1983, 9). He also notes that "many uses of *nagaś* indicate how tampering with the economic structures leads to oppression," citing examples of heavy tribute and debt (1983, 9–10).

Of the 31 instances of the use of *lḥṣ* (#4315) most of these deal with oppression. Hanks defines "*lahats* as the pain which the oppressed feel" (1983, 10–11). The root *ršš* (#8406) carries the literal sense of "to crush," grind or pound and so by extension the meaning of oppress (1983, 11). Of the 20 times the term is used in the HB (Isa 58:6; Amos 4:1) poverty forms the immediate context in 9 of these instances (1983, 11). *Dkʾ* (#1917) is probably "the strongest Hebrew word denoting oppression," carrying the literal sense of "pulverise, crush" (1983, 14). In the 31 instances of *dkʾ* and its cognates (e.g. Ps 10:10, 18; Isa 57:15) poverty is the context in 10 of these instances, and the emphasis is on "the fatal results of oppression" (1983, 14). "Oppression smashes the body and crushes the human spirit. That is, God's image is pulverised like a moth crushed under a boot heel" (1983, 14). In his summation of the meaning of the word, Hanks describes *dakaʾ* as the oppression which kills (1983, 14–15).

The term *ʿnh* II (#6700) is used 82 times in the HB, of which 14 occur in the context of poverty (Gen 15:13; Exod 1:11, 12; Deut 26:5). Hanks takes its key meaning as "oppression humiliates" (1983, 15–17). A dialectic exists between power and powerlessness, honour and shame. *Ṣar* II (#7640) carries the normal sense of enemy or enmity, but on four occasions the NIV renders *sārâ* II as "oppressor" (e.g. Amos 5:12). Thus, Hanks includes the root as "oppression expresses enmity" (1983, 17–20). *Ṣārâ* I (#7650 is found 46 times in the HB, and again it is the NIV that translates some instances as oppression (e.g. Neh 9:27). Hanks renders the meaning of the term as "oppression impoverishes" (1983, 20–22). *Ṣwq* I (#7439 is used in the HB 31 times (e.g. Deut 28:53, 55, 57) of which poverty forms the context in nearly half of these cases. Hanks defines *ṣwq* as typical of descriptions of siege, hence "oppression besieges" (1983, 22–25).

Hanks (1983, 26–31) goes on to include a further ten roots in which dictionary definitions include oppression, but which numerically are not as common as the first ten, and he adds a further ten roots that fill out the broader semantic field of oppression (1983, 31–33). Clearly, oppression was a major concern for the writers of the HB. This is all the more curious given its absence from many Bible Dictionaries and Encyclopaedias. In spending time on the semantic domain for oppression, my wish is to alert the reader to the underlying biblical understanding—oppression is essentially an abuse of power in a world where powerlessness and poverty went hand in hand.

7.3. *The Cycle of Oppression*

Oppression is a cycle, trapping both oppressor and oppressed. Such is the view which comes from Ecclesiastes. For example, Eccl 4:1 reads, "Again I looked and saw all the oppression (from the root *ʿšq* I #6943) that was taking place under the sun: I saw the tears of the oppressed—and they have no comforter; power was on the side of their oppressors—and they have no comforter." The repetition of the phrase "and they have no comforter" underlines the absence of hope for both oppressed and oppressor, drawing both into the cycle of oppression. Oppression, like violence, is a process in which the oppressors become trapped within their role as the oppressed oppressors who also need to be liberated, not least from their own fears.

Ecclesiastes 5:8[7] continues, "If you see the poor (*rwš* #8133) oppressed (*ʿōšēq* #6945) in a district, and justice and rights denied, do not be surprised at such things; for one official is eyed by a higher one, and over them both are others higher still." Officials have power and are in turn controlled by people with power, so that oppression has several tiers, with control won by a combination of legitimate and illegitimate exercise of power. Moreover, oppression feeds upon fear, with each player a victim of the fear of those above him or her. Ecclesiastes envisages a chain of abuse, starting with civil authorities, moving through the workplace and into the home.

7.4. *The Rich and Powerful*

In the HB, the non-poor are described by a plethora of terms, of which rich and powerful are an example of groups used in contrast to the poor. In the Psalms, other contrasting groups are the wicked (Pss 10:2; 82:4), evildoers (14:4), the strong (35:10), robbers (35:10), the violent—in the guise of the wicked armed with bow and arrow (37:14), people caricatured as wild beasts (74:19) and those who condemn the poor unjustly (109:31). Poverty is clearly more than just an economic category for the HB and reciprocity (usually negative) is implicit in nearly all of these contrasts.

Graphically, the psalmist in Ps 73 describes the wicked as prosperous (v. 3), sleek and sound of body (v. 4), wearing pride and violence (v. 6), "their eyes gleam through folds of fat" (v. 7 NRSV), "they threaten oppression" and their slander reaches even to heaven (v. 9). Yet they are perceived to be blameless (v. 10), and God seems not to care about what they do with their lives (v. 11). They seem to be unshakeably secure and wealthy (v. 12). This stereotype of the wicked as wealthy, healthy, secure, well-fed and influential, yet given to the abuse of power is striking. The crux lies in the last attribute and not in the earlier ones.

In the thinking of the ANE, the exercise of power by one person over another implies what Mann (1986, 5–6) terms a distributive aspect. Using the notion of a "zero-sum gain" Mann (1986, 6) argues that new power wielded is power taken away. For one person to gain power over another person, that other person has to lose power. In the realm of personal power, there is a fixed amount of power that can be spread among the participants (1986, 6). Isaiah 5:8 is a fine example of such thinking. Such thinking implies imaginary limitations on aspects ranging from honour to good harvests, and includes nice homes. If one person is seen to be excessively "blessed" in any of these aspects, the community might become concerned that there is a corresponding withdrawal from other members of the community of these things (1986, 66). Hence the prophetic invective.

The wealthy oppressors in Amos (cf. Andersen and Freedman 1989, 309) are given various names. They are Israel (Amos 2:6; 5:1), cows of Bashan (4:1), those living at ease in Zion, or who are complacent on the hill of Samaria (6:1), headmen (6:1) and one specific individual, namely the priest of Bethel, named Amazia (7:10). The mark of such people is power and prestige. They do not struggle for their existence, but live comfortably and at ease, safe from the daily grind of hard labour and fear of starvation.

The prophet Amos speaks of the ruling elite as those who are "complacent in Zion," or "feel secure on Mount Samaria" (Amos 6:1) so underlining the apparent absence of concern among these people. Amos calls these people "leaders" (*rōʾš* I, #8040). Hunger and thirst are not real threats to such people, and the personal experience of the violence of oppression is unknown. Yet Amos implies that the security of such people is based on false assumptions, and the future will bring a change of fortunes (v. 3). Their beds are inlaid with ivory; they feast off choice lambs and fattened calves (Amos 6:4), play musical instruments, like harps (6:5), drink wine by the bowlful, and use the finest lotions (6:6). Effectively, Amos draws attention to the deep gulf that exists between rich and poor at the most basic of levels, diet. He uses the comfort of the ruling elite as a foil for the implicit discomfort of the peasant poor, as once again the practice of balanced reciprocity is seen to have broken down.

Amos (4:1–3) targets women among the ranks of the oppressors (cf. Isa 3:16–17). They are the "cows of Bashan" (v. 1), which could be treated as a superlative (so Mays 1969a, 72), a cultic allusion (Jacobs 1985) or as an insult. The first is probably the best answer, since the implication is reasonably clear. In a land where famine reigns (Amos 4:6–9) the powerful are well-fed, like the cattle that graze the steppes of Bashan. However, the male-authored commentaries carry the stereotypes to excess. Mays (1969a, 72) speaks of "the women of quality in Samaria, the pampered darlings...ruling the society of Israel from behind the scenes with sweet petulant nagging for wealth to support their indolent dalliance." Lang (1985, 91) refers to "some well-to-do women [who] do not care much for a slim body" and "female dipsomania." Equally disparaging is Gossai who writes of "the over-eating and over-drinking [which] is particularly repugnant in these women" (1993, 273). These are striking examples of secondary abuse arising from the interpretations of the text—this time against women (cf. Yee 2003).

In the light of such vicious caricatures of women, Sandersen (1992) has reacted quite justifiably. Instead of critiquing the modern interpreters of the prophet, however, she has turned against Amos himself for condemning women without promoting their place among the poor. In defence of Amos, that is not entirely true given the reference to "the girl" in 2:7b. The relative powerlessness of women, however, is not regarded by the prophets, nor is the double oppression faced by peasant women, who are subject both to a political/economic system of abuse by the powerful, and to the strictures of the paternalistic system of the time.

Instead, Amos indicates that among the wealthy, both men and women are deeply involved in oppression. To suggest that the women are only the indirect perpetrators of oppression (so May 1969a, 72) is to misunderstand the basic nature of an oppressive society. Amos draws a direct causal link between the demands of the women and the oppression of the poor. In spite of the fact that the Hebrew is a confusing mixture of masculine and feminine verbs and endings (see Andersen and Freedman 1989, 415–21 for details), the culpability of the women remains, and they will be punished along with their male counterparts.

7.4.1. *Priests, Prophets and Leaders*

Wealth does not make one wicked, nor health, nor even power, but rather, it is the abuse of power. Such power is inclusive of religious, economic and legal dimensions. Andersen and Freedman (1989, 307) referring to the time of Amos speak of "a three-way alliance of priests, merchants and magistrates, with most of the personnel drawn from a few large and influential families." This is common also to Micah, Zephaniah, Hosea, Jeremiah and Ezekiel as the following examples show.

Micah targets the religious leaders when he cries out, "her leaders judge for a bribe, her priests teach for a price, and her prophets tell fortunes [prophesy] for money" (3:11). Shaw (1993, 110) suggests that titles like *rō'š* I (#8040) combined military and legal authority. The value system of the powerful has been switched around, and yet these are probably those who claim both honour and esteem from others. The oppressors are defined narrowly in Mic 2:3 as "this family," suggesting strongly that a single family is the target of that oracle (Wolff 1990, 78). The prophetic tirade should be understood, then, as targeting the members of this one family who are in the process of seizing control of peasants and their land (vv. 3, 8, 9), rather than as a general reference to either the aristocracy of Jerusalem (Shaw 1993, 79; Wolff 1990, 80) or to landlords generally (Hilliers 1984, 33). The process envisaged is not necessarily that of driving peasants off their lands, but rather, I suggest, of seeking to control more and more peasants through control over their villages.

Zephaniah pronounces doom upon the priests of Judah and Jerusalem (1:4) who do violence to the law (3:4), on the prophets (who are treacherous men—3:4) and on the royal house (1:8), accusing them each of violence and deceit (1:9). Thus, he too sees a three-fold alliance of prophets, priests and kings. Together these groups make up the aristocracy of the time. They live in the fortified towns and cities (Lang 1985, 91–93) as the leaders within the community and the rulers of the land. More generally, there is simply a group referred to as the strong or powerful (cf. Gossai 1993, 296–300).

Jeremiah reserves some of his toughest words for the priesthood. In God's name he warns, "Has this house [temple], which bears my Name, become a den of robbers to you? But I have been watching!" (Jer 7:11). The Hebrew term for robbers is *pārîṣ* II (#7265) found only once in the HB (Domeris 1997f, 3:686). For Jeremiah, the priests, instead of acting as the patrons of the poor, are feeding off them just as a gang of bandits might prey upon innocent villagers in the rural areas. The temple of Jerusalem has become an integral factor of the oppressive superstructures of the time. Indeed, even the prophets and priests are guilty of practising deceit (Jer 8:10b). The corruption runs deep. The people who have "stolen wives and fields" (Jer 8:10a) will lose their own. In Jer 21:11–14 and 22:1–6, the prophet challenges the civil leaders and the house of the king by warning them against oppression. They were meant to rescue the victim from oppression and robbery but they have failed to do so. The word used for robbery is from the root *gzl* (#1608; cf. Jer 21:12; 22:3) and implies robbery with violence (Domeris 1997c); violence is also inherent in *ʿōšeq* (#6945; cf. Jer 22:17) the term for oppression used here.

Like robbers in their den, the powerful believe that they are invulnerable. Jeremiah is specific in his targeting of the royal court (e.g. Jer 21:11—royal house of Judah…house of David). The prophet appeals for justice and concern for the weak, in a threat from God; "Administer justice every morning, rescue from the hand of his oppressor the one who has been robbed, or my wrath will break out and burn like fire because of the evil you have done—burn with no-one to quench it" (Jer 21:12).

Hosea castigates the leaders of Ephraim and Samaria for their various abuses of power, calling them rebels, companions of thieves, lovers of bribes and those who chase after gifts (Hos 7:1–4). In Hosea, the oppressors are also the ruling elite. Ephraim, a synonym for Israel's leaders, boasts of great wealth, and, in effect, defies God to show that they have sinned in the accumulation thereof (Hos 12:8). The religious system of the HB, both temple and local shrines, while designed to benefit the whole community, was easily co-opted by the priestly aristocracy to serve their own interests. Such an abuse of power leads to some of the most memorable of the prophetic invectives. Consider, for example, Hosea's comment, "As marauders lie in ambush for a man, so do bands of priests; they murder on the road to Shechem, committing shameful crimes" (6:9). Language used of the elite to describe the actions and atrocities of social banditry are here applied to the elite themselves. This use by the prophets of such verbs underlines the actions against the poor as the equivalent of banditry (Domeris 1997b, 1997i; cf. Andersen and Freedman 1989, 320).

In an oracle against the princes of Jerusalem, Ezekiel writes of their abuse of power ("to shed blood") and their oppression of the aliens or mistreatment of the fatherless and widows (22:6–7). The key phrase is "uses his power," indicating the clear connection understood between oppression and the abuse of power, the powerful against those without power. Ezekiel compared the officials to roaring lions (v. 25) and wolves (v. 27) who tear their prey, devour people, take treasures, make widows, shed blood and kill people for unjust profits (vv. 25–27). As in Jeremiah, terms like ʿōšeq for oppress (#6945; cf. Ezek 18:18; 22:7, 12, 29) and gzl for robbery with violence (#1608; cf. Ezek 18:18; 22:9) are present. Such violence is endemic to situations where power is abused. The shepherd leaders of Israel have failed to care for the flock. "You eat the curds, clothe yourselves with the wool and slaughter the choice animals" (Ezek 34:2). In place of strengthening the weak, healing the sick or binding their wounds, or seeking the lost, the shepherds have "ruled harshly and brutally" (34:4).

The prophet Ezekiel contrasts two groups within the ruled, the strong (powerful) and the weak (Ezek 34:12–21). God will judge between one sheep and another, the rams and the goats (v. 17). God asks, "Is it not enough for you to feed on the good pasture? Must you also trample the rest of your pasture with your feet? Is it not enough for you to drink clear water? Must you also muddy the rest with your feet? Must my flock feed on what you have trampled and drink what you have muddied with your feet?" (vv. 18–19). Therefore, God will judge; "See, I myself will judge between the fat sheep and the lean sheep. Because you shove with flank and shoulder, butting all the weak sheep with your horns until you have driven them away" (vv. 20–21). The weak and poor (lean) are driven off by violence, their pastures and streams are spoiled by the wastefulness of the powerful. In place of a sharing of resources, an equality of access, the strong in the community take what they want and spoil what is left.

The Wisdom literature includes a similar pattern in its critique of the civil and religious leaders as the following examples indicate. The book of Proverbs, for example, develops a sustained polemic against rulers and lawmakers, who use their power to oppress the poor. Proverbs 28:3 adjures, "A ruler who oppresses the poor is like driving rain that leaves no crops." Proverbs 30:14 picks up a similar theme when it speaks of the wicked, "whose teeth are swords and whose jaws are set with knives" and whose purpose is to scourge (devour) the poor (*ʿānî*) from the earth, the needy (*ʾebyôn*) from among humankind. Savagery and violence are overt, but the metaphor has to do with speech (teeth as swords), and so one should think of those who in court and in the promulgation of laws, create a situation of structural violence.

The sages clearly grasped and expounded the notion of structural oppression. Wicked rulers (Prov 28:12) drive the righteous into hiding by means of excessive and oppressive taxes (cf. v. 28; 29:2, 4). The Hebrew speaks literally about the one who is "eager for contributions." McKane (1970, 637–38) understands these verses as critical in general of the levy of taxes. One might also understand a reference to the practice of gift-giving that was incumbent upon peasants as a way of servicing their client–patron relationship. The whole community is unbalanced by the actions of such people (1970, 625). Finally, Proverbs reminds the reader that the king who deals out justice is secure in his throne (29:14), but where the wicked are in power, there sin reigns supreme (29:16). Reciprocity is unbalanced and oppression is king.

7.5. *Forms of Exploitation*

The ruling elite, both former peasants and others, controlled the destiny and lives of the peasant majority through a variety of mechanisms, including rents, taxes and labour obligations. In the light of our understanding of peasant survival strategies, let us examine the relevant biblical texts in the ANE and generic peasant contexts before moving to consider the manner in which oppression might wreak havoc in these areas.

7.5.1. *Rents*
Peasants, the world over, invariably have to pay a portion of their surplus in rent, whether for protection or for use of land. Various components made up a typical rental. For example, the peasants in Syria of the early twentieth century were expected to pay pure rent, which did not include payment for productive services (such as tools or water supplies) (Warriner 1957, 59). Depending on the extent to which some of the rental found its way back into the agricultural process, the system might be a

good or a bad one. Warriner argues that the system in Syria was a bad one, in so far as the landowner was a pure rent receiver and did not invest in the land: "The cultivators, on a low subsistence margin, have neither the means nor the incentive to invest: they are the labourers, rather than tenants, who work for a variable return, and cannot increase it by working harder or farming better" (1957, 59). She compares the system to the absentee landlord of nineteenth-century Ireland, where the owner neglected his functions (soil fertility and fixed capital) by reason of his absence: "The evil of this system is not absenteeism as such, but the lack of any investing or managerial function. The object of the system is to avoid the costs of management and investment" (1957, 59).

What the situation regarding rent was like in biblical times is unclear. With the establishment of the states of the divided monarchy and the subsequent demands upon the Highland villages, presumably rents would have formed an important means of acquiring wealth on the part of the urban elite and the state/temple. While the pattern in time came to resemble the Syrian system described by Warriner (1957), initially, it must have been comparable to some form of share-cropping, in which peasants experienced a balanced form of reciprocity (cf. Deist 2000, 166–68).

The Prophetic texts are eloquent about what appears to be a collapse of this reciprocity. We would probably not be far wrong if we imagined the peasants in ancient Israel, over the centuries, experiencing varying degrees of exploitation with commensurate levels of rental and taxation all done with some measure of legality. At some point all this began to change and the prophets reacted. So in Amos, the prophet speaks of the peasants being forced to give up their hard-earned grain as fines or rent (Amos 5:11a; cf. 2:8). The noun *maś'ēt* (#5368) has the basic sense of gift or ration, but here in Amos may imply excessive rent (so Andersen and Freedman 1989, 500). The NRSV reading is worth considering, which speaks of people who "levy taxes on the poor and extort a tribute of grain from them." Such extortion of grain suggests not just a form of tenancy, in which the peasants rent land and pay a portion of the income as rental, but an abuse of that form (cf. Soggin 1987, 88, on the basis of the Acadian cognate). The basic sense of fairness, to which Wolf (1966, 16) and Gottwald (2001, 174) alluded (see above), has been breached—and any pretence at positive reciprocity has vanished.

7.5.2. *Pledges and Fines*
The economic system in Israel, apparently, was easily manipulated by the powerful. Amos gives some examples when he speaks of pledges and fines. The strong are pictured as lying down on garments taken in pledge while drinking wine taken as fines (Amos 2:8). The location of both

actions is a sacred site, either a hill shrine or a temple. King (1988a, 137–61; 1988b) connects Amos 6:4–7 with the Marzeaḥ festival, and perhaps this is the context also for Amos 2:8. In essence the festival was a joyous social occasion in the locality of some or other deity. The people recline (rather than lie down) on cloaks, and eat and drink. The wine, taken in fines (v. 8b), links directly the enjoyment of the powerful and the suffering of others, especially if such fines, while legal, were indirectly an abuse of power. "Their god" has an ironic ring (Mays 1969a, 47; cf. King 1988a, 137–38) but clearly this is not the God of Israel, who is committed to justice—the God of the prophetic minority.

As a social occasion, the Marzeaḥ festival is to be enjoyed by the well-to-do, but for Amos (2:6–8) the occasion is marred by abuse (Gossai 1993, 249). These cloaks (pledges) are illegally being used as the picnic blankets of the rich (v. 8a). By law they should have been returned to their owner before nightfall (Exod 22:26–27 [25–26]; Deut 24:17; Job 22:6; Prov 20:16; 27:13), presuming such a law to have been in force at this time (cf. Mays 1969a, 47). A direct parallel from the time of Josiah is found in the Yavneh Yam inscription where a peasant appeals for the return of his cloak (*ANET*, 586; Gottwald 2001, 199). An Egyptian text "The Protests of the Eloquent Peasant" (*ANET*, 407–10) relates the lengthy process undertaken to right such a wrong (Gottwald 2001, 234).

7.5.3. *Taxation*
Part and parcel of the problem of taxation for peasants was the power of the tax collector. The following modern parallels illustrate something of the terrible power exerted by tax collectors in the Near East and the levels of violence which form part and parcel of the lives of the poor of all ages.

Tax collectors, in early twentieth-century Syria were local notables, heads of tribes and villages (Warriner 1957, 61). Commenting on the situation, W. Thomson wrote:

> The tax-collector extorts from the peasants nearly all of the produce of their lands in return for the doubtful advantage of having them stand between them and the officers of the Government. This system of tax-gatherers greatly multiplied the petty lords and the tyrants who eat up the people as they eat bread.... Village sheiks and collectors shared in the spoils. The peasant was delivered bound hand and foot to the tax-collectors, since he had not the slightest protection against their tyranny (up to 50% of produce, paid in kind), which exposed him to endless oppression, and was at times not able to rescue enough to save him and his household from the prospect of starvation.... The emergence of the large estates and their acquisition were brought about for the most part through the out sourcing of the tax collection (to tax-collectors), a regular practice in all

the lands of the East in various periods of their history, including the
tithe. (quoted in Granott 1952, 56–57)

Turning from these modern twentieth-century parallels, we enquire
into the situation for biblical Israel. Negev (1972b, 16) deduces that the
systematic system of taxation for Israel started with the united monarchy
as attested by the list of stewards (2 Sam 8:16–18; 20:23–26; 1 Kgs 4:1–
19). Whatever we conclude about that earlier period, taxes may account
in the later centuries for the abundance of the la-melekh (literally, "for the
king") jar handles. These were storage *pithoi* marked on the handles with
a winged scarab or solar disk and inscribed with the words la-melekh.
Each seal carries the name of one of four towns Hebron, Socoh, Ziph and
Mmsht (an unidentified place). All the jars were made of the same clay
indicating a common origin within the Shephelah (Barkay 1992, 346).

Barkay dates these jars to the eighth century for two reasons. First, the
distribution of the handles "corresponds to the borders of the Kingdom of
Judah in the eighth century and not to its extended borders in the time of
Josiah in the seventh century, which include parts of the coastal plain and
the former kingdom of Israel" (1992, 348). Secondly, the discovery of
complete la-melekh jars at Lachish and Tel Batash from the time of
Hezekiah, and the absence of such jars in the later stratum (up to the
destruction by the Babylonians), fixes the date of the usage of the jars
(1992, 348). Barkay concludes that "it is clear that the la-melekh jars
were linked to the royal or military administration of Hezekiah. The four
cities appear to represent the four regions of the Kingdom of Judah at
this time" (1992, 348).

Stamped handles of the rosette style succeed the earlier la-melekh
handles found at Lachish and appear to have been used for the same purpose. The preponderance of la-melekh handles have been found at Jerusalem (some 300, one found by me in 1983) and Lachish (some 400; so
Barkay 1992, 348). While the exact purpose of the stamps remains uncertain, the most likely answer is that they had to do with the collection of
taxation (Holladay 1998, 393). Na'aman (1986b), however, ventures a
connection between the stamped handles and Hezekiah's security preparations in the face of the Assyrian threat of 701 B.C.E. Another possibility
is that they are to be related to Assyrian tribute (see below).

Borowski (1987, 78–83) deduces that portable commodities like oil
and wine were most likely to be taxed. Most storage in Iron Age Israel
was based in village centres (see above) but there were some large storage facilities found in Jericho, Megiddo, Lachish and Tell Beit Mirsim
from the ninth and tenth centuries (1987, 79), or better ninth and eighth
centuries (following the Lower Chronology). Storage jars abound in the

storehouses of Dothan, leading Free to conclude that, "this was a centre for collecting taxes in wheat, oil and other commodities" (1960, 7).

Isaiah 3:12–15, albeit a text with several variants, probably has relevance here (see Gossai 1993, 284). The key verb is *ngš* ("exploit"), with the subject as supplied by the LXX being tax-collectors. Isaiah accuses the state of excessively exploiting the common people. Similarly, Amos 5:11a (cf. Amos 2:8) is appropriate here since the Hebrew resounds with the underlying strains of institutional violence, hence Wolff's suggested rendering of *ngš* as "to levy extortionate taxes" (1977, 230). The peasants are forced to pay excessive taxes, in spite of their daily struggle for food, so undermining their precious reserves (Mays 1969a, 47; Dearman 1988, 28–30) and rendering them vulnerable to extreme forms of poverty. As with the rental, the issue is not the tax itself, but the excess. Positive reciprocity is under threat of abuse.

Relating to the Persian period, Neh 5:1–5 mentions the pledging of fields, vineyards and houses. This should be understood as the onset of the borrowing of money in order to pay the king's tax, which would lead finally to both the loss of children as forced labourers (pledges) and the loss of lands (Deist 2000, 181). The Jerusalem temple appears to have played a role in the collecting of civil (for the central treasury) and religious (for temple expenses) taxes, if Schaper (1995) is correct in his assumption that the Persians followed Babylonian practices. Here in this new economic order, following the advent of coinage and the market economy, negative reciprocity works hand in hand with other abuses to create a prison of debt and exploitation. The plight of the poor, especially the poorest of the poor, has worsened considerably.

Aside from taxes, it seems that the Judean peasants over the centuries were subjected to further additional demands including duties and levies. Our best evidence comes from the New Testament period so we can only speculate for earlier times. Josephus makes mention of market duties (*Ant.* 17.205.18–19). From Palmyra comes information about tariffs, which included levies of sheepskins, salted fish, wheat, wine, straw and herbs (Schottroff and Stegemann 1986, 9). What had begun as simple rents and obligations in Iron Age Israel/Judah had probably escalated over the centuries with dire consequences for the ordinary population of the land.

7.5.4. *Tributes to Foreign Nations*
From the later records, it is clear that Israel and/or Judah paid tribute to the Assyrian rulers Shalmaneser III in 841 B.C.E., to Tiglath-Pilaser in 744 B.C.E., to Sennacherib in about 700 B.C.E. and to the Neo-Babylonians in 598–597 B.C.E. (Gottwald 2001, 192–98), prior to the destruction

of Jerusalem in 586 B.C.E. The source of these tributes would have been, first and foremost, peasant surplus. Presumably it is the landlords who are referred to as the "men [people] of means" and "people of the land" (cf. 1 Kgs 14:25–26; 2 Kgs 16:6–8; 18:14–16).

Deist points out (2000, 180) that no specific details are given as to the manner of the collection of such tributes. By contrast there are details given for the Persian period. Schaper (1995, 537–38) mentions three types of tax on the basis of the text of Ezra: the mandattu, stored in the temple and taken to Persia in silver and in kind; the biltu, a form of poll tax paid in service; and ilku, a form of property tax. These taxes point to a highly developed and differentiated tax system, coupled with storage and redistribution (Albertz 2003, 335–45). Darius I fixed taxation rates for all the provinces, in a move which curtailed the ability of the Persian nobility to exact taxes at a substantial profit (2003, 345–57). Whatever the rate, such taxes when coupled with poor agricultural conditions and negative reciprocity added to the burden carried by the peasants of Judah (Olivier 1994a, 180–85; 1994b).

In a very insightful article, Zwickel argues that the pressure of Assyrian tribute led to the creation of state vineyards—attested to by stamped jar handles—and increasing strain on the ordinary peasants of Judah as their surplus disappeared across the borders where it would be of no avail in hard times (1994, 575–82; see also Holladay 1998, 393). Following the Assyrian invasions in the late eighth century, there was a large influx of refugees from neighbouring Israel into Judah, with consequent impact on peasant livelihoods, along with the demand for tribute. Zwickel (1999) suggests that these factors may underlie comments made by Isaiah (3:14–15; 5:8–10; 10:1–2) and Micah (2:1–4). Local officials apparently are abusing their power and the peasants are suffering as a result.

7.5.5. *Interest on Loans*

Peasant debt occupied a peripheral role in pre-exilic Israel, as suggested by its marked absence from the prophetic tirades (see below). From the late Babylonian and early Persian period, debt played an increasingly debilitating part in the lives of the peasants of Israel, with the swing towards market economies, as evident in the rise of trade, the use of coinage, and other indications of the economic transition (Stern 1998, 434–37).

The HB uses two different Hebrew words for interest, namely *nešek* (#5967) from the root "to bite" and *tarbît* (#9552) meaning to increase wealth through the accumulation of interest. Both of these terms indicate the power of interest rates to break the backs of the peasant poor in post-exilic Israel. Ezra–Nehemiah is a vivid testimony to the changing modes of production (Neh 5), and to the vicious consequences of the cycle of debt of that time (see below).

The world of ancient Israel, as we have seen, worked within the notion of limited good (cf. Malina 1981; Mann 1986, 66), which meant that there was seen to be only so much material good to go around. Hence the sages were concerned that the acquisition of wealth should not be too much at the expense of another, while acknowledging that all acquisition is ultimately at someone else's expense. Interest was an obvious way for increasing wealth at the expense of others. Proverbs 28:8 warns, "He who increases his wealth by exorbitant interest amasses it for another who will be kind to the poor." Scott (1965, 64) uses the expression "patron of the poor," which underscores the patron–client notion basic to the verse. Scott's "exorbitant interest" emphasises the abuse of the system and the collapse of reciprocity (1965, 166; cf. Ezek 18:8; 22:12).

7.5.6. *Tithes*

The peasants of Israel were subject to the demand of tithes and to other religious obligations levied by the priestly aristocracy and the staff of the temples (Lev 27:30–33; Deut 14:22–29; Sir 35:8–12; De Vaux 1973, 140–41, 380–82, 403–5). The line between tithes and taxes is sometimes exceedingly thin. Tithes might be used for temple expenses (Num 18:21–32) or for state expenses (cf. 1 Kgs 8:15–17; Ezek 45:13–17; 1 Macc 3:49; 10:31). There is often an implication of compulsion about tithes as when Hezekiah collected tithes and stored them in the temple (2 Chr 31:5–6; cf. 2 Sam 6; 1 Kgs 12:25–33). Under Nehemiah and Ezra's reforms a tax-tithe was instituted for the maintenance of the temple and to support the priestly class (Neh 10:33–40). One can only speculate about the extent to which such tithes were an additional burden on the backs of the people. If anything was likely to cause peasant debt in the pre-exilic period, it may well have been such religious obligations (Wolf 1966, 16; cf. Noth 1962, 187). These were in addition to the other demands, but unlike them were underpinned by social and religious obligation.

7.6. *Forms of Injustice*

The HB perceives oppression at multiple levels, but focuses on the forms of oppression which impact most forcibly on the lives of the peasants of Israel, both before and after the Babylonian Exile. I stress that the contexts of the Prophets, Law and Wisdom genres are not limited to the pre-exilic times, not least by virtue of the fact that they were preserved and edited in the post-exilic times. Indeed, I suggest that the abuses may have been even more obvious in those later times.

7.6.1. *Injustice in the Markets*

The pre-exilic kingdoms of Israel and Judah knew only the most primitive of markets in the absence of the fully fledged market economy that would emerge under the Greeks (see below). Yet there was concern even before then. Early proverbial literature is not blind to the evils of oppression. Amen-em-ope 17:8 prohibits the making of false measures (a bushel of two capacities), since the bushel is the "eye of Ra," and such cheating is seen as an "abomination" (quoted in McKane 1970, 439). Similarly, Proverbs declares that false scales are an abomination to God (Prov 11:1; 16:11; 20:10, 23) and Deut 25:13–15 follows suit. The market (whether the primitive markets of the Iron Age or the sophisticated markets of the Persian and Greek periods) is one of the areas in which peasant and the elite (whether landlord or merchant) interact, and so is an area vulnerable to the abuse of power.

The market is thus also of concern for the Prophetic literature. Amos laments the fact that people rush the hours of sacred times (literally festivals and Sabbaths; cf. Andersen and Freedman 1989, 814.), when trade was apparently forbidden, so as to sell grain and wheat (Amos 8:5). Moreover, they do not trade honestly, but are instead "skimping the measure, boosting the price, and cheating with dishonest scales" (v. 5b). The poor are being unjustly exploited (cf. Deut 25:13–16) in the market place. Hosea explicates just such economic injustice—"the merchant uses dishonest scales; he loves to defraud" (12:7). Indeed, according to Amos (8:6), the peasants are being sold "the sweepings of the wheat," which Mays (1969a, 144–45) identifies as the chaff and trash left after winnowing which was then re-mixed with clean grain and sold to the poor in these hard times. The poor were particularly reliant on the market in times of famine and drought, when their own supplies were exhausted.

Amos accuses his hearers of making the shekel smaller and the ephah larger (8:5). The shekel is a stone weight and forms the basis for Israel's system of weights (see De Vaux 1973, 203–6). Andersen and Freedman (1989, 807) suggest the scale is tampered with by moving the fulcrum. Alternatively, the actual weight, a stone sphere, is modified. The ephah is the measure (dry) for grain (Scott 1959) and this is being made smaller. Amos is referring to peasants who are cheated both while buying and selling grain. Commonly, a peasant might farm in barley, but prefer to purchase wheat for the making of bread. As peasants bring their grain for barter, over-heavy weights are in use. When they buy seed or food, smaller measures are employed. The peasants are being robbed both in their sale of crops (against rental or debt), and in their purchase of commodities (for rations and seed).

Paying attention to similar economic offences, Micah writes, "Am I still to forget, O wicked house, your ill-gotten treasures and the short ephah, which is accursed? Shall I acquit a man with dishonest scales, with a bag of false weights? Her rich men are violent; her people are liars and their tongues speak deceitfully" (6:10–12). Economic exploitation, violence and injustice combine within such a dirge. Similarly, in a later period, Ezekiel castigates the princes of Israel. They are told "Give up your violence and oppression and do what is just and right…. You are to use accurate scales, an accurate ephah and an accurate bath (liquid measure)" (45:9–10). The text then goes on to detail the standards for all such measures, including the shekel and the mina (45:11–12).

7.6.2. *Injustice in the Courts*

The second arena of injustice takes place within the legal system, another area in which peasant and elite interact. Conventionally, the leaders of the community dispensed justice. In urban areas this took place in the annexes of the city gates. From the prophetic laments it seems that this system of justice has succumbed to corruption. Mays (1983, 13) aptly comments that "those who were rich could afford more justice than others."

Exodus 23:3–6 deals with the issue of lawsuits. Two points are made. Verse 3 forbids showing favouritism to the poor (*dal*), while v. 6 adds; "Do not deny justice to your poor people (*'ebyônîm*) in their law-suits." The use of two different Hebrew words is suggestive. Understanding *'ebyônîm* as the needy and often indigent would suggest that the issue is one regarding powerlessness. These *'ebyônîm* are both poor and powerless and, therefore, likely to be trampled underfoot or simply ignored, in the practice of community justice. The denial of justice is more than a bad verdict; it is the denial of actual access to the courts. They receive no justice because no one is even willing to hear their complaint. Their cries for help fall on deaf ears, and the sense of powerlessness is reinforced. The first command, regarding the *dallîm* (peasants), suggests a possible over-reaction by the landlords—while the powerless should be protected (v. 6), ordinary peasants should not by right be given more leeway in the court (v. 3); the latter situation is in any case unlikely.

Leviticus follows the second command but elaborates, by forbidding any "partiality to the poor or favouritism to the great" (19:15). The juxtaposition of poor (*dal*) and great (*gadol*) is significant. In this instance, the power dimension, which divides peasant and landlord, is being underlined.

Amos 2:6c speaks of "selling the poor for sandals or silver." This may refer to slavery (see below) but it is possible to read the text in the light of an abuse of justice. Debt leading to slavery is not an idea that is explicit within the writings of the prophets. Another suggestion is that Amos is using "selling the poor" as an analogy. The reference to sandals and silver is then a reference to bribery, which is clearly attested throughout the prophets (e.g. Isa 1:23; 5:23; 33:15; Mic 3:11), and is found in all the main literary genres of the HB (e.g. Exod 23:8; Deut 10:17; 16:19; Job 6:22; Prov 17:23). Garbini (1977) refers to the Kilamuwa inscription: "A girl he sold for a sheep and a man for a garment" (KAI 24). We have a similar expression in English regarding being "sold down the river," which in modern parlance means being betrayed. It is the right of the poor to a fair hearing in the courts that are being sold, rather than the poor themselves.

The judges are also taking bribes (McCarter 1980, 209–10). Both Speiser (1940, 18) and Gordis (1950) saw a linguistic connection between the verb *mkr* ("sell") and the noun *ma'alam* ("bribe"), while Soggin (1987, 47), linked the shoes and bribes together, based on 1 Sam 12:3 in the LXX (cf. Sir 49:19), "From whose hand did I take bribes or shoes?" Similarly, in Amos 8, sale of persons could be seen as an analogy. The focus in that pericope is upon the market place (1987, 134–37). By their cheating, the powerful are buying the rights of the poor to fair market practices, so that they may profit. The analogy forms the common basis both for the notions of bribery (Amos 2) and for unfair market practices (Amos 8).

The objection raised against the practice of bribery nearly a century ago falls away. Driver (1913, 88–89) had argued that sandals were too paltry a sum for bribery. However, third-world experiences, where thieves kill for the sake of a few dollars, undercut such first-world naivety. A good pair of sandals in the ancient world might be a handsome prize in a situation where few people could afford shoes for their feet. Regarding the sandals as a paltry sum also ignores the parallel in silver (Amos 2:6b), which is hardly paltry and I might add that such a parallel, if anything, underlines the value that sandals had in the ancient world, not least as a sign of status (Speiser 1940, 18).

The idea of the perversion of justice continues as Amos 2:7 speaks of the poor being turned out of "the way." Mays (1969a, 46) clarifies the language—"Turn aside is a locution for the perversion of the legal procedure" and "way is a synonym for justice" (see also Wolff 1977, 133). The NIV renders the verse as "to deny justice to the oppressed" (see also Andersen and Freedman 1989, 317; Deut 1:19; 24:17; 2 Sam 15:2; Isa

29:21; Prov 17:23). The same idea recurs in Job 24:2–4 (Pope 1965, 160). Mays writes "the courts [are] used as instruments of exploitation. The concern of Israel's legal customs for justice had been displaced by a crass commercial spirit. The courts had become places for profit by the strong, rather than as places designed to uphold the protection of the weak" (1969a, 48). Similarly, Gossai suggests that those who serve as judges are those whose position in society is secured by wealth or owner-ship of land, so that "as long as the individual is economically depressed the opportunity to serve does not arise. Decision-making is being shaped by the power and wealth and not by the circumstance and evidence of the case" (1993, 292).

Amos returns in ch. 5, to the abuse of the legal system of the time. Justice is poisoned and righteousness is thrown down (5:7). Andersen and Freedman (1989, 484), render the passage metaphorically as a funeral scene, "justice is buried," but include the notions of judgment and vio-lence. The NRSV places v. 7 directly before v. 10 allowing for a continu-ity, so that Amos immediately goes on to speak about those who "hate the one who reproves in court" (v. 10a). Andersen and Freedman (1989, 498) suggest that the Hebrew term for "reproves" is a legal term for a "third party or advocate who takes up the cause of the poor against the rich, and thus is hated." In such times, even the one who tells the truth is despised (v. 10b). The legal scenario is further explored in Amos 5:12b, "you oppress the righteous and take bribes and you deprive the poor (*dal*) of justice in the courts." In this overtly legal context "the righteous" might better be rendered as "the innocent." The innocent become the victims of a legal miscarriage. So injustice prevails.

Ezekiel targets the law courts (see Ezek 22:12a where men accept bribes to shed blood). In his discussion of individual responsibility, found in ch. 18, the model of a righteous person is one who does not oppress people, who returns pledges, who instead of committing robbery gives food to the hungry and provides clothing for the naked. In place of excessive interest rates or indeed any rates at all, such a person lends to those in need. The righteous person does no wrong (in the court) but instead judges fairly between one person and another (Ezek 18:7–9). The contrasts are interesting. Oppression is juxtaposed with the return of pledges; robbery with giving food to the hungry; charging excessive interest with lending fairly; and finally doing wrong with judging fairly. Positive reciprocity avails at every point in this description.

Injustice in court is the theme of several proverbs. So Prov 22:22 urges, "Do not exploit the poor (*^cānî*) because they are poor (literally, "put down or humbled"), and do not crush the needy (*dal*) in court."

Indeed, God will fight on their behalf (v. 23). False witness is condemned out of hand (19:9). In Proverbs 17:15, the release of the guilty and condemnation of the innocent are seen as abominations. Proverbs 17:26 alludes to the practice of beating condemned prisoners. Bribes as a means to perverting the cause of justice is decried in Prov 17:23, although in 17:8, the contrary view is heard (McKane 1970, 512). A moral ethic shines out in that the righteous are concerned about the well-being of the helpless (Prov 29:7). They champion the cause of the poor (Scott 1965, 168). Fair and just rule is summarised as to "judge fairly; defend the rights of the poor and needy" (Prov 31:9).

7.6.3. *Unfair Labour Practices*

Jeremiah, whose ministry straddles the late sixth century and the early fifth century, makes mention of a secretary in charge of conscripting the people of the land (the *am-ha-aretz*) or the peasantry (52:25), akin to the minister of the corvée of Solomon's time (1 Kgs 12:18). Apparently, the practice of not paying labourers went wider than the state. Jeremiah writes, "Woe to him who builds his palace [literally, 'house'] by unrighteousness, his upper rooms by injustice, making his countrymen work for nothing, not paying them for their labour" (22:13). Similarly, Malachi speaks against those employers who "defraud labourers of their wages, who oppress the widows and the fatherless, and deprive aliens of injustice, but do not fear me" (Mal 3:5). As with so many other abusive practices, children and the very poor are the most likely to suffer most in such situations. Wages are unpaid and children starve.

Certain categories of persons are often more vulnerable to oppression, injustice and poverty than others. Poverty studies have long indicated the particular vulnerability of women and children (Fenyves, Rule and Everatt 1998). Amos bears out this inclination when he speaks of an abused young woman. The reference to a father and son who use the same girl (Amos 2:7b) is taken by some commentators to be an allusion to the practice of temple prostitution, in the light of ritual "lying down besides every altar on garments taken in pledge" (v. 8). In support of a notion of cultic prostitution, Andersen and Freedman (1989, 318), turn to quoting Herodotus (1.199) and Code of Hammurabi (CH 178 and 182).

What is therefore being condemned, in this view, is the practice of temple prostitution (Cutler and MacDonald 1982, 35). However, to date there is simply no clear evidence for the practice of temple prostitution in ancient Israel (Grabbe 1995, 196; Barstad 1984, 21–23; Goodfriend and Van der Toorn 1992). Mays (1969a, 46) points out that the Hebrew term is not *qedesa* and he suggests that the maiden is a bond-servant or pledge who is being used as a concubine by both father and son. Legal texts (Exod 21:8; Deut 22:30) suggest that sexual access to such a person was the right of either the male head of the household or his son, but not both. The sexual "use" of the woman has, therefore, given way to "abuse." Instead of being taken as a second wife or concubine, with at least some security of status, she is being used by both father and son.

The context, focussing on the abuse of the poor, strongly suggests the lowly status of a servant or slave (Barstad 1984, 23; Soggin 1987, 48). The use of the definite article may imply a specific person (Andersen and Freedman 1989, 318) but a more likely answer is that we are dealing with a colloquialism. One should think in terms of the demeaning practice whereby adults, both men and women, are called "the boy" or "the girl" and other quasi-filial terms (Patterson 1982, 63–65) in some communities. In his attack on such abuse, Amos speaks out in the woman's defence (*pace* Sandersen 1992, 205–6). Here is one of the rare instances of the use of the female gender with regard to the poor (see Bird 1998, 52–78). The double oppression of women, both within and without of their household, is briefly apparent here. The young woman had been chosen (as the pledge for the loan) because of her gender, but then abused, because of her vulnerability, within that very situation.

Servants and slaves, whether in ancient Israel or elsewhere, are all too often the most likely victims of abuse. The so-called Suffering Servant of Deutero-Isaiah illustrates their vulnerability. In the classic Song of the Servant in Isa 53, the Servant/Slave of God moves in a world racked by pain and suffering. The Servant is shamed, pain-racked and afflicted by disease, stripped of honour and status (v. 3), oppressed for the sins of others (v. 5), maltreated (v. 7), arrested and sentenced (v. 8) and assigned a grave with the wicked (v. 9). Yet he will live and see his off-spring (v. 10). The metaphor is that of an abused and badly treated slave, whom God raises up and honours. Hanks calls him "God's Oppressed Servant" (1983, 74).

7.7. *The Violence of Oppression*

The violence of oppression is a theme within the HB that is graphically illustrated in unforgettable metaphors. Amos, for example, speaks of the powerful grinding the heads of the poor into the dust (2:7; 8:4). The reference is to the shaming of the poor (taking the head as a symbol of honour) including actual physical abuse. One paraphrase reads, "They smash them on the head, they shove them off the street and trample them in the dust" (Andersen and Freedman 1989, 316).

At times, the prophets use the language of robbery and plunder, depicting the powerful as warriors who plunder the poor. So Amos 3:9–10 draws attention to the unrest and oppression that occurs on the mountains of Samaria, and to the practise of hoarding "plunder and loot" in their palaces. Mays (1969a, 64–65) underlines the legal context. The poor, who are often accused of being robbers and thieves by the well-to-do, are instead the implied victims of the plunder of the rich and powerful. Cleverly, Amos juxtaposes these implied victims with the robbers and dividers of spoil, turning the business practices of the well-to-do into crimes of violence and abuse. The veneer of respectability is torn away and the true nature of the "business practices" of the strong is exposed for all to see. What the protagonists probably see as good business practices, Amos denounces as robbery. What the powerful see as the necessary disciplining of the poor becomes the violence of bandits. What the rich see as their God-given rights and privileges is seen by Amos as the foundations of their oppression of the poor. Amos concludes this section with the warning, "The plunderers will be plundered" (3:11). While the agent is not mentioned the implication is that God has declared war on the powerful (following Coote 1981).

Eliphaz (in Job) elaborates upon the social violence of oppression:

> Men [the subject is missing from the MT, so the LXX supplies "the wicked"] move boundary stones; they pasture flocks they have stolen [the LXX reads, "They seize flock and shepherd"]. They drive away the orphan's donkey and take the widow's ox in pledge. They thrust the needy from the path and force all the poor of the land into hiding. (Job 24:2–4)

Theft, economic exploitation and legal corruption join hands in these verses. The works of the powerful are exposed.

In their pursuit of power, such people do not hesitate to steal land and flocks from those who are weak. They take as pledges donkeys and oxen, which are needed in the agricultural process and so disadvantage the ability of the owners to repay the debt. The Code of Hammurabi specifies that the taking of pledges is forbidden from people in distress, and even more so when the person is a widow or orphan (CH 241). Pope (1965, 159) calls the action in Job 24:3 "doubly heinous" on that account. Job 24:3 speaks of the poor going "into hiding" and of "the hunting down of the poor." The violence of the passage is mirrored in the verbs used—stolen, drive away, thrust, and force. So the poor are violently treated and become, paradoxically, the criminals in a society where values are turned upside down, and might is right.

In Job 20:19, Zophar accuses Job of being one of those greedy people (cf. vv. 18, 20–23) who oppresses the poor and leaves them desolate and harassed, who seizes houses (or possibly robs houses—Pope 1965, 138), which he did not build. The Hebrew in Zophar's speech parallels oppressing the peasants and "leaving them destitute" with "seizing houses" (20:19). For such housing to be seized implies a collapse of the village community, and a driving out of certain peasants from the area. Destitution and homelessness is the common end. Peasant homes have been seized and others will be housed there and the "traders" profit all the while (20:18). Pope (1965, 138) translates, "he shall store his grain unused; his massed wealth he shall not enjoy" (Job 20:28). Positive reciprocity has collapsed, but for Job, God is not blind to such injustices.

Oppression of the poor, in the Psalms, is clearly portrayed as a social evil. Several Psalms speak explicitly about the poverty that results from the schemes of the wicked (e.g. Pss 8; 9; 10). The wicked are depicted as hunters out to trap their prey (Ps 10:9). Indeed, the language of the Psalms is filled with violent images. The wicked hunt down the weak (Ps 10:2), they ambush and murder the poor (v. 8), they catch and drag off the helpless (v. 9) and their victims are crushed and collapse under their strength (v. 10). The images highlight the "bully-boy" mentality of oppression. The psalmist laments those patrons and landlords who "devour the grain of Yahweh, they did not harvest" (Ps 14:4), and recalls the reader to the sobs of the poor and the groans of the needy (12:5).

Whether the oppression is structural or physical, violence is endemic to it (Tamez 1982, 24; Gutierrez 1973, 63). Isaiah 1:15 speaks of those whose hands are full of blood, implying perhaps the actual injury of the poor. More obviously, the prophet Micah laments those "who tear the skin from my people and the flesh from their bones; who eat my people's flesh, strip off their skin and break their bones in pieces; who chop them up like meat for the pan, like flesh for the pot" (3:2a–3). People are brutalised, dehumanised and consumed by the greed of the powerful. They are the animals, cut up, broken and ground down. Their bodies are abused, their minds destroyed. "All men lie in wait to shed blood; each hunts his brother with a net. Both hands are skilled in doing evil; the ruler demands gifts, the judge accepts bribes, the powerful dictate what they desire—they all conspire together" (Mic 7:2–3; cf. Hos 12:14).

Shaw (1993, 81–82) on Mic 2:2 stresses the real violence of the process that is manifest in the actions of the verbs. The coveting leads to taking by force with overtones of robbery. The Hebrew (*gazal*) for Shaw suggests military rather than economic force (1993, 82). Instead of reading Micah against a backdrop of peasants losing their land through debt, Shaw writes, "It is significant that there is no unambiguous reference to economic exploitation through foreclosures and usury. The taking of land…appears to be achieved mostly through acts of violence and harassment" (1993, 84). The point made here by Shaw is a critical one (see below). Habakkuk also equates oppression with robbery. He challenges those who pile up stolen goods and make themselves wealthy by extortion (2:6b). "Woe to him who builds a city with bloodshed and establishes a town by crime" (2:12).

Jeremiah offers a choice to his listeners:

> If you really change your way and your actions and deal with each other justly, if you do not oppress the alien, the fatherless or the widow and do not shed innocent blood in this place, and if you do not follow other gods to your own harm then I will let you live in this place, in the land which I gave to your forefathers for ever and ever. (Jer 7:5–7)

Justice is understood, as so often in the ANE, as not taking advantage of the powerless, including using violent behaviour (spilling innocent blood). Andersen and Freedman (1989, 815) speak of the passive acquiescence and ultimately connivance of civil and ecclesiastical authorities, with city merchants in the abuse of the poor.

7.8. *The Distortion of Religion*

Religion itself comes under the purview of the prophets, not as a separate category, but as a continuum of the distortion of justice and righteousness (Gossai 1993, 246). Wolf (1966, 16) speaks of those peasants whose wealth sets them apart from the neighbours, and who instead of using this wealth for the wider community, begin to ignore social obligation and community celebrations. Wealth is expended on purely selfish ends, and the cult becomes a game in which the elite pursue their own interests and intentions. The Little Tradition of the peasants stands in opposition to the Great Tradition of the aristocracy (Carney 1975, 198).

For Israel, the religion of the peasants was probably focussed on a form of ancestor veneration (cult of the dead) as a study of some 300 internments seems to indicate (Bloch-Smith 1992). One of the key indicators of Israelite sites is the presence of small terracotta figurines, which appear in abundance in urban Judah after the eighth century and up until the fall of Jerusalem (Kletter 2001). They have been related to the goddess Asherah (so Kletter 2001, 212–14) but the connection remains tenuous. Their context suggests that they represent the religion of the elite, but this also is not certain. There is much about Israelite religion, the greater and the lesser traditions, which remain unexplored—clearly a study awaiting further attention. What is clear is the tension between the established religion and the prophetic invective. That these words were edited in the post-exilic period strongly suggests that their relevance to that time was firmly established. The continued plight of the poor created the context for the popularity of the Prophetic writings—the non-poor delight in observing their own faults in earlier generations.

The cult, according to the prophets, has become enmeshed within the web of social crimes, and so the prophets call for its cleansing, if not for its abolition (Gossai 1993, 265–71). In one of the most radical of all the oracles attributed to him, Amos reports God as saying,

> I hate, I despise your religious feasts; I cannot stand your assemblies. Even though you bring me burnt offerings and grain offering, I will not accept them. Though you bring me choice fellowship offerings, I will have no regard for them. Away with the noise of your songs! I will not listen to the music of your harps. But let justice roll on like a river, righteousness like a never-failing stream. (Amos 5:21–24)

Religion without justice is an obnoxious odour in the nostrils of the Almighty. In the words of Amos, we have a powerful condemnation of the hegemony of a state, where religion is used to mask injustice and to disguise oppressive laws. Elsewhere, Amos speaks of those who rush the Sabbath days in order to return to their business of cheating the poor (8:5), so that "the poor who need the Sabbath to rest and survive another day" (Gossai 1993, 289), become instead the victims of an abusive situation, into which religion has been co-opted. The sense of community has been destroyed (1993, 289). No matter how spiritual the religion of the oppressors may seem to be, as long as injustice reigns in the land, such religion is a sham, and God rejects it.

The poor in the lands of Israel and Judah lived at the mercy of the sacrificial system. When drought and plague threatened, they turned to sacrifice to gain the favour of God or the gods. Taking the last of their hard-earned supplies, the peasants would buy a sacrificial animal or bird, and bring this to the temple or hill-shrine. While one might wish to applaud their recognition of God as the one who could help them, the potential, on the part of the religious leaders, to abuse the simple faith of the poor was great (cf. Hos 6:9; Jer 7:11).

Amos, like Jeremiah, appears to reflect the belief that the sacrificial cult stems from a source other than Yahweh (Amos 5:25) Perhaps this was one of the marks of the Yahweh-alone party, a religious sect that opposed the popular syncretistic cult (Domeris 1999). Such a reaction against the sacrificial cult may be justified if the cult itself was seen to be oppressive. For example, God is heard to say, "For I desire mercy, not sacrifice, and acknowledgement of God rather than burnt offerings" (Hos 6:6). Jeremiah 7:22 has God declare that he did not give the forefathers of Israel laws concerning sacrifices (cf. Carroll 1986, 216; Domeris 1999). Isaiah of Babylon (Isa 58) continues in the same vein. The house of Jacob has abandoned the just laws of God (v. 1); while overtly "mortifying themselves" and donning sack cloth and ashes (vv. 3–5), their hypocrisy is revealed in their quarrelling and strife (v. 4). God demands a different standard of fasting! "Is not this the kind of fasting I have chosen: to loose the chains of injustice and untie the cords of the yoke, to set the oppressed free and break every yoke?" (v. 6). The cult is not to be part of the burden of oppression and impoverishment, but should instead be a voice that cries for justice (Amos 5:21–24).

Micah explodes the myth that Yahweh can be bought, or co-opted into any system, no matter how valuable or costly the sacrifice may be (6:6–8). God has shown what is required of human society—not elaborate religious rituals, but "to act justly, and to love mercy and to walk humbly with your God" (6:8). The Hebrew says literally "to do justice," which has the double implication of acting justly and doing away with injustice. Micah rejects the appeal to a personal piety that ignores the fact of one's living in an unjust society. The divine imperative is to challenge injustice, while living justly. Too many people opt out of the struggle for justice by retreating into their own world of personal ethics. Doing justice is a costly activity, but this is the price which God requires.

Deutero-Isaiah spells out his ethic of concern. "Is it [true fasting] not to share your food with the hungry and to provide the poor wanderer with shelter; when you see the naked to clothe him, and not to turn away from your own flesh and blood" (Isa 58:7). The practice outlined here is not a significant departure from what peasants might expect from the landowners. The rules of reciprocity require that in return for taxation and rental, the owner will take care of his or her peasants in times of hunger, and will clothe and house them, including his/her family.

7.9. The Abuse of Power

An Ethiopian peasant was once asked why he did not remove the stones that littered his field. He replied that to do so would make his field attractive to the powerful, who would then take his land from him (Brand 1987, 144). In similar vein, Prov 13:23 refers to the vulnerability of the poor. It reads, "A poor man's field may produce abundant food, but injustice sweeps it away." McKane (1970, 462) speaks of oppressive exactions. Scott highlights two interesting ANE parallels, which urge, "Guard thyself against robbing the oppressed and against overbearing the disabled" (*ANET*, 422a, cited in Scott 1965, 138) and "Be not greedy for the property of a poor man" (*ANET*, 409b, cited in Scott 1965, 138). Even when a peasant has a good crop, he or she may not have the power to protect it.

Power corrupts, and absolute power corrupts absolutely. In no instance is this truer than in the domain of legislation. Isaiah of Jerusalem cries out, "Woe to those who make unjust laws" (Isa 10:1) followed by the familiar litany—depriving the poor of their rights, withholding justice from the oppressed, making prey of widows and robbing the fatherless (vv. 1–2). Not only is the judicial system corrupt, but the legislators conspire to change the rules. In similar vein, Habakkuk laments, "Therefore the law is paralysed, and justice never prevails. The wicked hem in the righteous, so that justice is perverted" (1:2–4).

The rich rule the poor, and the borrower is slave/servant to the lender, state the sages (Prov 22:7; cf. 6:1–5). Both McKane and Scott underline the power of the rich over the poor. The analogy of servant or slave is a powerful one for the stranglehold of debt (McKane 1970, 566), while the use of the verb "rule" carries the sense of "govern and control." Scott (1965, 127) uses the term "dominate," which brings out the essence of the language more forcibly.

The manner in which oppression is used alongside other Hebrew verbs is enlightening. So in Ps 44:24 [25] oppression is paralleled with misery or affliction. In Ps 107, the writer speaks of being humbled (put down or shamed) by oppression (v. 39). In Ps 72:14, the supplicant calls out to be rescued from oppression and violence. In Ps 12:5 [6], we hear of the oppression of the weak and the groaning of the needy. Quickly we realise that oppression is situated within the framework of power. Those with power oppress those without power (cf. the strong in Ps 35:10). The power that wealth brings is well illustrated in Prov 10:15: "The wealth of the rich is their fortified city, but poverty is the ruin of the poor." As wealth underlies the power, protection and honour of the rich, poverty causes the poor to fall and to stay as the fallen, the weak and the powerless.

Eliphaz, one of the "comforters" in the book of Job, exposes aspects of the typical imbalance of power. Job 22:6–9 reads:

> You demand security from your brothers for no reason; you stripped men of their clothing, leaving them naked. You gave no water to the weary and you withheld food from the hungry, though you were a powerful man [literally, "man of arm"; see Pope 1965, 150], owning land, an honoured man, living in it. And you sent widows away empty handed and broke the strength of the fatherless.

Here in Job, the contrast is between those who wield power with honour, and those who abuse power. For example, in Job 35:9 we read, "Men cry out under a load of oppression; they plead for relief from the arm of the powerful." Oppression here is the sheer abuse of power and the collapse of positive reciprocity.

In the ancient world, as today, certain categories of people are more vulnerable to abuse than are others. Job opens up the plight of the fatherless in a way no other book of the HB does. Without a redeemer to protect them they are among the most vulnerable. Their strength may be broken (Job 22:9), they may be seized as debt labourers (24:9; see Pope's emendation, 1965, 158), they have none to assist them (29:12), they struggle for food (31:17) and they are vulnerable to both physical and legal abuse (31:21). Without some powerful patron in the gate, the pleas of the fatherless, the weak (and silenced) would go unheard (Pope 1965, 205; cf. Job 29:12). The fatherless of Job's time and the street children of our own led similar lives, whether they live in Rio de Janeiro or Johannesburg. Poverty and violence, even violent death, are common realities. Whether they are the refugees of ethnic cleansing in some third-world country or just runaways from abusive homes (in a first-world country), injustice and abuse are simply part of their lives.

These texts paint a picture of a dislocated world. On the one hand, we find power, controlling peasants and their land and honour, and, on the other, hunger, thirst, debt, obligation, and shame. In the mind of the writers, and in the sight of God, evil is the abuse of the poor, and righteousness is the care of the needy. In this world the opposition is primarily between those with power and those without; between those who have access to land and those who do not; between those with honour and those without. Poverty and wealth are simply two of the many adjectives used to give flesh to these oppositions.

7.10. *The Shaming of the Poor*

In my model of poverty, I will show how shame and powerlessness work hand-in-hand against the well-being of the poor. Poverty is frequently described from the perspective of the non-poor as failure. To be poor is to have failed in some way. The poor have failed to achieve economic success, to find work, to show initiative, to break free from the cage of poverty. In the society of the non-poor, to be poor is therefore to be shamed, to admit to failure in the eyes of that world. This is the stigma of poverty, the sign of the wound. It is an inflicted sign, for the poor do not naturally feel shamed by their poverty, nor do they see themselves as failures, until they are conditioned to do so by the wider society of the non-poor.

If the poor are not naturally shamed, where then does this shaming arise? Here, then, is another answer to the root cause of poverty—the social stigma of shame. Shame may be a weapon, used against the poor. Powerlessness goes a long way towards explaining the erosion of the resistance of the peasants to poverty, but it is ultimately the shaming process that keeps the poor in poverty. The recognition of this process is to unearth the elements of the social construction of poverty and to realise that while the basic pre-conditions for poverty arise in the world of the poor, the root causes of poverty are to be found in the world of the non-poor. Yet if blame is found it is most often placed on the shoulders of the poor and they find themselves stereotyped. The Wisdom writings are best known for their stereotypes (Matthews and Benjamin 1991).

7.10.1. *The Stereotype of the Lazy Poor*

The interpretation of the collected wisdom of Proverbs and Sirach hinges upon their social location, among the ruling elite (Whybray 1974, 1990; Grabbe 1995, 163–76) and their didactical purpose (Pleins 1987, 61). While some of the proverbs may have originated in more common situations, in their written form they are the preserve of the educated elite (Lemaire 1984). Sirach acknowledges that "the wisdom of the scribe depends on the opportunity of leisure" (38:24).

The understanding of both wealth and poverty is consequently affected by the elitist origins. Scott (1965, 84), for example, argues that in a passage like Prov 10:15 there is no suggestion that the division of a community into rich and poor is seen to be unjust, or questionable. He continues, "Wealth, by which is meant not vast riches but substantial prosperity, is considered the result of diligent work (vs. 4) and of the Lord's blessing on an upright life (vs. 22). Poverty, conversely, is regarded as the fruit of indolence (vs. 4)" (1965, 84). However, to take this as a general maxim regarding the essential origin of poverty is to do a disservice to the didactic intention of the sages.

One of the results of the didactic nature of the books for the education of the elite is the presence of stereotypes. In Proverbs and Sirach these include the Adulterous Wife, the Virtuous Woman, the Lazy Man and the Fool (Domeris 1995). The sluggard lives in poverty, because he is lazy (Prov 6:6–11; 20:4). One can recognise his property from afar, because of the state of neglect and the weeds in the fields (24:30–34). The stereotypical lazy man serves as a didactic model for the young elite. They might become like him if they do not work hard. Poverty will come upon them like an armed warrior (24:34). Hyperbole makes the threat more real. The metaphor trembles on the edge of becoming myth. Proverbs seemingly propagates the view that poverty is essentially a consequence of laziness—the "fruit of indolence" (Scott 1965, 84). In fact, as Malchow (1982) shows the collection offers various paths into poverty, including oppression and injustice (e.g. Prov 14:31; 22:16; 29:13). These paths pose no real threat for the ruling elite—laziness, on the other hand, does.

Just as wealth and honour may be linked (Ps 3:16; 8:18) the reverse is also true. Oppression involves the process of being shamed, made miserable and sorrowful (107:39). The loss of social esteem is endemic to oppression. Tragically, people who are oppressed may begin to believe the lies of their oppressors and even to blame themselves for their own state of being broken. They begin to believe in their own inferiority, and in the myth of their inability to quest for honour; they abandon their own claim to equality. They are doubly shamed, both by their enemies and by the false image of themselves.

7.10.2. *The Stereotype of the Oppressed Poor*

Wisdom literature knows another type of the poor, namely, the oppressed poor. This category is often underplayed but forms an important counter to the lazy poor. Proverbs 14:31 states that, "He [she] who oppresses the poor (*dal*) shows contempt for their Maker, but whoever is kind to the needy honours God." Behind this proverb are the peasant poor and the notion that while poverty strips of all dignity, practical care for the poor is a way of honouring God. Indeed, God the supreme patron is shamed or honoured according to one's treatment of the poor. God's identity with the process, and with the poor, is significant. God is seen to invest real value within the poor, recognising as a basic right the right to be honoured, and as an abuse the tendency to shame the poor.

Shame and honour are options both for the powerful and the powerless, but the tendency is towards the shaming of the poor. This is what the sage attempts to guard against. A similar proverb is Prov 17:5, which reads, "He who mocks the poor shows contempt for their Maker, whoever gloats over disaster will not go unpunished." After violence, the experience of the poor is one of shame. Their enemies malign them but God will save them (Ps 12:5). Metaphorically, but also in a real sense the very location shames them, for the poor inhabit the dust and the ash heap (Ps 113:7). Dahood (1968, 130) has "dung hill," reminding one that the poor are often forced to scavenge through the garbage of others. They are often dirty and their honour is dragged in the dust. The psalmist appeals for them to be honoured by God (Ps 74:21) rather than to sit in shame as if in ritual of mourning (Dahood 1968, 208).

7.11. *The Marginalisation of the Poor*

The term marginalised arises from the context of the third world as a label for those people whom society had swept into its darkest corners. Quite often the expression "the marginalised" is used in concert with the poor, as distinct but complementary. In understanding the concept of the marginalised it is necessary to understand the operation of negative values like shame and powerlessness. To be marginalised is to be driven to the boundaries in society, or even across these boundaries into the realm of the outcast. Here in this peculiar half state live those whom society has decreed undesirable, the outcasts. In this amorphous group there are few common factors other than a common experience of social isolation. The process of marginalisation is testimony to the power of the non-poor (those who are not marginalised) and ultimately to the process of the social construction of poverty, which underlies this present work.

Bechtel (1991) describes the shaming process as a means of social control, as a form of pressure to preserve social cohesion and reject deviancy (including the poor) and finally as a means of domination by one group over another allowing for the manipulation of the social status. The shaming of the poor often leads to what may be termed as a progressive process of marginalisation by the non-poor.

The marginalised are those who experience the double effects of the pressures of shame and powerlessness. They are a narrower category than the poor, although often they may include large groups of the poor. To be marginalised is to lose, first of all, one's sense of place in society and to be relegated to the margins in the ordering of power. This, in turn, means to be shamed because one has been taken out of any pretence to the regular ordering of honour. Among the ranks of the marginalised we meet a variety of persons, including prostitutes both male and female, beggars and street urchins, certain categories of labourers or occupations, certain criminals and people who have been publicly ostracised. In the ANE one might add widows, the fatherless and the resident aliens to the list. Finally, we have the physically and psychologically challenged whose numbers would have made up a significant section of the marginalised, more so because there seems no legal or ethical protection for them.

In Ps 10, the fatherless are grouped with the victim (v. 14) and with the oppressed (v. 18). In 68:5–6, the fatherless is found in company with the widow, the friendless and the prisoner. In 82:3, the fatherless are linked with the weak, the poor and the oppressed. In 94:6, the fatherless are linked to the widow, the alien, and to oppression (cf. v. 5). In these verses, one gains not just a sense of the semantic domains, but of the social context of poverty and oppression, and the categories of people who make up the social construction of the marginalised in ancient Israel (cf. "the people of the land" in New Testament times; Finkelstein 1962, 2:754–67). Townsend (1988) proposes that while Job and Sirach especially recognise the debilitating impact of poverty, the solution (throughout the Wisdom corpus) is conditioned by the giving of charity, rather than the changing of society (as in the Prophetic corpus). Nevertheless, the various Wisdom references to oppression and injustice across the corpus should not be underplayed.

Women are particularly vulnerable to becoming members of the group of the marginalised (Tamez 1989). Ruether speaks of the betrayal of women even within a society that harbours a prophetic tradition in conflict with the ruling elite (1990, 24–33). In any society where honour plays a role—and by honour, one normally refers to male honour since women have little recourse to achieving any form of status, other than by marriage, which is through association with a man. Normally unable to achieve honour in their own right, women must avoid bringing down shame on their own heads and the heads of the males of their family. All of this contributes, in honour-bound societies, to the vulnerability of a woman. She must walk a narrow path through the sinking sands of potential shame with great care. So it is not surprising to discover that the majority of the marginalised in most, if not all societies, are women and female children.

Poverty is a form of disaster. To mock people in the midst of disaster is to fail to render assistance, and worse, to humiliate. The poorest of the poor are those who have no hope. Their eyes are empty. They are the living dead. Job 5:16 speaks of the precious hope of the poor, and the emptiness that life without such hope represents. Appositely, Proverbs enquires "who can endure, if the spirit is crushed" (Prov 18:14). Integral to a full understanding of poverty is the realisation that when the spirit is damaged, one's whole capacity to function as a human and to fight back against oppression is undermined. Jesus would call such people "the poor in spirit," meaning those people stripped of spirit (Domeris 1990). In the words of Trudi Thomas, "This week, I saw an old man bludgeoned by poverty into…vacant apathy, alive only because he was not dead; who only said when asked what was wrong, 'I am hungry'" (quoted in Wilson and Ramphele 1989, 103).

7.12. *Conclusion*

The HB clearly associates poverty with oppression and injustice. This is why the theory of the social construction of poverty is so fitting. For the peasants of Israel, their struggle for survival is tainted by the experience of being disempowered. Reciprocity has changed from positive to negative and as a result the poor suffer. The poor are abused and become the victims of injustice, of violence and shaming. They are alienated and marginalised and live under the spectre of death. The horror of poverty is unmistakable, yet so rarely described in the secondary sources commenting on the biblical texts.

At the heart of oppression lies a well of fear. Such a fear is almost inconceivable to those who live in comfort and security today, yet to those who have experienced real oppression that fear is a tangible experience. One can smell it, feel it, and sense it, like a deep pain in the stomach, a taste of nausea in the mouth. Raw pain! The wise man stays silent in such evil times (Amos 5:13a). One does nothing to attract attention for fear of the violence, physical or verbal, which that would bring. Oppression is indeed an evil time.

I have spoken in terms of the collapse of the ethic of positive reciprocity opening the way to injustice and oppression. I suggest that the process began in Iron Age Israel/Judah and intensified in the post-exilic period. What some scholars (Coote 1981; Gossai 1993; Lang 1985; Premnath 1988) perceived to be a change contained within the Iron Age, we will demonstrate was instead spread across the centuries into the Persian, Greek and Roman periods. This is the focus of the next chapter.

Chapter 8

THE IMPACT OF THE POST-EXILIC
ECONOMIC CHANGES

8.1. *A New Perspective*

From the outset of this study, I have indicated my concern about the treatment of the economy of Israel and Judah, which has tended to ignore the fundamental differences between pre-exilic and post-exilic times. In this chapter, I break with some of the established thinking about the peasant plight in pre-exilic times, suggesting that much of this is anachronistic and a result of collapsing two separate economic systems into one. Solid archaeological data exist for viewing the Exile in Babylon as an economic watershed, with particular implications for the peasant economy of Judah. One might draw a continuous line from the peasant economy of the divided monarchy back into the Late Bronze period of the El Amarna, and the peasant economy of that time. To all intents and purposes, from the peasant perspective little changed. Not so with the period beyond the monarchy, through the time of the Exile and beyond, where massive changes took place in virtually every area of peasant life.

In his review of the economy of ancient Israel, Hoppe (2004, 8–13) assumes that debt leading to land loss and slavery were major problems in Iron Age II for the divided monarchy and had been so from the time of Late Bronze Age Canaan. Moreover, this was a pattern that continued more or less unchanged until Roman times (2004, 10–13). Wolff argues that the ruling elite of Israel (in Iron II) have coveted the fields of the peasants and their homes and, by manipulation of the law (fraud), rob people of their land and so of their inheritance (1990, 78). In similar vein, Coote (1981, 32) uses the term "mulct" in the sense of the seizing of patrimonial lands, for the creation of large estates through exorbitant interest and fines during the eighth century B.C.E. (cf. also Gossai 1993, 285). Micah 2:2 (cf. Shaw 1993) and Amos 2:6 are often used as proof texts for such annexation through fines and debt seizures (Speiser 1940, 18; De Vaux 1973, 169; Mays 1969; Chaney 1986, 68). I do not contest that such oppressive actions eventually took place. Rather what this chapter will argue is that the time-scale is wrong.

The whole are of the economy of the monarchy remains one of the most neglected chapters in biblical research yet it is pertinent to almost every area of the subject of poverty. As in all ancient economies, we can only approach the process of reconstruction through the medium of a suitable societal model. In this instance, I have chosen to make use of five key indicators developed on the basis of the writings of the political theoretician Kautsky (1982). In the process, I will adduce the evidence that has led me to consider the Exile as a moment of major significance in the history of peasant Judah and Israel.

8.2. *Five Key Indicators in the Economy of the Monarchy*

Kautsky (1982) compares two stereotypical forms of empire, namely aristocratic empires with commercial empires. Where commercial empires are based on trade and commerce, aristocratic empires are located within agrarian economies, in which these aristocrats control both land and peasants (1982, 6). Kautsky highlights certain key indicators that enable the reader to locate a particular state closer to one or other of these stereotypes. This is the most important aspect of his work, because regardless of the value of the titles he gives to his stereotypes, these indicators remain valid.

The typical aristocratic empire includes such varying societies as the Babylonians, Egyptians and Persians (Kautsky 1982). Kautsky details various characteristics. The leadership of an aristocratic empire are born into positions of power. Wealth is conceived of in terms of land, with large landowners being drawn entirely from the ruling aristocracy; only minor roles are played by trade and commerce (1982, 5–6). Aristocrats use systems of patronage and military might to control their peasants giving them the right to taxation, through a highly decentralised form of government (1982, 6). The aristocrats fulfil a dual role of warrior and exploiter, and their value system is commensurate with this role, as is the economy at large (1982, 6). In peasant eyes, aristocrats are "distant, alien, utterly different and incomprehensible beings. They are after all members of a different society, who are housed, fed and dress differently, whose language and religion is different, who think differently and behave differently" (1982, 274).

Government is for aristocrats, who look down on peasants as lesser mortals (Kautsky 1982, 273–74). He writes that the aristocrats consume the peasant surplus in preference to investing it and increase their wealth by the simple expedient of increasing peasants under their control (1982,

7). All these descriptions are interesting, but what is essential for our purposes are the key indicators for an aristocratic empire which are an absence of commercial estates, together with lesser roles played by the market, trade and debt and a strong emphasis on the relationship between peasants and the ruling elite (1982, 5–6).

The commercial empires are those empires where trade has achieved a major part in the economy. Kautsky includes Greece, Rome, the Chinese Empire and Medieval Europe, and distinguishes these sharply from aristocratic empires. Kautsky excludes Persia, but I would argue that it belongs in this category on the basis of the economic transformation brought about during the Persian period, not least the innovation of banking (Neufeld 1960). In such empires, Kautsky writes, the land becomes alienable and a commodity under the influence of commercialisation (1982, 290). Not only is land alienable, meaning that peasants run the risk of losing their lands, but debt is a major cause of such loss. "Moreover cash crops become a way of making lands more profitable for the owner than simple subsistence farming. The patchwork of peasant lands makes way for the large estates of commercial farmers" (1982, 290–91).

Kautsky included pre-exilic Israel in this model as an aristocratic empire (1982, 64). Here in this chapter, I will give reasons for agreeing with this decision and at the same time use the same key indictors to show why post-exilic Judah over the course of the centuries changes fundamentally. I shall examine each of his key indicators, which he uses to separate aristocratic empires from commercial empires (namely, land tenure, labour, trade, markets and debt) and use these as the distinguishing markers for Judah before and after the Exile. Regardless of the value of his stereotypes, the key indicators remain a solid basis for comparison. I must emphasise that I am looking for trends and not a perfect fit. I begin with the key indicator of land tenure.

8.2.1. *Land Tenure*

In looking at the key indicator of land in ancient Israel and Judah, one may expect to see a move from small subsistence farmers to large-scale estates. What is important is the timing of this event. That it eventually happened is not open to debate; that it happened in the eighth century B.C.E. will certainly be challenged.

Much of the work on land in ancient Israel (e.g. Brueggemann 1977) finds its focus at the textual and ideological level. So one might begin with Deuteronomy's description:

> The Lord your God is bringing you to a good land, a land with streams,
> springs and underground waters gushing out in valley and hill, a land

with wheat and barley, vines, fig trees, and pomegranates, a land with olive oil and honey. It is a land where you will never suffer any scarcity of food to eat, nor want for anything, a land whose stones are iron ore and from whose hills you will mine copper. (Deut 8:7–9)

God is deemed to be the only true landowner, the ultimate patron, and Israel is the peasantry (tenants) who work the land as we read in Leviticus: "The land must not be sold permanently because the land is mine and you are but aliens and my tenants (25:23)." What, then, of land tenure?

In addressing issues of land tenure, one is often met with discussions on inheritance. Inheritance in the ANE (cf. Davies 1993) varied between equal allocation for all heirs (Hammurabi) or preferential division (Old Babylonian) especially in the case of the eldest son (Middle Assyrian, Nuzi) or both (Neo-Babylonia). Inheritance in the HB was apparently patrimonial and based on primogeniture with the first-born receiving a double portion of the land in comparison with the other heirs (cf. Deut 21:15–17). The status of first-born might be a conferred one (Deist 2000, 265). In some cases, an heir might be appointed as administrator over the land, which was then communally held, rather than fragmenting the land among the heirs (Westbrook 1991, 118–41).

Generally, across cultures, peasants might inherit the right to work specific farming land from their parents. It was their right to work the land, which was passed down in inheritance and not private ownership itself until the Roman period (Bloch 1961, 115–16; Rodinson 1973, 64). An Aramaic document from Egypt (Kraeling 6, dated to late fifth century B.C.E.), which deals with the inheritance of an estate as recorded by a father, clearly spells out that it is a life right of usufruct that is to be given to his daughter (Szubin and Porten 1988). A cognate term is used of the grant of usufructum given by Hezekiah to the priests of Jerusalem in the late eighth century (2 Chr 31:19).

Indeed, understanding the land tenure of the HB is far from simple. Unlike New Testament and Mishnaic times (Lang 1985, 98 n. 27), what, in practice, owning land in pre-exilic or post-exilic times means is far from clear and few texts even touch on the subject (Borowski 1987, 21–22).

The theoretical material is quite clear—until the time of the Romans, control over land took precedence over what we today call ownership. Kautsky argues that the issue of who owns the land, in an aristocratic empire is less important than the question of who controls both the peasants and the land (Kautsky 1982, 72–75; cf. Carney 1975, 148; Eisenstadt and Roniger 1984, 62). "The peasant, unlike the farmer, does not regard the land as capital and commodity. He has what anthropologists term 'inherited use-ownership' of it…. One had family land as one had one's name. It was not held by an individual but by the family, past, present and future…. It was an accident of life" (Kautsky 1982, 273).

Often peasants "simply went with the land," when it changed hands (Meillassoux 1991, 90). Polanyi (1957) speaks of the "legal fiction" that attended many of the ANE contracts, in that the land itself was not for sale, but rather there were negotiations around rights of access and use. The land "just is and is not produced to be sold" (1957, 72). Alienation of land, therefore, becomes a very complex practice, since so many diverse interests are embedded within a single piece of land (Kautsky 1982, 102; cf. Hilton 1973, 71). Moreover, arable land is the most important economic factor in the life of the peasant poor (Gossai 1993, 275).

All this is in contrast to later Roman practice with its "fixed proprietary exclusiveness" (Bloch 1961, 115–16; Rodinson 1973, 64). Legally therefore, land ownership in monarchic Israel and land ownership in Roman Palestine cannot be equated. In fact, Lang notes that "the first unquestionable attestation" for the sale of land in Israel is a contract document found in Egypt dating from 515 B.C.E. (1985, 98 n. 27). Deist concludes that it was only in the Persian and Hellenistic times that "property could be sold by deed and for money" and no longer treated as "the fixed share of the household" (2000, 144).

What, then, was the practise in pre-exilic Israel and Judah? Neufeld suggests that while "laws and customs presupposed that every man was owner of his own property" in biblical Israel, indications are present that "the practice existed of periodically cutting up common land" (1960, 32). A reasonable conjecture is that farming land was reallocated by village officials to individual families from time to time to be cultivated (Kaufman 1984, 280; Neufeld 1960, 32; Job 20:29; 1 Sam 22:7). Psalm 16:5–6 reads, "Lord, you are my allotted portion and my cup; you maintain my boundaries; the lines have fallen for me in pleasant places; I am well content with my inheritance" (see Weinfeld, 1995, 178; Warriner 1957, 208). An interesting Paleo-Hebrew inscription, from Late Iron Age Judah, contains the plea of a widow to a local official. In the inscription she asks for a field that had been promised to her husband, but was instead given to her brother-in-law (Becking and Wagenaar 1998, 185–93).

How might this regular allocation of land have been conducted? Since the Bible is largely silent, we should consider a modern parallel taken from an African context, if only for general comparison.

The practice of land distribution of the Bapedi in modern Africa provides a suitable illustration of how such a system still works in practice (Letsoala 1987, 17–28). All land, within the confines of a particular village, is deemed to belong to that village. Use of the land (usufruct) is therefore at the behest of the leadership of the village. Strictly speaking, such land can be neither bought nor sold, since its ownership, for all practical purposes, is invested in the actual community. An African expression is appropriate here: "Land belongs to a vast family of which many are dead, a few are living and countless numbers are still unborn" (1987, 21). The chief of the village, with his council of elders, distributes the land according to the needs of particular families, or individuals. A person may make application for a grant of land. This is usually done through the offices of a mediator, so that a young person might make application, through a family member or mentor, to the council of elders.

Depending on a variety of factors, such as the amount of land available, the quality of the land and the specific needs of the community and of the applicant, a suitable piece of land is chosen (cf. Letsoala 1987, 21). People do not live on their land, but within the actual site of the village, for security reasons and for the development of community, so that in making a grant of land, older people, who have trouble walking, might receive a grant of land nearer to the village than their more energetic counterparts. Only by relinquishing membership of the community does one forfeit the right to one's land (1987, 21) and this seems to be exemplified in the biblical case of Naboth (1 Kgs 21). How similar or different this was from the practise in ancient Israel is an open question.

Turning to the HB, we have in Jeremiah what is sometimes called a purchase of a field (32:6–15). Yet it is anything but a purchase. The field clearly belongs to a relative and so Weber (1952, 24) quite correctly refers to this action not as the purchase of land, but as Jeremiah's "reclaiming of his lot from among his people" (cf. 37:12; and see Carroll 1996, 618–25). Like the Bapedi, Jeremiah approaches the community leaders to lay claim to what is his land by right as a member of that community.

I shall suggest that there was another significant difference. What the archaeological data for the post-exilic period in Judah especially during Greek and Roman times indicate is a move away from the traditional peasant small-holdings, which had been the norm since the Bronze Age (Holladay 1998, 393; Stern 1998; Anderson 1998) to large estates.

The archaeological evidence first adduced by Dar (1986, 3–6) draws attention to the large size of some farmhouses in Israel of the Late Iron Age, which he associates with extended families and not rich landlords. These might have been single- or double-storied dwellings occupying anything from 400 to 1200 square metres of which less than half was the actual dwelling and one third was courtyard. In spite of Dar's conclusion, some scholars followed the view that these houses were indicators of large estates (cf. Herzog 1992a, 1992b; Weippert 1988; Netzer 1992).

Holladay disagrees completely and his conclusion is worth quoting in full:

> The point to be stressed here…is that as far as present evidence goes—and there is a lot of evidence—the pattern of residence in four- and three-roomed houses clearly designed to house livestock, process crops and store agricultural produce on a family-by-family basis (as opposed to redistributive mechanisms involving communal store facilities) is… unvarying from Early Israel down through the late eighth century highland and Shephelah materials (little has been published from the lowlands) typified by the Lachish Level III material culture complex…. As far as we presently know, similar residence patterns continued, though less well documented in terms of excavated remains, on down to the final destruction of the Judaean state in 586–582 B.C.E. (1998, 392–93)

The archaeological verdict is clear. There are no indications of palatial residences or large estates until the Exile.

Holladay speaks of the absence of worker barracks: "During this entire space of time we know nothing about one- or two-room hovels, or worker barracks or the like, and we do know enough to render the likelihood of discovering large numbers of the latter highly improbable" (1998, 392). Not only are there no palatial residences, there are also no barracks, which one would expect for housing the labourers of the large estates, at least until Persian times. Once again, the interpretation of the archaeological data rules against the plethora of large estates, such as characterised the later times.

In Persian and Greco-Roman times, land become part of a market based (commercial) economy (Deist 2000, 144) under the economic impetus of the Babylonian and Persian Empires (cf. Kessler 1994, 413–20). Holladay writes:

> only in the drastically reduced populations of the Exile, the Persian and Hellenistic periods, with their drastically altered housing arrangements, e.g., the agricultural estate utilizing the ruins of the Assyrian palace-fort at Hazor, is it possible to witness the rise of the sorts of agricultural estates which seemingly persist into Hellenistic and Roman Palestine. (1998, 392–93)

Dar (1986, 11, 19) refers to the size of a particular oil press dating from the Persian period (2 metres in diameter) and the size of the threshing floors of a farm in Samaria (500 square metres). The latter examples are consistent with the rise of large estates in the Persian and Greek periods (Holladay 1998, 393).

A line must be drawn between the patchwork of peasant lands of the Iron Age I and II and the later rise of the large estates that would mark the Persian, Greek and Roman times. Viewed from this perspective, the Exile (not the eighth century B.C.E.) forms the watershed in land tenure. The earlier prophetic concern was about positive reciprocity and not changing forms of tenure or land loss arising from debt default. Nor were the prophets concerned about slave labour.

8.2.2. *Labour*

The second of Kautsky's indicators is labour (1982, 6–8), with the tendency in commercial empires to make use of slave-labour instead of peasant labour. This raises another of the important areas of comparison between pre-exilic and post-exilic Judah. We begin with some general comments on labour and poverty before we come to this comparison.

One of the critical areas of impact of the world of the non-poor upon the poor is that of labour. Millions of people are poor because they are unable to find work. Wilson and Ramphele quote an African migrant worker as saying, "When you are out of a job, you realise that the boss and the government have the power to condemn you to death. If they send you back home (and back home now there's a drought) and you realise you can't get any new job, it's a death sentence" (1989, 97). Labour can empower people, but it can also enslave. Patterson writes, "Slavery is one of the most extreme forms of relations of domination, approaching the limits of total power from the viewpoint of the master, and of total powerlessness from the viewpoint of the slave" (1982, 1).

Defining slavery has taken different courses. One avenue was to see slaves as property (chattel slavery) following upon the manner in which slaves were listed alongside furniture and possessions. In reaction, Patterson (1982, 17–22) argues that while various societies promulgated laws which dealt with slaves, including their sexuality, not least the laws of ancient Greece and Rome, there is no instance of slaves being considered other than as members of the human race. Slaves were people, and the literature of the ancient world accorded them all the virtues and faults of those born free. Slaves were just like other men, women or children, except that they were slaves. To define slaves as furniture (or some other category of being or property) or even to speak about chattel slavery ignores the vital fact of their humanity, albeit debased in the extreme. Indeed "the notion of property is important, but in no way one of the constitutive elements" (1982, 17), and Patterson concludes that "[a]s a legal fact, there has never existed a slaveholding society, ancient or modern, that did not recognise the slave as a person in law" (1982, 22).

Instead of property, the slave, according to Patterson, should be defined as a socially dead person, who experiences "natal alienation." "Alienated from all 'rights' or claims of birth, he ceased to belong in his own right to any legitimate social order. The slave was denied all claims on, and obligations to, his parents and living blood relatives" (1982, 5).

The world of the New Testament was the world of the Roman Empire, which divided people into two essential classes, free people and slaves. People were born into one or the other, and a complex rite of passage (enslavement or manumission) existed between the two worlds. Aside from this social division all others paled into insignificance (e.g. Finley 1960, 1968, 1980; Patterson 1982). Meillassoux (1991, 89–90, 223–35) distinguishes sharply between peasantry and slavery. Peasants were entitled, even expected, to use part of their produce to build up the next generation of workers. Slaves were not expected to make provision for offspring (1991, 89). Peasants belonged to the land, and if the land was exchanged, they simply went with the land (1991, 90). In comparison to peasants who actively looked for patrons, slaves were expensive, and in the absence of wars not easy to acquire in large quantities (1991, 92). Being born as the child of slave parents along with enslavement arising out of debt were the common ways in which people became slaves (Patterson 1982, 105, 120–32).

In the ANE, and the world of the HB, the main source of slaves was war, and several texts, including the Assyrian texts of Tiglath Pileser III, Sargon II and Sennacherib, refer to the capture of prisoners and property. Lists include various items of furniture, armour, precious metals and stones, followed by "palace-women, male and female singers, and elite soldiers" (cited in Cogan and Tadmor 1988, 337–39). Nevertheless, such slavery met only a small part of the labour needs of the ANE. In Finley's major work on slavery (1980), he categorically excluded the slavery of the ANE from his purview. Already in 1949, Mendelsohn had laid the foundations for such an understanding of the uniqueness of ancient Near Eastern slavery (1949, 1962). For Finley, slavery based on the model of the Roman period was exceptional rather than the rule, appearing only late on the historical horizon (1980, 77). More common, until the advent of the Roman Empire, was a form of what he describes as rural dependent labour, with slaves limited to urban contexts (1980, 79). In the rural areas, slavery made up only a very small section of a much larger group of forced labourers. Indeed, Patterson (1982, 27) states that most non-Western peoples have no word for freedom, and they do not distinguish in the same legal manner as do Western peoples between free and unfree persons.

The basis for the labour of ANE society was not slaves but tenant-farmers, share-croppers and artisans (Callender 1998, 68). The labour lists from Nuzi (Dosch 1987), Ugarit (Heltzer 1987) and the Babylonians (Dandamayev 1987) concur. Thus, Jeremiah also castigates the state for using forced labour in the construction of the royal palace, making people labour without pay (Jer 22:13). Biblical Israel never experienced the great gangs of chattel slaves which for Rome and Greece became the norm and would in time threaten the social order (De Vaux 1973, 80; Diakonoff 1987, 2). In place of such a permanent status, "those persons who survived the transformation from freedom to slavery were generally returned to semi-free, serf status" (Matthews 1994, 122, *pace* Westbrook 1998, 214–38). Matthews concludes that "Despite the increased numbers of persons taken in warfare, the idea of permanent chattel status, on the North American model (ca. seventeenth to nineteenth centuries C.E.), was unknown in the ancient Near East" (1994, 122). The closest the ANE came to regular slavery was what was known as the debt pledge.

The term debt slaves should be restricted to people who have been permanently enslaved for debt. Debt pledges, on the other hand, are people who are temporarily bonded as forced labourers or debt servants (Patterson 1982, 9) until their contract has been terminated (Meillassoux 1991, 39–40). Debt bondage is then the appropriate term for such contractual labour, even if, in terms of human suffering, the actual experience of the pledges may have differed very little from that of actual slaves (Patterson 1982, 9). When the HB refers to slave (*ebed*), its usual context is debt bondage, and its referent is to the pledge. Leeb's work (2000) on the social location of the Hebrew term rendered as "youth" (*na ʿar* and *na ʿarah*) implies someone who is a member of a household that is not their biological one—such as a debt pledge.

The ANE was home to a complex system of debt pledges, whereby humans might find themselves in bonded service, as a pledge. In classical Greece, this was called an antichretic loan (Eichler 1973). Such pledges were, in many ways, forced labourers, but in the light of Patterson's definition of slaves as permanently alienated (1982), they were not slaves. Patterson, himself, is careful to make a sharp distinction between debt bondage and slavery (1982, 34; also Postgate 1987, 263; Diakonoff 1987, 3; Chirichigno 1993, 54, 77). In the light of these observations, the practice of using the term debt-slaves (e.g. Chirichigno 1993, 53–54) or temporary enslavement (e.g. Postgate 1987, 263; Diakonoff 1987, 3) to refer to debt pledges is both confusing and inaccurate.

The process of taking pledges was a complex one, as is attested to by the various legal codes in the ANE. Sometimes at Nuzi, it is mentioned

that the pledge will receive food and clothes from the house for which he
or she works (Dosch 1987, 230–31). In the Laws of Hammurabi (LH
114–19) there are references to the taking of human distraints (*niputum*),
either voluntarily or by force. Such pledges may work within the household, and so pay off either the interest or the principal debt (Zaccagnini
1976; Maidman 1976, 137). In the Neo-Assyrian documents, it appears
that the pledged peasants remained in their own dwellings but were
obliged to work in the fields of their creditors, who were often absentee
landlords and lived in the cities (Postgate 1987, 263). Other pledges were
described as "residing in the house of their creditors" (Postgate 1987,
263).

Various legal devices are evident for the ANE, which are designed
to protect the debtors and their pledges. In the Middle Assyrian Laws
(MAL 48) we read that a creditor may not give the daughter (distress) of
a debtor in marriage without the consent of her father or guardian. The
Laws of Hammurabi (LH 48) hold that if the debtor loses a crop (by rain
or floods) he or she does not pay interest that year. The creditor may not
take an ox as a pledge since this is would seriously impact production,
but can take a dependent (LH 115–16). Protective features for peasants
who were leasing land were not uncommon. So in Old Babylon, leases of
land to peasants took account of fallow years, while peasants might have
recourse to law in the wake of bad harvests caused by unavoidable natural disasters (CH 45–47; Klengel 1987, 162–63). Finally, laws protected
the welfare of the pledge. If a creditor kills the pledge, then his own child
may be put to death (LH 116). Chirichigno (1993, 65–66) concludes on
the basis of such laws that pledges were probably often ill-treated and
abused. His reasoning follows the belief that legislation implies the presence of some abuse. The extent of such abuse, after the introduction of
protective measures, is, however, open to debate.

For the states of Israel and Judah, forced labour and not slavery was
the order of the day. Callendar states that the emerging consensus is "that
slavery in the ancient Near East differed markedly from that found in
classical Greek and Roman societies" (1998; cf. also Patterson 1982, 27;
Diakonoff 1987, 3; Matthews 1994, 112; Deist 2000, 267). Patterson
describes the ANE as a place where "the personalistic idiom was dominant," implying a social coherence which formed a single continuum and
so stood apart from the typical Roman understanding of a sharp juxtaposition of free and unfree persons (1982, 27). Thus, in the ANE, "everyone is *ba'l* or lord to someone and *ebed* or slave/servant to someone else"
(Diakonoff 1987, 1–2). Diakonoff concludes that "all of this makes us

doubtful whether categorisation of labor into slave or free can be meaningfully applied to ANE history" (1987, 3).

The reality was that the lives of the peasant labourers of the time of the monarchy, may have been little different from the later Greco-Roman slaves, but they did not experience the shaming and severe social dislocation that accompanied such slavery. So in this way also, the Exile and in particular the early years of the Greco-Roman Empire brought about a significant deterioration in the lives of the peasant majority. Poverty took on a new twist in its increased capacity to shame and to dehumanise through the appropriation of the tools of slavery and in particular slavery for debt. Debt had always been omnipresent, but now in this age, the prospect of enslavement for debt, with attendant loss of land usage, became real. Large estates required new forms of labour and new crops destined not for consumption by fellow peasants, but by a privileged elite, resident sometimes on the other side of the known world.

8.2.3. *Trade*

The third indicator utilised by Kautsky is trade, which in particular plays a major role in commercial empires (1982, 6–8). I would expect, therefore, in terms of our hypothesis, that trade would play very little role in the time of the divided monarchy and a major role after the Exile. In fact, this is precisely what the archaeological data indicates. Moreover, there is a marked decline in trade accompanying the transition from Late Bronze to the start of Iron I in Canaan. The reasons for this are not clear, but the net result is to underscore the absence of trade in the initial centuries of Iron II (tenth to eighth centuries B.C.E.). I begin with a brief history of trade in Israel in the context of the Middle East.

In the Middle East, inter-regional trade has long played an important role. Trade was in luxury items for the elite (such as the spice and silk trade to the Far East), which are relatively easy to handle, highly priced and worth transporting over great distances (Carney 1975, 102; Frick 1977, 201; Stern 1998, 436–37). A shipwreck (from the Late Bronze Age) off the coast of Turkey, reveals organic remnants of materials used in perfume manufacture, along with fig seeds, olive stones, grape seeds and cereals (Haldane 1990). Other shipwrecks off the coast of Israel dating to the Late Bronze Age have bequeathed a variety of items including tin, lead and copper ingots (with Cypro-Minoan characters) and stone anchors weighing several hundred kilograms (Misch-Brandl 1985). The western Mediterranean seems to have supplied Crete, Greece and the Levant with ingots of silver according to lead isotope analysis throughout the Bronze Ages (Dayton 1984).

Placed as it is at the meeting of Europe, Asia and Africa, Israel was a natural region for control of the trade routes including some of the major caravan and shipping routes. Trade waxed and waned over Israel's long history. As far back as the Chalcolithic period, signs appear of contact between Egypt and Cisjordan, in the form of Egyptian objects found in Canaanite sites (Ben-Tor 1992b, 93). A dramatic increase in such trade occurs at the beginning of the Early Bronze Age I (3200/3100 to 2950/2900 B.C.E.), as the discovery of a large number of Egyptian artefacts, especially ceramic objects, testifies (1992b, 93–95). Similarly, in Egypt, storage vessels, manufactured in Cisjordan, make their appearance in the interior, at several sites (1992b, 94). The pattern continues throughout the Early Bronze Age, as indicated by the dispersion of the Canaanite Abydos ware, a fine pottery for the transportation of liquid products such as scented oils, and cosmetics, throughout Egypt (e.g. Sakkara) and as far north as Tell Judeidah in northern Syria (1992b, 107). Some trade continued throughout the Intermediate Bronze Age (ca. 2400–2200 B.C.E.), a time of general crisis and depopulation (Gophna 1992, 153).

During the Middle Bronze Age (ca. 2200 to 1870 B.C.E.), strong links connected Cisjordan and Egypt as the Execration texts indicate, and the continued presence of Egyptian artefacts, in both Cisjordan and Syria, are to be found (Kempinski 1992, 160, 176–78). During the Late Bronze Age (ca. 1550–1270 B.C.E.), imports from Cyprus (so-called Cypriot ware) become common in Cisjordan, along with Mycenaean, Syrian and Egyptian pottery (Gonen 1992a, 236–40). Gonen writes, "In tombs one might find Canaanite jars sealed with Cypriot bowls and Mycenaean vessels alongside Canaanite and Egyptian ones. Such phenomena testify to the flourishing trade among the disparate parts of the eastern Mediterranean basin" (1992a, 240).

An entirely different pattern is evident in Iron Age I (ca. 1200–1000 B.C.E.). Mazar writes, "One of the principal differences between the Iron Age I and the preceding period is the absence of extensive international trade, particularly with Cyprus and the Aegean. Finds from the Iron Age I reflect isolation and interruption of international relations" (1992, 300). Assyria and Babylon endured what can only be described as a dark age (Holloway 1997). The same pattern is evident in the Philistine city of Tel Miqne-Ekron, which abounded in imports from Cyprus, Egypt and Mycenae until these cease in about 1200 B.C.E. (Dothan 1995). For much of the Iron Age period, Palestine was relatively isolated and there is very little archaeological evidence for imports from the west until the end of the eighth century B.C.E. (Stern 1998, 434; Holladay 1998, 382 *pace* Gottwald 2001, 202–3).

Slowly, from the eighth century (the time of the new state of Judah) tentative signs of a revival in trade come to the surface. A revival in trade in basic commodities in some locations in Israel/Judah begins at this time and Judean exports appear in other parts of the Mediterranean basin. For example, large *pithoi* were found in ancient shipwrecks on the Mediterranean seabed and serve as the first indications of a renewal of trade in the Iron Age. These jars (mostly from Jerusalem) probably contained wine and olive oil. They exceeded a metre in height and may be dated as early as the eighth century B.C.E. (Barkay 1992, 353). Wine and olive oil were among the major items of export and import between Israel and her neighbours. Eighth-century texts from Samaria (24 in all) detail the ratios for the exchange of wine to olive oil (Rosen 1986–87). In the south, Singer-Avitz (1999, 3–59) finds that Beersheba was involved in limited trade with Philistine settlements from the eighth century onwards. The evidence is found in the higher percentage of "coastal type" vessels present in the debris (12.5%) as opposed to pottery from Lachish (2.9%) and Tel Beit Mirsim (3.1%). Trade items were mostly myrrh and frankincense (Singer-Avitz 1999, 55–59). In spite of these earlier indications, Stern concludes that it is only in the seventh century when the full indicators of international trade appear for the Central Highlands and Galilee (1998, 434). From the late seventh and early sixth centuries come a number of rosette seals indicative of trade, taxes or even preparations against possible Babylonian invasion found in Jerusalem (Cahill 1995).

The evidence from Tel Miqne-Ekron (a Philistine city) shows that, in the seventh century, the city functioned as the focus of the Assyrian economic activity for the region, specializing in olive oil and textiles, with evidence of imported Greek pottery (Gitin 1990, 1995a). Gitin suggests a production capacity of 1,000 tons of olive oil in a good harvest year, making Ekron the largest olive oil centre in the ANE (1990, 32–42). By contrast, the former territory of Israel (especially Lower Galilee) remains relatively deserted until as late as the Hellenistic and Roman periods (Gal 1998, 48–53). This would have been a result of the deportations of Tiglath-Pileser III of Assyria. In the south, Judah experienced a major growth in population (see above) throughout the seventh century and a rise in trade relations. From the seventh century onwards, in Neo-Babylonian Judah, we enter a time "characterized by extensive foreign relations, reflected in nearly every facet of local culture: language, religion and cult, dress, burial customs, and the products of material culture" (Barkay 1992, 357). Alongside trade, perhaps even in place of it at times, was the levying of tolls and taxes especially on the south Arabia trade route—one of the main routes in Iron Age II (Holladay 1998, 382).

Barkay writes that "close scrutiny shows that the real turning point in terms of material culture came only at the end of the sixth century when Persian authority was established, new pottery types appear and Attic ware was imported from Greece" (1992, 373). Here was the watershed for the economy in Judah, not least in terms of international trade (both imports and exports), which continued to grow and impacted on the economy of Israel throughout the Babylonian, Persian, Hellenistic and Roman periods. The wealth generated by such trade probably found its way into the pockets of the urbanites (Frick 1977, 135), further enhancing the social divisions within post-exilic Israel. Eph'al (1998) analyses the epigraphic and non-epigraphic sources for the second half of the Persian period (ca. 450–332 B.C.E.) and concludes that there was a significant non-Jewish presence evident in Judea. Oded's study (2000) of Judean and Israelite exiles in Mesopotamia from the eighth to the sixth centuries, based on epigraphic material, makes it clear that they were widely distributed among different cities, and rural areas. The Zenon papyri (ca. 250 B.C.E.) speak of "the Ptolemaic exploitation of Palestine through developing and supervising estates that exported oil and wine" (Gottwald 2001, 237). All this would have been conducive to trade.

We may conclude that the transition into a trade-based economy was a lengthy process, aided and abetted by foreign influences on the native peasant economy with the significant turning point being the end of the sixth century under Persian influence (Barkay 1992, 373). What is not mentioned is the impact that the rise of trade must have had on the ordinary peasants. While not all would have been negative, inevitably trade would have impacted the markets and created the sustainability for the large estates and their particular crops, which would have sounded the death knell for subsistence agriculture—the mainstay of the peasant economy in Judah.

8.2.4. *Markets*

The fourth of Kautsky's indicators is markets (1982, 6–8). If my hypothesis is correct, then markets would play a larger role after the Exile than before for Israel/Judah. The use of the term market is ambiguous, so I will define it here in terms of two types of market. The first is the earlier peasant type of market, which involves barter. The second is the commercial market, which is typical of the more advanced economy introduced by the Greeks. Israel experienced over time both of these markets.

Pre-exilic Israel would have operated on a system of barter since it lacked the facilities required for the emergence of a true market economy, namely, coinage, general literacy, accounting and banking skills (so

Deist 2000, 172; cf. Carney 1975, 176). Payments or loans were in kind (Stern 1998, 435–36), so weights are the dominant system. For example, the cost of sharpening a plough (1 Sam 13:21) is given in weight (a pym) a word inscribed on several stone weights from Iron Age finds (Millard 1986–87, 47).

Interestingly, two different shekel weights were used in Israel. Ronen (1996) suggests that the first was as a result of Egyptian influence and tribute requirement. Regarding he second, Kletter's study of the inscribed limestone weights from Judah (1998) puts their appearance as late eighth century, with the majority from the seventh century. This would coincide with the influence of Assyria and her demands for tribute. Most of the contexts in which weights are found are domestic and their uniformity indicate a pattern of state centralisation, whether Egyptian or Assyrian.

One learns from classical studies that generally in the rural areas, slaves and serfs had no use for the market system while peasants and tribesmen participated only rarely (Carney 1975, 177). In the urban areas, there would have been local merchants, whose task was that of supplying the needs of the urban population, namely food or fuel, and also seeing to the specific needs of artisans, by bringing in products like metal, wood and wool (following Kautsky 1982, 324–25). We know from the archaeological data for Iron II (Israel/Judah) that the peasants of Israel chose to store their surplus physically in household silos (Holladay 1998, 392–93). In addition, the peasants of Israel would have invested in livestock as a hedge against poor harvests, but one which was often costly to maintain (Grigson 1988, 248). While the prophets clearly referred to injustices in the local markets, whether the incentive behind such markets was trade or tribute, is unclear. We need to remember that coinage and the market system were yet to be invented (Deist 2000, 172).

With the demands of foreign tribute, the economy of Judah came under severe pressure. In the seventh century, Judah was obligated to contribute to the Assyrian economy through tribute derived from the peasants. The usual agricultural surplus was converted into luxury goods (e.g. grape and olive by-products), challenging the limits of the barter economy (Olivier 1994b). Amounts measured as weighted bars of metal, probably refer, in the first instance, to equivalents in barley or some such crop; but in other instances, clearly silver or bronze ingots were in use (De Vaux 1973, 195–209).

Lists of tribute paid to foreign invaders such as that paid out by Jehu to Shalmaneser III and Hezekiah to Sennacherib refer to a profusion of luxury items, including gold and silver (Gottwald 2001, 202). In pre-exilic times, silver is the preferred metal for precious objects; in Persian times, with the introduction of gold coins, gold begins to take over from silver as the more valuable commodity (Kessler 1986). Several hoards of precious metals (silver and gold) have been found in both Middle Bronze and Iron Age loci. Do these indicate a movement towards a monetary economy (so Gitin and Golani 2004)? Kletter answers in the negative, since the objects lack uniform shape and size and there are the much earlier Middle Bronze parallels (2003). He concludes that a monetary economy did not exist prior to the production of regular shape and size coins (Kletter 2004).

In the early part of the Persian period (sixth to fifth centuries) coins were struck as and when needed by the monarchs, priests or cities—as with the first Judean and Samarian coins (Mildenberg 1996). During the last quarter of the fourth century (330–321 B.C.E.), the first standardised and centralised imperial coinage came into existence in Babylon (Mildenberg 2000, 98–100), but it was only in the later Roman times that coins would become commonplace in Judaea.

Once coinage was in place, it was left to the Greeks of the fifth century to invent the market system, refining its requisite mechanisms in the centuries that followed (Carney 1975, 177). Gallant defines this market as "a system of exchange in which the participants are a supply crowd offering certain goods and a demand crowd wanting those goods, all of whom are free to choose the counterpart with whom the exchange will be made" (1991, 198 n. 14). Prior to this, the peasant market was a very different place for the population of Israel and Judah (Deist 2000, 172)—comparable to the difference between a rural market in the third world today and its equivalent in the First World. By the Hellenistic period, the first indications of large estates emerge—the usual supporters of a market-based economy (Holladay 1998, 393). Without coinage, the market system, full-scale trade and the demands arising from large estates, the market met primarily the small-scale needs of the peasant majority.

In this economic review, I have stressed the importance of the Babylonian Exile as the economic watershed for Israel/Judah—this is certainly true in terms of markets (Stern 1998, 434). Markets would have played a limited role in pre-exilic Israel in comparison with post-exilic times. However, this is not the impression some writers convey. For example, Gossai uses phrases like the "flow of money," the "flow of capital" and "entrepreneurs" (1993, 276; cf. Lang's "rent-capitalism" [1985, 87–88, 94]) for the markets of eighth-century Israel. These ideas are clearly anachronistic. Carney points out that the extended households of antiquity not only lacked an entrepreneurial ethic but were actually "antipathetic" to such an ethic (1975, 150).

The post-exilic period witnesses the full potential of the market system and begins the rapid erosion of the old peasant existence. The wealth evident in the Persian period (Barkay 1992, 304) indicates the increased pressure placed on the peasant majority—a fact which is rarely noted. The faults and flaws that were implicit in the old economic order cracked wide open under the impetus of the new economic order. Poverty was no longer just the peasant struggle with the environs. It had become a war between poor and non-poor, as debt assumed proportions hitherto unimagined in the pre-exilic society of ancient Israel.

8.2.5. *Debt*
The fifth of the indicators used by Kautsky (1982, 6–8), is debt, which we have already touched on (see above). In commercial empires, debt plays a much bigger role than in aristocratic empires, since in the former, peasant debts are rare and usually related to social or religious obligation rather than commercial ventures. We would expect, then, that debt assumes a larger role in post-exilic Judah, but what does the evidence say?

Debt had long played a significant role in the life of the people who in antiquity populated the ANE. So much is evident from the multitude of written records (Maloney 1974). Interest prior to coinage was in kind. The second-millennium documents from Nuzi refer to bad harvests and the consequent indebtedness of small land owners, while making mention of the high interest rates (Dosch 1987, 224). However, such indebtedness appears not to have led to the loss of land because in Nuzi, at least, laws protected the ownership of peasant lands (1987, 225). The reasons for the debts are not mentioned, but one might presume causes like bad harvests or the more common social and religious obligations.

In ancient Israel, debt, at least in the Iron Age, would have been accrued in the fulfilment of ceremonial obligations (based on Wolf 1966, 16) and because of seed (*pace* Hyatt 1971, 233; Wenham 1979, 321). This, at least, is the opinion of Lang, who points to such needs as family or ritual obligations, clothing and other non-agricultural expenses. Commenting on Exod 22:24, Lang observes that "Credit is not given in order to allow for production, but to help someone…out of an actual emergency. In other words, credit is given for consumption" (1985, 99 n. 30). Several decades ago Noth had spoken of the peasant borrowing money "for pressing needs, and not to finance himself in commercial undertakings" (1962, 187).

In spite of the small-scale nature of much of the debt, exorbitant interest rates were the norm, both in ancient and modern times. Lang (1985, 86) quotes mid-twentieth-century Syrian rates at 40–60 percent per

6-month period, or 5–8 percent per month, and compares these figures with the Jews of Elephantine in Egypt (Persian period) with an average of 5 percent per month or 60 percent per annum. Among the thousands of contracts found in the ANE, interest might easily reach 50 percent, with the average in Babylonia, Assyria and Syria being 20–25 percent on silver and 33⅓ percent on grain (Mendelsohn 1962, 4:385).

What was the situation in Israel and Judah? Certainly we know that by New Testament times it was a major problem (cf. the parables of Jesus) and as Josephus makes clear (*J.W.* 2.14.3), was a contributing factor leading up to the Jewish Revolt (66–70 C.E.) (see Domeris 1993). In his review of the economy of Ancient Israel, Hoppe (2004, 8–13) assumes that debt and land loss were major problems from Late Bronze Age Canaan, with an intervening period of freedom until the problem erupted again under the united and divided monarchy. This pattern, Hoppe believes, continued more or less unchanged until Roman times (2004, 12–13). Premnath (1988), Coote (1981), Chaney (1983, 1986) and Andersen and Freedman (1989, 309) argue that starting in the eighth century or earlier, it was the debt cycle that brought about foreclosures on agrarian lands. Andersen and Freedman speak of the poor, in the time of Amos, being "forced off their land, enslaved and denied access to the courts" (1989, 309).

The issue of debt is addressed in the Pentateuch on a few occasions, but not in such a way as to enable one to gain a clear notion of the extent of the problem or of the nature of the debt and its causes. In the Jubilee laws we read of the loss of land arising from poverty (Lev 25:25–28)— but debt is not mentioned here and we have already offered a way of understanding these laws in the light of the returning exiles.

Debt is referred to obliquely in the laws regarding the charging of interest. The issue of interest is first raised in the Covenant Code, which some scholars believe formed one of the pre-exilic strata of the Pentateuch (cf. Albertz 1994, 261; Schwienhorst-Schömberger 1990). Here in Exod 22:25 (cf. also Lev 25:36–37; Deut 23:19–20) there is a warning against charging interest to the ʿānî. In this context the term ʿānî should be rendered as "the indigent poor" or "the oppressed." The verse implies that such people have few if any resources with which to pay back interest, and will struggle even to repay the original loan. Rather than assuming some level of generosity, the law might simply imply that the loans to the ʿānî are small and the interest therefore insignificant. Remember the conversation in Chapter 1, with the little girl whose grandmother "borrowed food."

The message of Exod 22:25 is often repeated (cf. Lev 25:36–37; Deut 23:19–20; Ps 15:5; Ezek 18:8, 13, 17; cf. Maloney 1973). All of these references indicate the potential abuses of the system. The prophets, while condemning bribery, false scales and false evidence, rarely make mention of debt. Gossai (1993, 281) writes, "It is noteworthy that there is only one instance in the eighth-century prophets against usury, and this is a disputed one (Isa 3:12)." Isaiah 3:12, according to the MT, reads as follows: "My people, I will make youths their officials; My people, women will rule over them." The crux of the translation lies with the term rendered "youths" which is an *hapax legomenon*, and which impacts on the correct reading of the second part of the poetic parallel, and the reference there to "women." The LXX has "exactors" in parallel with "extortioners." The Targums have "gleaners" paralleled with "creditors." Finally, the Vulgate muddies the water with "exactors" opposite "women." Kaiser translates the verse as "My people—every one of their governors is a plunderer, and usurers rule them!" Gossai, in spite of his description of the verse as disputed (1993, 281), goes on to speak of "money-lenders and usurers" (1993, 284). More reasonably to my mind, Oswalt concludes, "At this remove dogmatic conclusions are not possible" (1986, 138 n. 12). Certainly, this verse cannot carry alone the weight of a theory of significant debt for the eighth century.

Elsewhere later in the traditionally dated Prophetic corpus, there are a few allusions to debt or interest rates, which need consideration. Referring to the exilic period, Ezekiel writes "you take usury and excessive interest and make unjust gain from your neighbours by extortion" (22:12b). Beyond simply usury, Ezekiel stresses the sin of charging excessive interest, at the expense of one's neighbour. Indeed, Ezekiel (22:12) compares the charging of interest to the taking of a bribe. The reference to "neighbour" suggests that once again we are dealing with debts arising from social and religious obligations, and not from commercial ventures. Habakkuk has a curious but inconclusive reference to either creditors or debtors suddenly arising against one (2:7). That concludes the prophetic evidence, which certainly militates against the view that debt was a major concern of the prophets of Israel, compared to poverty and oppression.

In the historical writings, debt is mentioned once within the account of Elisha, who comes to the aid of a peasant widow; she stands to lose her children as a result of debts incurred by her husband (2 Kgs 4:1–7). A miraculous supply of oil, however, pays off the debt and leaves the family provided for the future (v. 7). The reference to "losing" the sons, is probably another reference to debt bondage, rather than to slavery. In effect the boys would become debt pledges, a normal ANE occurrence. The disaster for the widow was that these boys were her livelihood, especially since she is deprived of the labour of her husband.

Debt features slightly more often in the Wisdom material of the writings. The rich rule the poor, and the borrower is slave/servant to the lender state the sages (Prov 22:7). Overall, Bleiberg suggests that the Wisdom literature (as with its Egyptian counterpart) encourages the virtues of a bureaucrat, rather than those of a merchant, which suggests a redistributive economy rather than a commercial society (1994). Proverbs 6:1–5 is a warning against falling into debt, especially if the creditor is a foreigner (cf. Deut 15:2–3; Scott 1965, 56). Job makes mention of the "infant of the poor" who is seized as a debt pledge (for a debt—NIV insertion into Job 24:9) in parallel with the child snatched from the breast; he places the ox of a widow in parallel Perhaps donkeys belonging to the orphan (fatherless) (Job 24:3). Since children regularly became debt pledges in the ANE, I assume that this is the situation here—but that the issue is the tender age of the child.

Interest rates were clearly an issue for the sages. Proverbs 28:8 warns, "He who increases his wealth by exorbitant interest amasses it for another who will be kind to the poor." Scott (1965, 164) uses the expression "patron of the poor," which underscores the patron–client notion basic to the verse. The combination of two Hebrew terms (*nešek* #5967 and *tarbît* #9552), rendered here as "exorbitant interest," is, according to Scott, a standard phrase for extortion that includes general usury but also rents (1965, 166; cf. Ezek 18:8; 22:12). The underlying value has to do with honour, which comes from charity. Since the poor are involved, the actual amounts may well be small, although probably significant from their perspective.

In the historical writings, in a rare insight into post-exilic Israel, Neh 5 describes the following: the peasants (v. 1) complain to Nehemiah that they have been forced to give up their children as debt pledges so that they may have food to eat (v. 2); furthermore they have mortgaged their fields, vineyards and homes to buy grain during the famine (v. 3); finally, some have had to borrow money against their crops so as to pay the Persian tax (v. 4) (cf. Watts 1983, 440). This is the clearest reference to the problems arising from debt in the HB and it is located in the Persian period. Debts here are related directly to consumption during a famine and to tax. The patrons who should have taken care of their peasants have failed to render positive reciprocity. Now the fields, vineyards and even homes of the peasants are endangered and there are already debts due against the future harvests. All in all, this is precisely the situation imagined for the eighth century (Hoppe 2004, 12–13; Premnath 1988; Coote 1981; Chaney 1983, 1986; Lang 1985, 95; Andersen and Freedman 1989, 309). I suggest that the HB correctly locates the process in the

Persian period instead (so Stern 1998, 434–37; 2000, 166–68; Deist 2000, 181). In spite of Grabbe's opinion (2002) that Judah under the Persian and Hellenistic periods experienced a more equitable distribution of power; the reverse appears to have been the case. In agreement with Deist (2000, 181), I believe that commercial debt first became a major problem only in these later periods.

Against Lang (1985, 95) who believed that debt caused a change in the eighth-century economy, I refer to his own citation of Karl Marx. Marx writes, "Usury...does not change the mode of production, but clings on to it like a parasite and impoverishes it. It sucks it dry, emasculates it and forces reproduction to proceed under ever more pitiable conditions, hence the popular hatred of usury, at its peak in the ancient world..." (1981, 731). He goes on to add "In Asiatic forms [which for Marx includes Israel], usury can persist for a long while without leading to anything more than economic decay and political corruption" (1981, 732). If Marx is correct in his evaluation of the role of debt, then some other cause must be responsible for changing the modes of production in Israel. I have suggested instead two causes, namely, foreign tribute, which led to a collapse in positive reciprocity, and the post-exilic inventions of coinage in the Greek market system.

8.3. *Conclusion*

The lives of the poor were irrevocably altered through the rise in the post-exilic period of a fundamentally different economy. I have identified five key indicators namely land sales, labour, trade, markets and debt, each of which become fully apparent only in the post-exilic period. What this also indicates is that as the economy changed, so the forms of exploitation changed. Indeed, when one considers these five indicators, it is clear that the post-exilic period brought about a definite change for the worse, when viewed from the perspective of the common peasant.

The struggle for survival among the subsistence farmers of the geographical entity known today as Israel and the West Bank has never been easy. In this book, I have traced the peasant journey from Late Bronze to Roman times. The peasants of Canaan became the peasants of Israel, and eventually also of Judah. They suffered secondary abuse through the tribute demands of the Assyrian and Babylonian overlords and their successors. They suffered primary abuse at their hands of their own elite, in the form of negative reciprocity and ultimately various forms of oppression and abuse. The post-exilic period (Persian, Greek and Roman periods) continued the journey with the introduction of a market economy, the rise of large estates and cash crops and Greco-Roman slavery. Debt, land loss and permanent slavery would become in these later centuries the hallmark of a form of poverty unknown in earlier pre-exilic times. For this reason, one can maintain the view that the poor of New Testament times and the poor of the time of Amos, while intrinsically identical, faced different weapons of war in their struggle for life and well-being. The power of the non-poor increased significantly over the centuries.

Fortunately, the HB was not completely inured to the cries of the poor. Various legal provisions, as elsewhere in the ANE, were in place. In the penultimate chapter, I consider some of these provisions and raise the difficult question of their effectiveness.

Chapter 9

LEGAL AND OTHER RESPONSES TO POVERTY

9.1. *The Alleviation of Poverty*

In this penultimate chapter, I consider some of the responses of the HB
to the problem of poverty. The HB is clearly aware of the phenomenon
of poverty, viewing it as an undesirable state (cf. Deut 15:11), but one
may justly ask whether it offers tangible hope for those caught in its grip.
The full details of Israel's legislation regarding the poor are now lost. As
Cassuto (1967, 262) reminds us, the statutes of Torah are not to be con-
fused with Israel's secular legislation. Typically, as with other ANE
codes, the HB deals in detail only with specific subjects (Cassuto 1967,
263) the choice of which is conditioned by the underlying ideological
intent.

These law codes of the ANE (especially their prologues) are couched
in idealistic terms, so I should guard against assuming from a given law
or edict, that it was necessarily practicable or regularly invoked. What
these law codes indicate, at best, are examples of the types of laws
enacted, and the states of being or actions that were considered either
good or bad. Typically, within the prologues to the law codes, general
appeals are made to the populace and judgments are made upon previous
rulers, in light of their lack of compassion regarding the poor. So in the
inscription of Esarhaddon, we read that Babylon was destroyed because
of its oppression of the poor, corruption and bribery (Weinfeld 1995, 99).
These are clearly designed to enhance the status of those presently in
power at the expense of their predecessors. The agenda of the poor is
being co-opted by the powerful. With these cautions in our ears, I turn to
some of the better known ANE law codes.

9.2. *The Laws of the Ancient Near East*

The ANE is the site of the oldest law codes so far discovered. Ranging
from as far back as 2000 B.C.E., there are law codes from Babylonian
rulers, Egyptian pharaohs and Assyrian monarchs showing a high degree

of continuity with each other. A study of these various collections provides vital background for an understanding of the biblical collection of
legal texts. In particular, Fensham has demonstrated that the ethic of
concern for the poor, widows and the orphan is a familiar feature in the
legal material of the ANE including the HB (1962; see also Lohfink
1991). The category of orphan here is better rendered as "fatherless" and
refers to the offspring of a woman who is a widow, hence the common
pairing of widow and orphan. While provision for the poor falls far short
of a proper welfare system, one may still think in terms of principles.

In a typical ANE society, men served the function of protector and
guardian of their wives and children. In the event of their death, one of
the other males in the family would be expected to take on this role. So
the eldest son succeeds his father as patriarch and protector of his mother
and siblings. Two values underlie this pattern. The first is honour and the
second is a fear of shame. The honourable man is the one able to protect
and care for his family. The shameful man is unable to perform these
tasks. Altruism functions as a subordinate value to these higher imperatives. Care for widows and the fatherless is essentially the duty of the
dominant males as fulfilled in the carrying out of their role as a protector
of the community. Failure to make provision for a widow in the community would be seen as a shameful action. Conversely, honour and prestige
comes to the man who publicly demonstrates his care and concern.

In the patriarchal society of the ANE, the king is the ultimate patriarch.
Hence, in the preambles and postscripts to the various law codes, the
honour of the ruler is a common feature. As the ultimate patriarch, it is
expected of the monarch that he should show concern for those in need
of his protection. Indeed, the categories of widow and orphan/fatherless
together with the poor generally appear to have become a mark of honourable concern, a kind of distinctive mark for the dominant male in his
role as protector. The following examples, drawn from major ANE codes,
give attention both to the concern for the weak and the various provisions put into place and arising out of such concern. The former and not
the latter tend to predominate throughout the ANE codes (Lohfink 1991).

9.2.1. *The Laws of Ur-Namma*
The Laws of Ur-Namma, king of Ur, lands of Sumer and Akkad (dating
from 2112–2095 or to his son Shulgi, r. 2094–2047 B.C.E.; see Roth
1995, 16) commence with the words, "I did not deliver the orphan to the
rich. I did not deliver the widow to the mighty. I did not deliver the man
with but one shekel to the man with one mina (i.e. 60 shekels). I did not
deliver the man with but one sheep to the man with one ox" (Roth 1995,
16). The preamble exposes not only an interesting set of contrasts (e.g.

orphan and rich/mighty) but also some sense of the prevailing social tensions within that society. Setting the orphan and the widow against the rich and mighty indicates that the fundamental problem is best understood in terms of the use and abuse of power. The claim implies that there is a real possibility for that society of the rich abusing the orphan and the mighty exploiting the widow. In terms of a peasant community, there is envisaged the possibility of a collapse of positive reciprocity between the patron of a community and the lowest ranks of the village who look to him/her for protection.

The process behind the verb "to deliver" indicates that the king is supposed to serve as the ultimate protector of the weak against the strong. The writer clearly believes that such giving up of the weak is in conflict with the role of the king as the patron and benefactor of all citizens. The weakest members of his kingdom household are meant to be able to rest in safety. What the reality is remains unknown. In this way, the preamble resembles the praise songs of a traditional praise singer in African society. For this reason, one has to take such claims as reflecting the social expectations of the king. As a typical aristocrat, he offers protection to those of his domain, in return for allegiance and prestige. His competition is at the level of other aristocrats (the rich and mighty) and so he presents himself ideally, if not actually, as the champion of the marginalised. Token gestures to elevate his honour are expected from time to time.

The preamble continues with the king claiming, "I did not impose orders, I eliminated enmity, violence, and cries for justice. I established justice in the land" (Roth 1995, 17). The latter claim is a common one, and needs to be tested against the actual records for the reign. It can neither be taken at face value, nor as a guarantee that justice prevailed. The rhetoric about freedom and justice that emanates from the most brutal of modern regimes is adequate caution. The actual code of Ur-Namma, in spite of the claims of the preamble, lacks any laws dealing explicitly with the poor, widows or orphans. This tends to be the pattern throughout the ANE, with a brief mention of the poor within the prologue, but largely or entirely absent within the actual legislation (Lohfink 1991).

9.2.2. *The Code of Hammurabi*
The code of Hammurabi (ca. 1750 B.C.E.) is introduced by a reverent preface, which reads, "Hammurabi, the pious prince, who venerates the gods, to make justice prevail in the land, to abolish the wicked and the evil, to prevent the strong from oppressing the weak, to rise like the sun-god Shamash over all humankind, to illuminate the land" (Roth 1995,

76–77). The stylistic features of the passage are obvious, akin to a typical praise song. The caution against the strong oppressing the weak is suggestive of the basic societal tension. The categories are not developed, but the aspect of power is clearly the significant demarcation. There is evidently a clear and present danger of the strong (powerful) oppressing the weak and the king's role is seen to rest upon the prevention of such exploitation.

The protective role of the king is very apparent also in the epilogue. Hammurabi claims, "I made the people of all settlements lie down in safe pastures; I did not tolerate anyone intimidating them. The great gods having chosen me, I am indeed the shepherd who brings peace, whose sceptre is just" (Roth 1995, 133). There are obvious parallels here with the biblical Psalms especially Ps 23. The notions of justice and peace are seen to work in unison. The work concludes, "In order that the mighty may not wrong the weak, to provide just ways for the waif [orphan] and the widow, I have inscribed my precious pronouncements upon my stele and set it up" (1995, 133).

Within the actual law code (LH), the plight of the poor is only indirectly addressed. In LH 48, we read, "If a man has a debt lodged against him, and the storm-god Adad devastates his field or a flood sweeps away the crops, or there is no grain grown in the field due to insufficient water—in that year he will not repay grain to his creditor; he shall suspend performance of his contract and he will not give interest payments for that year" (Roth 1995, 90). What is important is the concession within the system for acts of God. If there is no income then the debt is held back and no interest levied.

Similar protective legislation is found in LH 17 which reads, "If an obligation is outstanding against a man and he sells or gives into debt service his wife, his son, or his daughter, they shall perform service in the house of their buyer or of the one who holds them in debt service for three years; their release shall be secured in the fourth year" (Roth 1995, 103). There is considerable debate about whether this law was ever put into service, and Chirichigno (1993, 72) argues that it may represent no more than an ideal. Nevertheless, it stands as an interesting forerunner for the biblical Sabbatical laws, considered below. So too does LH 118, which deals with a slave who is sold to repay a debt, with the proviso that the three year clause may then be extended. If the slave is a woman (LH 119) who has borne children to her owner, she may only be redeemed by the payment of the full debt to the merchant (Roth 1995, 103)—an option not accorded her in biblical law. Effectively this law protects the "marriage" of the woman.

9.2.3. *The Code of Eshnunna*

One law, from the Laws of Eshnunna (LE) from ca. 1770 B.C.E., deals with redemption of a house sold in times of impoverishment. Rather than a time limit (like the Jubilee laws), the legislation here requires that whenever the new owner comes to resell the house, the original owner has the right to repurchase his old house. The provision for redemption underlines the close links that exist between a family and their home, as well as the critical value of owning one's own place. Probably this has to do with the homes of the elite rather than that of the average peasant; there is no corresponding provision regarding the sale of farm land or fields, which is in line with the general ANE practise of joint tenure.

9.2.4. *The Middle Assyrian Laws*

The Middle Assyrian Laws (ca. 1076 B.C.E.) deal in detail with various social issues including some of the most striking laws on social provision for the vulnerable. For example, there is the concern voiced about boundaries and the punishment of a man who alters the borders of his property to incorporate his neighbour's land (MAL B8 and B9 in Roth 1995, 179). Included also is a useful definition of a widow's freedom (A33). "If her husband and her father-in-law are both dead, and she has no son, she is indeed a widow; she shall go wherever she pleases" (1995, 165). I note here the patriarchal tendency to define women by their relationship of subservience to a dominant male. Only if there are no dominant males (husbands, fathers or father-in-law, or sons) is she a free woman, able to go and live where she wishes. At the same time, however, she may often be extremely vulnerable.

Another concern of the Middle Assyrian Laws is the married woman who is destitute, through the imprisonment of her husband (in war) by a national enemy. Depending upon her place in the community, provision should be made at the hand of another family member or the palace. If the land of her husband is insufficient to take care of her needs, then she shall declare it to the judges of her community. After consultation with the mayor and aristocracy of that area, she shall be assigned both a house and a field for a period of two years. At the end of this time she may then legally be declared to be a widow and so free to marry again (MAL A45 in Roth 1995, 170–71). Two things are present here: the first is the general care for the woman and secondly the double provision of a house in a town or village, plus a field.

In the case of a woman who is neglected by her husband and so becomes destitute, the law holds that she should first hire out her sons as labourers. If she has no sons, she may remarry, but only after five years

(MAL A36 in Roth 1995, 165–66). How she survives in the interim is unclear. The husband is judged dishonourable by his failure to provide for his wife.

Although the laws are inadequate as they stand, of all the law codes, clearly the MAL contain the most comprehensive of mechanisms for ensuring the well-being of members of society who through no fault of their own become vulnerable. Taken as a unity, the ANE law codes challenge the idea that the Laws of the Pentateuch demonstrated a greater concern for the poor than their cousins in the rest of the ANE (so Fensham 1962).

9.3. *The Laws of the Pentateuch*

The HB represents one more set of ANE texts, in which justice is measured in terms of care for the widow, the fatherless and the alien. The Pentateuch, in its present form, is a composite document made up of several different genres, including some collections of laws and ethical imperatives (Rendtorff 1984). Like the other extant codes of law in the ANE, the Pentateuch represents only a portion of the laws, enforceable at different times during the history of ancient Israel (Cassuto 1967, 263). No indication is given as to why some laws were included and others left out, but as before we may assume ideological grounds. Similarly, there is no indication which laws were actually promulgated and enforced and which laws represent simply idealist intentions. Finally, the dating of the various laws is extremely uncertain.

To speak about the rights of the poor (cf. Kevers 1985; Schwantes 1977) is anachronistic. The whole idea of rights is very much a modern concept and so really not applicable to the biblical period. What the poor had, at least in the time of the HB, was a modicum of protection offered by patrons, temple, state or village elders. Welfare was primarily that which was normal between peasant and landlord—namely, some form of reciprocity. With the poorest of the poor, where there was little chance of reciprocal returns, there was probably very little meaningful generosity. Help was given to those poor peasants where there was some promise of future rewards in the form of rent, tax or tithe or where there was some honour obligation in place.

9.3.1. *The Village Environment*
Various texts in the HB deal with the provision for the poor. That we have the semblance of a welfare system rather than one that is fully fledged itemised in the Pentateuch is obvious (Kaufman 1984).

Nevertheless, such a semblance indicates directions that provision for the poor might take. The basic unit of existence within the rural areas is the village. In normal practise among peasants, villages are responsible for the needy within their ranks. No one should starve while the community has access to food. This ethic of caring for one's own community is integral to most peasant communities, and rarely needs to be legislated. Only with the impact of urbanisation, or some form of ranked society within the village, would it become necessary to make a legislative issue out of such a common-sense practice.

The reality of a ranked society lies behind the biblical legislation regarding high interest rates. I have already dealt with the issue of debt, pointing out that in the Iron Age villages of Israel, debt was for consumption or social obligations and not for investment in future crops. Prior to the market economy of the Hellenistic period, large loans in which fields and lands were mortgaged were uncommon, although a portion of a crop might be pledged.

Hyatt (1971, 243) stresses that the biblical injunctions on loans was not against high interest, but against any form of interest whatsoever (cf. Ps 15:5; Prov 28:8; Ezek 18:8, 13, 17; 22:12; Neh 5:6–12). The provision, moreover, is not against the charging of interest per se but specifically against charging interest to this one particular category of person, the ʿānî (Maloney 1974). While other ANE law codes decry the excesses of interest (LE 18a–21; LH 48–51), none match the absolute prohibition of interest on loans to the poor (Wenham 1979, 321). So we need to take particular note of this innovation, tying it to the prophetic concern with positive reciprocity. Chaney (1991) confirms that debt easement also served the interests of the ruling elite, perhaps even to win the support of the peasants by one group temporarily out of power. The El Amarna evidence suggests that the reason may have been as simple as avoiding a peasant revolt.

Skotte uses the notions of "safety nets" to describe the provisions in the HB (1988, 87–92) designed to catch the poor. An example is found in Exod 23:11, where fallowing is related to provision for the ʾebyôn (poor or marginalised) of the villages, albeit framed within the Seven Year laws (see below). When land is unploughed, whatever grows there is for the benefit of the poor. So care for the poor and care for the land work together, and with the practice of bi-annual fallowing, vacant fields would be a permanent feature. Leviticus follows similar lines, specifically the material within the Holiness Code. Here, the laws require that the gleanings of the harvest and the edges of the fields should be left for the poor and the alien (Lev 19:9). Similarly, Lev 19:10 legislates against picking the grapes which have fallen from the vine, or going over the vineyard for a second time. The remains are to be left for the poor and the aliens (cf. Gowan 1987, 345–46). These laws may represent peasant customs going back over millennia.

The HB includes legalisation that deals with the relationships between client and patron. In Exod 22:26–27, the patron is required to return a cloak, taken in pledge, by sunset. For Noth and Childs returning the cloak at nightfall was impractical (Noth 1962, 187; Childs 1974, 479), nevertheless, what else did the peasant have to offer? The cloak was probably one of the most valuable of their paltry possessions, and served not just as a covering for the sake of decency, for both men and women, but also as a bed-covering at night. To deny a family such protection, especially in winter, was to allow them to run the risk of hypothermia, and at the very least to undermine their ability to work properly the next day. The right to sleep warmly, therefore, is a basic human right according to the Covenant Code. God will hear the cry for help, because he says "I am compassionate" (v. 27c).

Aside from these general laws, there are the Ten Commandments and two programmes found within the HB, namely the Seven Year laws and the Laws of Jubilee. These programmes actually pose more questions than they answer, so one can do little more than describe how they may have functioned in ancient Israel.

9.3.2. *The Seven Year Laws*

The Sabbatical or Seven Year laws (Exod 21:2–6; 23:10–11; Lev 25:18–22; Deut 15:1–18) cover a variety of concerns including the release of debts, setting free of slaves or other forced workers (bond servants) and the letting fallow of a field (Wright 1984). Mayes (1979) considers that Deuteronomy has extended the original agricultural context of the Seven Year laws into the economic context. Here, in Deut 15, it is applied for a fixed period, with the debt release being scheduled in terms of a general amnesty as opposed to a fluctuation from one field to another (Mayes 1979, 247). Noth (1962, 190) observes that whether the Sabbath Year is to be observed in unison or for each piece of land in rotation is unclear. Fields, in order to retain any reasonable degree of fertility, would have been allowed to remain fallow far more often, perhaps even every second year (see above). Hence, the seventh year becomes a double fallowing (Hopkins 1985, 200–201), but that would mean that the rest of the fields are worked two years in a row.

Evidence of the actual enforcement of the Seven Year laws occurs in the periods following the Exile (De Vaux 1973, 174–75), namely Persian (Neh 10:31), Hellenistic (1 Macc 6:49, 53), and Roman times (Josephus, *Ant* 13.8.1; 14.10.6). The precise dating and working of the system will probably never be finally explained, but at least the principle of a Sabbath for the land, slaves and debt is clear. The fact that these laws occur in the post-exilic period when so many things where changing to the detriment of the subsistence farmers of Israel, gives pause for reflection. Was there, then, a marked increase in landless people? Was this a response to the increasing debt, loss of land and escalation in debt pledges? My hypothesis would certainly suggest that the timing is significant.

9.3.3. *The Jubilee*

Jubilee appears by name only in Lev 25. Much debate has centred on whether or not the Jubilee was practised in the way in which it is detailed here (cf. Weinfeld 1995, 152–18). Chirichigno (1993, 302–43) argues that Jubilee was an extended form of the Sabbatical laws and of equal or near equal antiquity. Westbrook (1971) suggests that the Jubilee was an invention dating from the time of Nehemiah. North (1954, 204–7) argues that the laws are better suited to the idealism of the Mosaic period. Weinfeld describes the passage as "permeated with idealistic-utopian elements," although its background is clearly rooted in the ANE (1995, 156). Wenham (1979, 318) argues that it remained an ideal, perhaps from the time of the Exile onwards, or even that it was never enforced. The questions abound. When were the Jubilee laws promulgated and why were they introduced? Whose interests did they serve? Were they ever formally observed or do they simply represent and idealistic solution? What is their relationship with the Seven Year laws?

The ANE has several interesting parallels to a Jubilee remission of debt, and setting free of slaves (cf. Chirichigno 1993, 85–92). For example, Nuzi law mandates a maximum debt period of 50 years (Weinfeld 1995, 153). On notable occasions, various rulers proclaimed a remission of debt, such as the Babylonians (Chirichigno 1993, 85–92). These releases apparently were not designed to be regular events, but were rather reactions to dire need in the land (so Chirichigno 1993, 86). Usually there were also good political reasons for the move, other than compassion for the poor and indebted. Olivier's study of the Edict of Ammisaduqa (Old Babylonian) reveals that while it promises economic redress, the actual results fall short (1998). The interests of the elite remain paramount, with the intent probably being a short-term relief to stave off the possibility of peasant unrest.

In principal, the Jubilee law mandates that at the end of seven sets of Sabbatical Years, not only should all Jewish debt pledges be released (Lev 25:39–40), but lands (outside of domiciles in cities—25:29–30) should be returned to their original owners (25:13). In Lev 25:25, provisions are made to keep the land within the broader family. The ethos of buying or selling of land indicates the market economy of the late post-exilic period. In v. 35, further provision is made for the poorer members of the community. Such an obligation should be automatic, so that the legislation strongly suggests a collapse of the community ethic. Leviticus 25:39 deals with debt pledges and rules that when someone is forced to labour to pay off a debt, instead of being treated as bond-labourer, the person should be considered as either a tenant farmer or a free labourer, and treated appropriately.

Wenham discerns the primary purpose of Jubilee as preventing the "utter ruin of debtors," but its failure to be observed led to the creation of a society divided between "rich landowners" and a mass of "landless serfs" (1979, 317). I have already shown that peasantry was the order of the day for monarchic Israel, who were hardly "landless serfs," and that debt played little or no role in the loss of property before the market economy of the Persians and Greeks. Would Jubilee have served any purpose before this time?

Wenham (1979) is one of the writers who believe in the pre-exilic dating of Jubilee. He writes that "about once in a man's lifetime the slate was wiped clean. Everyone had the chance to make a fresh start...the Jubilee would have restored some semblance of equality between men, thereby recapturing something of the relationship that existed between men at their creation" (1979, 317). Here, however, it is necessary to introduce a hermeneutic of suspicion. The Jubilee laws do not deal with the remission of debt but rather with the right of families to lay claim to their land lost through debt. Moreover, the Levites are seen to be a privileged group within the legislation (Lev 25:32–34). The actual needs of the poor seem to be peripheral.

The privileging of the Levites, the exclusion of houses within cities and the length of the period (forty-nine or fifty years) has led to the view that the real issue is the return of the elite priestly exiles (Gottwald 1997, 36–38). At the beginning of the Exile, the Babylonians distributed land among the poorest of the poor (2 Kgs 25:12). The majority of the population remained in Israel, as Barstad's "myth of the empty land" (1996) so adequately demonstrates. Archaeological exploration of the Negev, the Benjaminite region and the Judean hills, including the area around Jerusalem, demonstrates continuity in agricultural practices throughout the sixth century (Barstad 2003). So clearly the peasant economy continued intact, which indicates the presence of some native ruling elite presumably along with Babylonian overlords.

An interesting question may be posed: What if at the close of the Exile certain of the elite (perhaps the priestly aristocracy) fashioned the Sabbatical regulations in such a way as to reclaim their own lost land, and so, in the process, recreated the notion of Jubilee? This would be in line with Josiah's co-option of the Passover rituals (Nakanose 1993). In both cases the powerful take over the agenda of the poor to use for their own benefit, whether this be the family celebration of Passover, or legislation to keep land in the family. Haggai (1:1–11) attests to the resettlement of elite groups in the area of Jerusalem. By the time of Ezra and Nehemiah (150 later) we find that peasants are in the grip of poverty and debt (Neh 5)—the Jubilee has succeeded but not in the way most people would have imagined. Instead it has allowed the returning Exiles to reinstate themselves as the overlords of the peasant majority. Their land claims, which may or may not have been legitimate, become the basis for demanding a share of the peasant surplus. The Jubilee's apparent ethic of concern for the poor has been subverted.

In spite of this abuse of the Jubilee principle, there remains within the basic notion much that is good. The idea that debt in particular and loss of land should be controlled in the interests of the poor is a noble ideal. Considering the plight today of many of the poorer nations of the world, the writing off of national debts in perhaps the only hope for the future. The history of Israel warns us that even today the powerful might use even such a release to their benefit, as some poor nations have discovered—they were released from debt but at an enormous cost to their freedom.

9.3.4. *The Ten Commandments*
Located within the Covenant Code, the Ten Commandments are probably the most familiar of the laws of the HB. What is not so well known is the extent to which these laws dealt with the protection of the poor and marginalised, and the way in which they pertain to land policy (Gottwald 1985, 210).

Power and its use lies behind the legislation that deals with the Sabbath. The observance of the Sabbath occurs either as a prohibition against work (Exod 20:7; Lev 23:7) or as a command to observe the festival (Exod 23:12; 31:15; 34:21; Lev 23:3). As prohibition, the law reaches back to the tradition of Israel's own experience of bondage (cf. Exod 20:2), and as such stands in opposition to the notion of forced labour. It may be of some considerable antiquity (DeWitt Knauth 2000). In a world where forced labour was commonplace, the rules regarding the Sabbath as a day of rest for all people strikes a notable chord (Pixley 1987, 134). Exodus 23:12 explains the motivation for the Sabbath day of rest. On this day, all workers, whether animals or humans, ought to refrain from physical labour so that they might be refreshed (cf. Exod 20:10). Servants, slaves and aliens are explicitly included in the prohibition, thus firmly forging the connection with all forms of labour.

The relegation of the alien to a position below the animals speaks volumes. Such people have always been open to abuse, exploitation and racial prejudice. Nevertheless, the Covenant Code signals the need for even aliens to relax and to be refreshed. That such people need protection from oppression and mistreatment is itself a testimony to the existence of such practices. Brueggemann concludes, "The Sabbath is a sociological expression of a new humanity called by God. Sabbath is the end of grasping and therefore the end of exploitation. Sabbath is a day of revolutionary equality in society" (1982, 35).

In the commandment against taking human life, Pixley argues that we are dealing strictly with death by malicious intent (1987, 137). In a world where certain categories of people were more vulnerable than others, however, such a dictum has evident implications for the poor and the marginalised. In the commandment against stealing (Exod 20:15), there is possibly a deeper sense of stealing the liberty of a fellow human, by enslaving such a person for one's own use or for selling them (Alt 1959, 333–40; Noth 1962, 165–66). Again there is an application for vulnerable people.

The commandment against false testimony (Exod 20:16) has a general implication for all legal processes (Hyatt 1971, 215), but in the prophetic indictments it has a particular focus upon the abuse of the legal rights of the poor. Once again, the heart of the issue is that of the abuse of power. Even the law against coveting (Pixley 1987, 139) is probably directed against the powerful, who use their privileged resources to take possession of what belongs to their weaker neighbour. Noth (1962, 165), by extending the notion of coveting (20:17), includes both the desire and the action of illegal acquisition, and suggests that the theft of a person's freedom recurs here. In his view (1962, 166), while the eighth commandment centred on adult males, the tenth commandment focussed on women and children. Both Hyatt (1971, 215) and Childs (1974, 423–24, 427) are critical of Noth's suggestions. What is uncontested is that the commandment against coveting addressed the issue of power over another person or their property (Gottwald 1985, 210); theft or other more devious forms of gaining possession is included (*pace* Hyatt's restriction of the notion to an inner feeling [1971, 216]). Much less likely is Chaney's theory of the tenth commandment as a proscription against latifundialization (1982, 1985; Premnath 1988), unless we place it in the context of the Hellenistic period where large estates are clearly indicated (cf. Holladay 1998, 398).

9.3.5. *Equality Before God*
Reference to the poor occurs also in Exod 30:15, where we read of the tax payment of half a shekel; this immediately alerts us to a Persian or

Greco-Roman date when coinage was commonplace. This half shekel is a religious tax and is to contribute to the functioning of the temple (De Vaux 1973, 403). Hyatt (1971, 293) dates the tax to the Persian period (cf. Neh 10:32 where the tax is a third of a shekel), viewing the reference in Chronicles (2 Chr 24:6, 9) as anachronistic. The stipulation reads that neither should the peasant poor (*dal*) give less nor should the rich (*ʿšr*) give more. Since it was a system of tax for the cult, the rich, by paying more, were not justified in laying claim to a greater number of cultic rights (Noth 1962, 236). The tax increased in the later periods to the half shekel of first-century Judaism (Matt 7:24).

Reference to the poor also occurs in Lev 1:21–22, where instructions are given regarding the re-integration of the person who has been deemed cured from leprosy. Leprosy in ancient Israel was the umbrella term for a wide variety of skin infections (De Vaux 1973, 462–64). In effect it was a social category, equivalent to an isolation ward. People deemed by the community to be socially unacceptable due to a particular skin ailment (contagious or not) were sentenced to live on the outskirts of the community, ostensibly in the interests of the well-being of the community at large. Just as a ritual exclusion probably attended their excommunication, so their reincorporation into the community demanded a rite of passage.

A sacrificial gift of three lambs, flour and oil, was to be brought to the priest, in a public declaration of the desire to be reincorporated within the community. The priest, if satisfied with the cure, anoints the supplicant with oil and offers the lambs as a burnt offering, against the present defilement. The man or woman too poor to afford the three lambs could substitute a single lamb (Lev 1:21) and two turtle-doves (v. 22). Thus, the expense that might force an individual into debt is at least partially avoided. One is reminded that in the pre-exilic period, debt arose primarily as a result of social and religious obligations. At the same time, however, there remains a cost, which the person must meet in order to be reintegrated as a socially acceptable person. Clearly demarcated is the line separating ritual cleanliness from profane. The preservation of such lines was deemed to be of vital importance for the sake of the community. As with so many of the previous instances, the principle behind this legislation is more powerful than the actual legislation.

9.4. *Widows, Orphans and Aliens*

The HB often links together widows, orphans and aliens (see Gowan 1987 and bibliography there). So Exod 22:24 contains one of the curses typical of other ANE covenants and agreements: "God places himself directly in the role of protector" (Childs 1974, 478); if the people abuse the aliens, widows and orphans in their midst (vv. 22–23), God will allow the enemies of Israel to prevail against them. The ethic of concern for the weak is intrinsic to the well-being of the whole community (Gowan 1987) and includes the disabled (Lev 19:14; Deut 27:18; cf. Job 29:15). Sneed (1999) adds a caution. We cannot assume a correlation between the ideal of these texts and the reality experienced by widows, orphans and aliens. Rather, he argues that the texts reflect far more the interests of the elite than any form of overt altruism; the issue is the honour of the patron. Ultimately, however, widows, orphans and aliens are vulnerable people in all societies.

9.4.1. *The Widow*

Women were already vulnerable within the society of ancient Israel, so that widows were doubly vulnerable (Prov 15:25; 1 Kgs 17:9–24; 2 Kgs 4:1–7; Job 24:3). Rock exposes the danger of being either a widow or an orphan, and living outside of the protection of an adult male (as either husband or father) and so prone to exploitation, especially exploitation of land or labour (1997, 1998; see also Noth 1962, 186). Widow implies a woman, who has not only lost her husband, but is also outside of the protection of an adult male (Gowan 1987; Hyatt 1971). Leeb (2002) adds a further qualification of being past the age of child-bearing, since not all women who have lost husbands are described as "widows." Frick (1994b) cautions that in spite of her perceived powerlessness, a widow beyond child-bearing years might still have exercised a level of choice as some modern anthropological parallels indicate. The elderly widow in Africa, for example, plays a considerable role in the face of HIV/AIDS pandemic today.

Widows might lose their claim to land (Prov 15:25) without the protection of a male who also had access to the courts and councils of the elders. They might be abused, raped, abandoned and ill-treated in many different ways (cf. Job 24:3), simply because they were vulnerable. Scarce wonder that care of widows became the bedrock of ANE law codes—a measure of justice in the land (Fensham 1962, 138–39). Naturally, these vulnerable people also create the opportunity for patrons to extend their honour.

In Exod 22:22, the people are warned not "to take advantage" of widows. The Hebrew, however, uses the verb *ynh* ("oppress or afflict," #3561) with the sense of the physical and psychological violence. I suggest a translation like "abuse them." The very existence of this instruction shows that people are using their power to marginalise and to abuse widows. The abuse of widows is a common theme in the Prophetic literature (Jer 7:6; 22:3; Zech 7:10; Mal 3:5). The example of the widow's plea in the Paleo-Hebrew inscription from Late Iron Age Judah is a case in point (Becking and Wagenaar 1998, 187–93). The text, if genuine, witnesses to a widow asking for the field which had been promised to her husband, but given to her brother-in-law (Shanks, Stieglitz and Lang 2003).

Exodus 22:22 [21] continues with a warning: "If you do [abuse them] and they cry out to me, I will certainly hear their cry." God's nature, as the one attentive to the cry of the oppressed and abused among humankind, is deeply rooted in the book of Exodus. Where the Egyptian sun-god used his single eye to search out injustice, the God of Israel is the hearing God, who is attentive to the smallest cry of distress which comes to his ears (cf. Exod 2:23). The implicit threat of the vengeance is clear (Noth 1962, 186) as we come close to the heart of God.

9.4.2. *The Orphan*

Orphan in the HB means minor children who have no father or male guardian (Ringgren 1982, 3:1075–76), hence the preferred rendering as "fatherless." The usual connection of widow and orphan in the ANE texts (Fensham 1962) may be understood, then, as widowed women who have only very small children, and lack the protection of an adult male who is a close family member. Exodus 22:22 forbids the abuse of the fatherless, but it is the book of Deuteronomy, which along with the widow and the alien, raises the care of the fatherless as a critical issue (Deut 10:18; 14:29; 16:11–14; 24:17–21; 26:12–13; 27:19). Job has several references to the abuse of the fatherless. People cast lots for the fatherless (Job 6:27), the fatherless are crushed (22:9), their donkeys are driven away (24:3), they are snatched from the breast (24:9), they have no helpers (29:12) and they are subject to violence (31:21).

The psalmist speaks of the murder of the fatherless (Ps 94:6) and of Yahweh as the defender of the fatherless (10:14, 18). Finally, the prophets either point to the abuse of the fatherless (Isa 1:23; 10:2; Jer 7:6; 22:3; Zech 7:10; Mal 3:5) or appeal for their vindication (Isa 1:17; Jer 5:28; Hos 14:3). Once more, positive reciprocity and the honour of the patron are issues here.

9.4.3. *The Alien*

Gossai (1993, 130) distinguishes between two types of aliens mentioned in the HB. The Hebrew term *ger* is used to imply a person who was resident in a community, but who was signified as an alien, an outsider—a member of another people (Milgrom 1995). Such a person might be, like Ruth, related by marriage, or simply an immigrant from one of the surrounding nations. The alien is removed from his or her original kinship ties, and needs to discover a new form of kinship (Halpern 1988, 273–74). These ties involve protective ties (Noth 1962, 186), and even newly created genealogical and mythical connections (Halpern 1988, 274). The major point is that the *ger* is permanently resident in the land.

By contrast, the *nokri* is a temporary resident, and may be rendered as the "stranger" (Gossai 1993, 130). In the laws on loans with interest (Deut 2:20–21 [19–20]), it is the stranger who may be levied with interest (Neufeld 1960, 38–39; Mayes 1979, 248). This stranger is the "one who passes through Israel, perhaps on business; he is not integrated into the community, nor is he recommended to the charity of the Israelites" (Mayes 1979, 248). Similarly, Noth distinguishes between the resident alien and the stranger whom he thinks of as "merchants or foreign workers" (1962, 100). Snaith (1967, 165) separates the *ger* from the passing guest. Zwickel (1994) connects the presence of the alien (*ger*) and the hired worker with the influx of refugees following the destruction of the northern kingdom by the Assyrians, and in so doing alerts us to yet another form of pressure on the peasants of Judah.

The Covenant Code has three references to aliens. Exodus 22:21 reads, "Do not mistreat an alien or oppress him, for you were aliens in Egypt." The same instruction is repeated in Exod 23:9 with the further note, "You yourselves know how it feels to be aliens." Gowan (1987, 343) notes that the interest in the welfare of the alien is distinctive to Israel in the ANE (which is consistent with a post-exilic dating and the experience of being aliens in Babylon and other places). To oppress an alien, in this context, was tantamount to a denial of one's link with the past and a turning of one's back on the liberation brought by God.

Exodus 12:19 allows the alien who is circumcised to participate in the Passover meal (cf. Noth 1962, 100). The rules of Passover are to apply equally well to both alien and Israelite homes, with the proviso of male circumcision (Exod 12:48). Verse 49 stresses that "the same law applies to native-born and to the alien living among you." In this, the sacred and communal remembrance of deliverance from oppression, a place is found for aliens. Yeast and the lack of circumcision stood as the marks of an old order, out of which God had delivered the people, including aliens, who now found a home among those people.

Numbers has two references to aliens, all linked to one theme, namely equality before the law. Numbers 9:14 stipulates that the alien who celebrates Passover should follow the same rituals as the Israelites. The alien is also to obey the laws regarding sacrifice when he or she brings a food offering to God (Num 15:14–16). Provision for the alien is found in Lev 19:9–10 (cf. 23:22). A singular command is found in Lev 19:33–34, which reads, "When an alien lives with you in your land, do not mistreat [oppress] him. The alien living with you must be treated as one of your native-born. Love him as yourself, for you were aliens in Egypt. I am the Lord your God."

In most countries today, the instruction to love the alien as oneself would be met with astonishment. Aliens are so often treated with the deepest suspicion by the community at large. They are often the first to be exploited, to be cheated of whatever wealth they may acquire. In the inner city community, the alien often works long hours for a pittance, doing the kind of work that no-one else is prepared to do, living in the most primitive of conditions. They are the outsiders, deserving of none of the privileges of the community. Aliens in ancient Israel probably were subjected to similar abuses. Leviticus urges another ethic. The aliens are to be loved and treated as full members of the community.

9.5. *No Poor or Always the Poor?*

Deuteronomy 15 has two statements about the poor, which appear to be contradictory (cf. Hoppe 2004). The first of these is found in vv. 4–5, which read, "However, there should [will] be no poor (*'ebyôn*) among you, for in the land the Lord your God is giving you to possess as your inheritance, he will richly bless you, if only you fully obey the Lord your God and are careful to follow all these commands I am giving you today." The use of the term *'ebyôn* implies people in need of material help—they are the needy, those who are so poor that they are thrown upon the resources of others. They cannot survive without outside help. "Among you" suggests the closed walls of a community. Where reciprocity and an ethic of true community are operating, such people will be absorbed by the community, and poverty, to all intents and purposes, will disappear. So this invocation is about the need for community co-operation.

A related (albeit contradictory) sentiment appears in Deut 15:11 which reads, "There will always be poor people (*'ebyôn*) in the land." This sentiment is the better known of the two, since it is used in the New Testament (John 12:8). Mayes stresses that in the Hebrew the pronoun "your" is linked with all three nouns of v. 11, "emphasizing that it is to the community of Israelites living in their own land that the law applies" (1979, 249). The presence of the poor in this location demands a reaction from the people. "You are to be open-handed towards your brothers and toward the poor (*'ānî*) and needy (*'ebyôn*) in your land" (v. 11c). Here, the writer is implying that there will always be needy peasants within the community, because of the varied levels of fertility of fields and the vagaries of the weather.

Unfortunately, the laws listed above may have meant very little in the reality of the peasant existence in Israel. While recognising that I am not dealing with the full legal code for Israel, we note the absence of laws for the protection of reciprocity, controls on taxes and fines and protection against oppression and violence. At this basic level, the laws of the HB seem to have failed the poor in comparison even to the laws of Assyria and Old Babylon. The actual situation on the ground may well have been different.

9.6. *Conclusion*

While ideals regarding the eradication of poverty need to be translated into practical laws that impact directly on the material and spiritual well-being of the poor and marginalised, the success of these laws depends upon their being rooted in the culture of the non-poor. The ANE texts as a whole championed the need to protect the poor, widows and orphans. To these categories the HB adds that of the resident alien. To what extent one can speak about meaningful legislation for the prevention or even amelioration of poverty in either the ANE or the HB is open to question. At present there is an appeal to the kindness of the hearts of other peasants to allow some access to crops for the poorest of the poor; there is also a restriction on some forms of debt pledges but without punishments attached.

There is a positive side to this. While much attention has been given to notions of Jubilee as a counter to poverty, what makes the literature of the HB stand out, however, is not the legal documents but the cries of the prophets. Their emphasis on oppression and injustice against a background of the changing economy of Israel and Judah is critical to understanding the poverty not just of the HB, but also of the ANE. This biblical consciousness of oppression gave the HB a unique position within the texts of the ANE. Within the combination of the legal guidelines and the prophetic voice, one may discern a balance for directing a programme for the transformation of society and a cry to the heart of God.

In the final chapter, I develop a model for understanding biblical poverty and also lay down a set of guidelines for responding to poverty based on the chapters of this book. Here lie the lessons learnt in the previous pages, the wisdom gleaned over generations of peasantry and not least the glimmers of hope for an end to poverty.

Chapter 10

MODELLING BIBLICAL POVERTY

10.1. *A Thick Description*

Chapter by chapter, we have accumulated "a thick description" (cf.
Geertz 1973)—a multi-dimensional understanding of the process and
appearance of the poverty, which spectre-like, stalked the world of the
peasants of Iron Age Israel. In retrospect one is struck by the immensity
of the trials faced by the peasantry of Israel, caught as they were upon
the horns of a dilemma. On the one hand, there were the physical factors
of the environment—the reality of inadequate means (land, labour and
resources); households were unreliable sources of labour; allotments
were small; climates were harsh; droughts frequent; and farming methods
primitive. On the other hand there was the human factor—the power of
those who demanded their share of the limited surplus for rentals, fines,
debts, taxes and tithes. That they, the peasants of Israel, succeeded in
carving a life out of the Highlands and deserts is a testimony to the
human spirit and to faith.

Earlier studies of the poor of Israel tended to focus attention on the
changes brought about by the rise of the monarchy (Mendenhall 1975;
Gottwald 1986), including debt, and along with the loss of land and slavery arising out of debt (Lang 1985; Premnath 1988; Grabbe 1995). Apart
from Deist (2000) and Holladay (1998), little attention has been placed
on the impact of post-exilic innovations like coinage, the market system,
slavery and land tenure on the lives of the ordinary peasants of Israel. The
contribution of this work is to challenge the existing status quo through a
detailed study of the evolution of the economy of ancient Israel.

In the pre-exilic period, the major shift was the move into the Central
Highlands and the Negev desert, followed by an increase in patronage
and urbanisation. At some point in the later centuries of this period, there
was a general collapse in reciprocity, perhaps the consequence of foreign
taxation, which resulted in an increase in oppression and violence and to
which the earliest Prophetic texts draw attention.

In the post-exilic period, a different economic order came to the fore. Key changes included the introduction of coinage by the Persians and the introduction of the market economy by the Greeks, both of which opened the door to large scale peasant debt and loss of land. This was followed by the advent of large estates, as attested to by the archaeology, starting with the Greek period and resulting in further loss of land and a marked increase in day labourers. Forced labour and debt bondage were normative for Iron Age Israel, while life-long slavery became a major factor in the late Hellenistic and Roman periods. Finally, there was the introduction of the notion of private property under the Romans, which further exacerbated the plight of the poor. Any one of these changes would have had a major impact on peasant existence. Taken together, over the centuries, the cumulative impact was catastrophic. Scarce wonder that a series of revolts followed, particularly the Jewish revolt of 66–70 C.E., which has all the hallmarks of a peasant revolt (Domeris 1993).

For all these reasons, one cannot simply set Old and New Testament (or even the pre- and post-exilic) pictures of poverty side by side. Different situations prevailed under different economic constraints, which in turn demanded different responses; Amos, Nehemiah and Jesus lived in different economic times and the nature of poverty varied in consequence.

As the lives of the poor deteriorated over the centuries, the relevance of the great prophets like Amos and Isaiah probably increased, especially since these texts were collected and edited in the Persian and Hellenistic times (Gottwald 2001, 234). Why the later elite chose to safeguard these texts is unclear, unless it was to recognise their own sins, several generations removed.

The HB remains a testimony to the faith of the people who weathered the challenges across the centuries and offers us a unique glimpse into the pre- and post-market system worlds. Now in this final chapter, I offer a model of a society like ancient Israel to explain the impact on the lives of the peasants in Israel of different economic innovations.

10.2. *Modelling Biblical Poverty*

This work started as an exegetical study of poverty in the Hebrew Bible, akin to the recent study by Hoppe (2004). What changed the course of the book was the growing awareness of the multiple questions at the theoretical level. This fact prompted me to develop a model of biblical poverty, which would make sense of the peasant economy and its many challenges and which I would now like to share. I have found that poverty in the HB cannot be understood without reference to both the scale of power and the scale of honour. The poor of Israel frequently experienced both the loss of power and the burden of shame, and indeed the absence of these become the bars in the cage, which made escape from poverty so difficult for the majority of the poor. There were other interrelated problems as there are today, like bad nutrition, poor or no schooling, dysfunctional families, crime and substance addictions. These, however, were and continue to be the symptoms of poverty and not the root causes. The poor of Israel experienced the double oppression of powerlessness and shame—which present models of poverty do not develop fully.

An excellent place to begin is with Gerard Lenski's model of society (1984, 45), where he lists three key variables, namely power, privilege and prestige. These he sees as operating together to protect the interests of the powerful (the non-poor). Power is the primary variable (1984, 46) with privilege being a function of power and creating the potential for prestige (1984, 45). Allowing a feedback loop within the model, power in turn is reinforced by privilege (1984, 46). In developing our model of biblical poverty, I shall utilise Lenski's triad, but offer a modified understanding of the relationship of power and prestige, by using the notion of shame and honour, as particularly relevant for ancient Israel.

10.2.1. *Power*

Given the diversity of the sociological definitions of power (cf. Weber 1964, 152; Parsons 1968, I, 263; French 1985; Johnson 1995, 210), that of Giddens (1979) is most useful for our purposes. Wealth is expressed in terms of power over other people, and in privileged access to resources (1979, 91). Giddens (1984) delineated four sources of social power—ideological, economic, military and political relations (cf. Mann 1986, 2, 22–32). For Israel, prophets and priests correspond to the ideological relations, state and military formed the political and military relations respectively, leaving the economic power vested mainly in those who controlled the land—variously state-owned, temple-owned or individually owned. It is the complex interweaving of these realities that allows one to think in terms of a single axis of power in a single society as in our model (see below).

Power rests in this complex ordering of relations and institutions, to which humans respond in diverse manners. "Underneath, human beings are tunnelling ahead to achieve their goals, forming new networks, extending old ones and emerging most clearly into our view with rival configurations of one or more of the principal power networks" (Mann 1986, 16). People in ancient Israel looked not for individual freedom (in the Western sense of isolation from the influence of others) but rather "to become embedded in a network of protective power" (Patterson 1982, 28; cf. Sen 1999). Networking was one of the ways in which the non-poor formed power alliances and through which agrarians in need (e.g. famine) sought out patron–client and other peasant relationships (Patterson 1982, 80; Eisenstadt and Roniger 1984). These relationships revolved around power—"power will determine the distribution of nearly all the surplus possessed by a society" (Lenski 1984, 44). My study of the peasantry of Israel confirms my choice of powerlessness as the most important aspect in understanding the poor in ancient Israel, rather than economic disadvantage.

A clear interconnection but not equivalence exists between poverty and powerlessness (cf. Miller 1996, 581–82; Chambers 1997). Power and social position stood over against powerlessness and social exclusion, for "the socially vulnerable become the economically vulnerable" (Miller 1996, 575). In turn, powerlessness leads to other realities—the symptoms of poverty, including vulnerability to injustice and oppression—bringing us to the second of Lenski's categories, namely privilege or the lack thereof (Lenski 1984, 45).

10.2.2. *Privilege*
Privilege is defined as "possession or control of a portion of the surplus produced by a society" (Lenski 1984, 44). This is particularly relevant to the agrarian society of ancient Israel where patronage offered just such a privilege. As power increases so does privilege, although this is not a perfect continuum (Miller 1996, 575). To map out the distribution of privilege one has only to comprehend the power distribution (Lenski 1984, 44), which for a society like peasant Israel meant recognising the clustering of privileges around landowners and urban patrons. Agrarian resources conventionally include natural resources like drinking water, water for irrigation, natural sources of food (like game or wild plants), fertile lands and safe environments. They also include aspects like labour (free or under compulsion), fertile and hardworking women or men, tools and technology. The more limited the supply of resources, the greater is the degree of competition, the more obvious is the attendant power play, and, finally, the more important is privileged access.

10.2.3. *The Axis of Power*
The challenge, here, is to represent the power plays of peasant Israel in the form of a model. If one understands power as a vertical axis, absolute power would be at the top of the vertical axis of power and complete powerlessness would be at the bottom. Not all societies would include

these extremes, nor would there always be a great power differential. Some societies would have a shortened axis, and others may have a very long axis. In simple societies, one might speak about a "power elite" while in more complex societies one might have to deal with "elite pluralism" (the combinations of more than one elite group; cf. Johnson 1995, 211). Power elites draw their power from different sources, thus allowing for more than one group of elite to co-exist in a single society. For ancient Israel, power was vested in three groups, namely the military or state leaders, the priestly aristocracy and the prophetic circles and, in post-exilic times, large landowners and merchants.

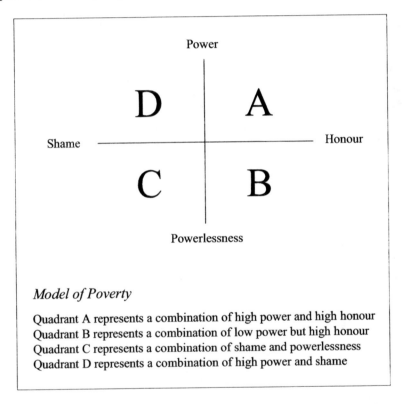

Model of Poverty

Quadrant A represents a combination of high power and high honour
Quadrant B represents a combination of low power but high honour
Quadrant C represents a combination of shame and powerlessness
Quadrant D represents a combination of high power and shame

The vertical axis A (the Power Axis) ranges from total power at the top to powerlessness at the bottom and represents diagrammatically an agrarian society like ancient Israel. As one moves up the axis, so one's power increases along with one's access to scarce resources like land usufruct, water, seed and tools. One could also add other resources like bases of social power, social networks (patronage), financial advantages and information. Giddens (1979, 91) reasons that power is not in itself a resource but rather that resources form the means by which power may be exercised. Peasant society was not monolithic, but was markedly stratified. These gradations that existed within peasant society meant that some had more power than others, and so were able to cope better with the challenges of the weather or their society. Thus, the fertile lands of one peasant might lead to a steady increase in personal power and prestige.

If this model stopped at the single dimension of power it would fail to reveal the full dimensions of biblical poverty. The HB also gives much weight to the notion of honour (prestige) and to its converse, shame. It might be assumed that aspects like honour and status follow naturally upon the increase in power. I suggest, however, that this is not always the case, and so it becomes imperative to introduce a second axis to the model.

10.2.4. *The Axis of Honour*

I propose here a model for the biblical world, which utilises a double set of variables, namely power (and powerlessness) and honour (and shame). I have chosen to represent these variables as a double set of axes. David Hamburg, president of the American Advancement of Science and the Carnegie Corporation of New York said in Cape Town in 1984:

> Poverty is partly a matter of income and partly a matter of human dignity. It is one thing to have a very low income but to be treated with respect by your compatriots; it is quite another matter to have a very low income and to be harshly depreciated by more powerful compatriots. Let us speak then of human impoverishment, low income plus harsh disrespect… To speak of impoverishment in this sense is to speak of human degradation which is so profound as to undermine any reasonable and decent standard of human life. (quoted in Wilson and Ramphele 1989, 5)

Two worlds lie side by side, each opaque to the other, the poor and the non-poor, and a cushion of less-poor people sandwiched between (Øyen 1996, 12). So in his studies of Zimbabwe, Scoones found that "prestige, respect, esteem, conduct, behaviour and local political influence may be significant in ranking a particular household and act to trade-off against potentially lower asset or income levels" (1995, 85). Chambers argues, therefore, for a notion of well-being as a broader category than wealth, and one more apposite for the complex varieties of the worlds of the poor (1997, 58). Well-being, while not always including wealth, certainly takes cognition of power, privilege and values like honour and dignity. In one instance, the "poorest" person in a Zimbabwe village according to the other villagers turned out to be the highest wage-earner, but who was poor since he was unmarried, without children and with few friends (Scoones 1995, 85).

Honour, and its converse, shame are part of a social idiom, which prescribes appropriate behaviour for members of society depending on their location in the hierarchy (Davis 1977, 98) and are recognised to be key values for the HB (Malina 1981; Bechtel 1991; Domeris 1995). Honour may be defined as a societal bequest (Pitt-Rivers 1968, 6:503) dependent on birth and achievement, or an arena of social conflict (Herzfeld 1980, 349), and even a power play (Gilmore 1982; Davis 1977; Dubisch 1993; Wikan 1984; Chance 1994) especially for male power (Abu-Lughod 1986, 1990). There is also a dark side—where honour in war meant rape and pillage and the fearful abuse of women and children (Keefe 1993; Niditch 1993; Thistlethwaite 1993) or in peacetime with its displays of consumption, which meant other people went hungry. Honour was so often gained at the expense of the humanity of others.

In spite of the tendency of the powerful to presuppose an absence of honour among those occupying the lower ranks of the ladder, this is not the case. Herzfeld speaks of the dishonour that on occasion attends the rich and conversely the honour that is found among the poor (1980, 342). So a poor person who is industrious, and a good father or husband, will have more honour than someone on the same level of power, but who fails in these regards. Poor people also keenly experience a sense of shame. Only when the experience of shame utterly destroys their sense of self-worth do they enter into the dark realm of shame, where honour and shame no longer exists.

Shame has a connection to power in that it functions as a social sanction (Piers and Singer 1963; Scheff 1987) not least in the HB (Bechtel 1991). This is true for both men and women, although the latter are the easier prey for such a punishment. The honour of women is deeply bound up with the honour of her father (and brothers) and later her husband (Stone 1996, 68–133). A woman who commits adultery shames her husband, and a daughter who loses her virginity outside of marriage shames her father. In both instances it is the honour of the man that is at stake, with the shaming of the woman the consequence of the activity (cf. Schneider 1971; Niditch 1993). With regard to the poor, shame increases the control of the powerful over the poor and powerless. Shame may become a form of structural violence (Jacobs 2003; McClenney-Saddler 2003), yet it may also be independent of the power line. Thus we need a separate axis.

The horizontal axis B (the Status Axis), which bisects the vertical axis, represents the honour/shame line, with the far right representing the highest honour and the far left, absolute shame. In a patron–client situation there is a constant ritualistic affirmation of the honour of the patron, such as in the giving of gifts and in the essence of the social intercourse acted out from day to day. Charity and the giving of charity or other forms of aid likewise inculcate a sense of honour for the donor, but may also add shame to the recipient—perceived failure of households to take care of their members (Pitt-Rivers 1977, 13–17).

The model thus represents the fuller dimensions of the biblical society, where shame and honour were key values alongside the competition for power. The model recognises the possibility that one may have both a high degree of honour and of power, or alternatively one may have one or the other. Honour exists even among those with little power. A person who is shamed experiences the sideways pressure of the shame/honour axis far more powerfully than any loss incurred in the simple competition for honour. The tighter the degree of social conformity expected within a society, the greater the degree of shame. The greater the potential for shame, the greater the pressure exerted along the shame/honour axis.

Among the pressures exerted by those with the greatest power, is a downward tendency, whereby the powerful prevent (or seek to prevent) the accumulation of power by those below them. In other words, power achieved has a correlation with power lost. As the powerful become more powerful, they do so at the expense of the less powerful—a very real trampling on the poor, as the prophet Amos would express it. Just as there is a downward pressure within the axis of power, with the people at the top exerting pressure on those below them, so there is also a sideways pressure, with those with more honour exerting pressure on those with less.

The value of this model lies in its attention to various forms of social pressure. With regard to the poor, we have drawn attention to the twin pressures, down the power axis and across the shame/honour axis. This dual force means that the poor are being driven from a place of powerlessness with honour to powerlessness without honour. The flow is uniformly in one direction with only rare opportunities for someone to swim with any success against the current. So the poor experience daily pressures designed both to render them more powerless and more shameful, and these are acted out in a score of disparate symbolic actions. For the most part, the powerful have a monopoly on symbols, and use them to their own advantage. Whether the symbol is a form of greeting, with particular titles and actions (e.g. genuflection), a style of dress (note the ornate garments of the traditional church leaders), or a place of abode, the message is clear: "You are the poor, and you do not belong in this world!" They are "the outsiders" within their own society, even the society in which they form the majority. It is to these and other symbolic actions that the prophets of old drew attention as they spoke of those who "trample on the heads of the poor as upon the dust of the ground" (Amos 2:7a).

Alienated from their natural resources, and deprived of honour and status, the poor become more and more dependent upon the non-poor and the social construction of poverty moves inexorably onward.

10.3. *The Way Forward*

So many studies of the poverty of the biblical world start and end in the ancient world, with little relevance for today. As an inhabitant of the developing world, I cannot allow this to be true of this study. To this end I conclude with five principles, which have arisen through the course of this work and which might be helpful in the present context of the readers.

The First Principle is that poverty is an extremely complex social phenomenon—an imposition on the poor by the non-poor; the deliberate creation of a subset within society, through the initial processes of labelling and demarcation, and the subsequent processes of disempowerment, oppression, marginalisation and alienation. In countering such poverty, there is no option but to seek a change within the very fabric of society—a righting of the essential elements that continue to perpetuate poverty and to form barriers for those who would escape its clutches. Failure to take this prior step renders all attempts at the eradication of poverty as being the equivalent of using Elastoplasts to treat cancer.

The Second Principle for understanding poverty in both the ancient world and today is—most of the poorest of the poor have been, and still are, peasants, especially peasant women and children. Peasant existence is a struggle for survival, which is made all the more unequal by the obstacles that powerful interests place in the way. Combating poverty means levelling the playing fields even if this is apparently unjust to those who have for centuries exploited the poor. Today the nations of the first world have a burden of responsibility to use their wealth and power to end the poverty of the two-thirds world, without seeking to expand their territorial interests through neo-colonialism and the neo-imperialism of twenty-first-century powers.

The Third Principle states that marginal agricultural areas are often home to great numbers of the poor, forcing them to eke out an existence on the edge of catastrophe, living daily with the reality of drought, starvation and the spectre of hopelessness. Land is the most critical element in the emerging and third-world economies and often the last to be addressed. Yet land holds the key to freedom, survival and honour—an arm that unites people with their ancestors and promises hope for off-spring as yet unborn.

The Fourth Principle states that while the poor have developed traditional ways of coping with famine, external human exploitation under-cuts these survival techniques, so exposing the peasants to increasing levels of poverty and need. While the bulk of the poor of the world continue to be peasants, emphasis on traditional methods of coping need to find space alongside modern methodologies like genetically modified crops; in the language of French (1985), to use "power-to" as in "the capacity to do things, to achieve goals especially in collaboration with others" instead of "power-over." Working with the traditional survival mechanisms of the poor is more effective than imposing a new set of mechanisms on the poor. One starts with the solutions of the poor to find the solutions to poverty.

The Fifth Principle states very simply that working to end poverty means also working to end indignity, powerlessness and shame. Without incorporating all these aspects, one may be guilty of recycling poverty and offering solutions such as those which have left whole communities as cultural orphans—disempowered, robbed of their culture and self-esteem (Vallely 1990). Yet in finding full and complete solutions to poverty, there is an added bonus—discovering that one is touching the very Heart of God.

The psalmist writes:

> They [the peasants of Israel] sowed fields and planted vineyards that yielded a fruitful harvest; God blessed them, and their numbers greatly increased, and he did not let their herds diminish. Then their numbers decreased, and they were humbled by oppression, calamity and sorrow; he who pours contempt on nobles made them wander in a trackless waste. But he lifted the poor out of their affliction and increased their families like flocks. The upright see and rejoice, but all the wicked shut their mouths. Whoever is wise, let him heed these things and consider the great love of the Lord. (Ps 107:37–43)

BIBLIOGRAPHY

Abu-Lughod, L. 1986. *Veiled Sentiments: Honor and Poetry in a Bedouin Society.* Berkeley: University of California Press.

—1990. The Romance of Resistance: Tracing Transformations of Power through Bedouin Women. *American Ethnologist* 17:41–55.

Ahlström, G. W. 1991. The Origin of Israel in Palestine. *SJOT* 2:19–34.

—1993. Pharaoh Shoshenq's Campaign to Palestine. Pages 1–16 in *History and Tradition of Early Israel: Studies Presented to Eduard Nielsen.* Edited by A. Lemaire and B. Otzen. VTSup 50. Leiden: Brill.

Ahlström, G. W., and D. Edelman. 1985. Mernephtah's Israel. *JNES* 44:59–61.

Albertz, R. 2003. Zur Wirtschaftspolitik des Perserreiches. Pages 335–57 in *Geschichte und Theologie: Studien zur Exegese des Alten Testaments und zur Religionsgeschichte Israels.* By R. Albertz. Edited by I. Kottsieper and J. Wörle. BZAW 326. Berlin: de Gruyter.

Albright, W. F. 1960. *The Archaeology of Palestine.* Rev. ed. Baltimore: Penguin.

—1975. Syria, the Philistines and Phoenicia. Pages 507–36 in Vol. 2, pt 2 of *The Cambridge Ancient History.* Edited by J. E. S. Edwards. 3d ed. Cambridge: Cambridge University Press.

Allan, W. 1965. *The African Husbandman.* London: Oliver & Boyd.

Alt, A. 1966. The Settlement of the Israelites in Palestine. Pages 135–69 in *Essays on Old Testament History and Religion.* Translated by R. A. Wilson. Oxford: Blackwell.

Amiran, R. 1962. Land Use in Israel. Pages 101–12 in *Land Use in Semi-Arid Mediterranean Cultures.* Edited by D. H. K. Amiran. Arid Zone Researches 24. Paris: UNESCO.

Andersen, F. I., and D. N. Freedman. 1989. *Amos: A New Translation with Introduction and Commentary.* AB 24A. New York: Doubleday.

Anderson, J. D. 1998. The Impact of Rome on the Periphery: The Case of Palestine-Roman Period (63 BCE–324 CE). Pages 446–65 in Levy 1998.

Anderson, P. 1974. *Passages from Antiquity to Feudalism.* London: NLB.

Anderson, B. W. 1988. *The Living World of the Old Testament.* 4th ed. London: Longman.

Angel, J. L. 1975. Paleoecology, Paleodemography and Health. Pages 167–90 in *Population, Ecology and Social Evolution.* Edited by S. Polgar. The Hague: Mouton.

Araya, V. 1987. *God of the Poor: The Mystery of God in Latin American Liberation Theology.* Maryknoll, N.Y.: Orbis.

Arnold, D. 1988. *Famine: Social Crisis and Historical Change.* Oxford: Blackwell.

Ash, P. S. 1999. *David, Solomon and Egypt: A Reassessment.* JSOTSup 297. Sheffield: Sheffield Academic Press.

Atal, Y. 1997. Involving the Poor: The Many Question Marks. Pages 18–24 in Atal and Øyen.

Atal, Y., and E. Øyen, eds. 1997. *Poverty and Participation in Civil Society*. Proceedings of a UNESCO/CROP Round Table. New Delhi: Abhinav.

Aufrecht, W. E., N. A. Mirau and S. W. Gauley, eds. 1997. *Aspects of Urbanism in Antiquity: From Mesopotamia to Crete*. JSOTSup 244. Sheffield: Sheffield Academic Press.

Avigad, N. 1953. The Epitaph of a Royal Steward from Siloam Village. *IEJ* 3:137–52.

—1986. *Hebrew Bullae from the Time of Jeremiah*. Jerusalem: Israel Exploration Society.

Avi-Yonah, M. ed. 1975–78. *Encyclopedia of Archaeological Excavations in the Holy Land*, vols. 1–4. Englewood Cliffs, N.J.: Prentice-Hall.

Avner, U. 1990. Ancient Agricultural Settlement and religion in the Uvda Valley in Southern Israel. *BA* 53:125–41.

Bammel, E. 1968. The Poor in the Old Testament. *TDNT* 6:888–94.

Barkay, G. 1992. The Iron Age II–III. Pages 302–73 in *The Archaeology of Ancient Israel*. Edited by A. Ben-Tor. New Haven: Yale University Press.

Barstad, H. M. 1984. *The Religious Polemics of Amos: Studies in the Preaching of Amos II 7b–8, IV 1–13, V 1–17, VI 4–7, VIII 14*. Leiden: Brill.

—1996. *The Myth of the Empty Land: A Study in the History and Archaeology of Judah During the "Exilic" Period*. SO 28. Oslo: Scandinavian University Press.

—2003. After the "Myth of the Empty Land": Major Challenges in the Study of Neo-Babylonian Judah. Pages 3–20 in *Judah and the Judeans in the Neo-Babylonian Period*. Edited by O. Lipschits and J. Blenkinsopp. Winona Lake, Ind.: Eisenbrauns.

Barton, J. ed. 2002. *The Biblical World*. 2 vols. London: Routledge.

Bar-Yosef, O. 1992. The Neolithic Period. Pages 10–39 in Ben-Tor 1992a.

Bar-Yosef, O., and A. Khazonov, eds. *Pastoralism in the Levant: Archaeological in Anthropological Perspective*. Monographs in World Archaeology 10. Madison, Wis.: Prehistory.

Basler, F. 1982. Weeds and Their Control. Pages 143–52 in *Lentils*. Edited by C. Webb and G. Hawtin. London: Commonwealth Agricultural Bureau and the International Centre for Agricultural Research in the Dry Areas.

Beaudry, M. 1994. L'urbanisation à l'époque du Fer. Pages 31–51 in *Où demeures tu? La maison depuis le monde biblique*. Festschrift Guy Couturier. Edited by J.-C. Petit. Saint-Laurent, Québec: Fides.

Bechtel, L. M. 1991. Shame as a Sanction of Social Control in Biblical Israel: Judicial, Political, and Social Shaming. *JSOT* 49:47–76.

Becking, B., and J. A. Wagenaar. 1998. Het "Huis van JHWH" en het "Verzoek van de weduwe": Enkele opmerkingen bij twee recent gepubliceerde oud-Hebreeuwse inscripties. *NTT* 52:177–93.

Ben-Tor, A., ed., 1992a. *The Archaeology of Ancient Israel*. Translated by R. Greenberg. New Haven: Yale University Press.

—1992b. The Early Bronze Age. Pages 81–125 in Ben-Tor 1992a.

—Tel Hazor, 1993. *IEJ* 43: 253–56.

—2000. Hazor and the Chronology of North Israel: A Reply to Israel Finkelstein. *BASOR* 317:9–15.

Ben-Tor, A., and D. Ben-Ami. 1998. Hazor and the Archaeology of the Tenth Century B.C.E. *IEJ* 48:1–37.

Bendix, R. 1978. *Kings or People: Power and the Mandate to Rule*. Berkeley: University of California Press.

Bendor, S. 1996. *The Social Structure of Ancient Israel: The Institution of the Family (beit ʿab) from the Settlement to the End of the Monarchy*. Jerusalem Biblical Studies 7. Jerusalem: Simor.

Bienkowski, P. 1989. Prosperity and Decline in LBA Canaan: A Reply to Liebowitz and Knapp. *BASOR* 275:59–63.

—1992. The Beginning of the Iron Age in Edom: A Reply to Finkelstein. *Levant* 24:167–69.

Bill, J. A. 1972. *The Politics of Iran: Groups, Classes, and Modernization*. Columbus, Ohio: Charles E. Merrill.

Biran, A., and J. Aviram, eds. *Biblical Archaeology Today 1990: Proceedings of the Second International Congress on Biblical Archaeology*. Supplement: Pre-Congress Symposium: Population, Production and Power. Jerusalem: Keterpress

Bird, P. A. 1998. *Missing Persons and Mistaken Identities: Women and Gender in Ancient Israel*. OBT. Minneapolis: Fortress.

Bisel, S. L. C. 1980. A Pilot Study of Aspects of Human Nutrition in the Ancient Eastern Mediterranean, with Particular Attention to Trace Elements in Several Populations from Different Time Periods. Ph.D. diss., University of Minnesota. Ann Arbor, Mich.: University Microfilms.

Bleiberg, E. 1994. "Economic Man" and the "Truly Silent One": Cultural Conditioning and the Economy in Ancient Egypt. *JSSEA* 24:4–16.

Blenkinsopp, J. 1997. The Family in First Temple Israel. Pages 48–103 in Perdue 1997.

Bloch, M. 1961. *Feudal Society*. Chicago: University of Chicago Press.

Bloch-Smith, E. 1992. The Cult of the Dead in Judah: Interpreting Material Remains. *JBL* 111:213–24.

—2003. Israelite Ethnicity in Iron I. Archaeology Preserves What is Remembered and What is Forgotten in Israel's History. *JBL* 122:401–25.

Bloch-Smith, E., and B. A. Nakhai. 1999. A Landscape Comes to Life: The Iron Age I Period. *NEA* 62:62–92, 101–27.

Boerma, C. 1979. *The Rich, the Poor—and the Bible*. Philadelphia: Westminster.

Borowski, O. 1979. Agriculture in Iron Age Israel. Ph.D. diss., University of Michigan. Ann Arbor, Michigan: University Microfilms.

—1987. *Agriculture in Iron Age Israel*. Winona Lake, Ind.: Eisenbrauns.

Boserup, E. 1965. *The Conditions of Agricultural Growth*. Chicago: Aldine.

—1981. *Population and Technology*. Oxford: Blackwell.

Botterweck, G. J. 1977. "*Ebyon*." *TDOT* 1:27–41.

Brand, P. W. 1987. "A Handful of Mud": A Personal History of My Love for the Soil. Pages 136–50 in *Tending the Garden: Essays in the Gospel and the Earth*. Edited by W. Grandberg-Michaelson. Grand Rapids: Eerdmans.

Bratton, M. 1987. Drought, Flood and Social Organization of Small Farmers in Zimbabwe. Pages 213–44 in *Drought and Hunger in Africa: Denying Famine a Future*. Edited by M. H. Glantz. Cambridge: Cambridge University Press.

Brenner, A. 1994. Who's Afraid of Feminist Criticism? Who's afraid of Biblical Humour? The Case of the Obtuse Foreign Ruler in the Hebrew Bible. *JSOT* 63:38–55.

Bright, J. 1980. *A History of Israel*. 3d ed. Philadelphia: Westminster.

Broshi, M. 1974. The Expansion of Jerusalem in the Reigns of Hezekiah and Manasseh. *IEJ* 24:21–26.

—1980. The Population of Western Palestine in the Roman-Byzantine Period. *BASOR* 236:1–10.

—1993. The Population of Iron Age Palestine. Pages 14–18 in Biran and Aviram 1993.

Broshi, M., and I. Finkelstein. 1992. The Population of Palestine in Iron Age II. *BASOR* 287:47–60.

Brown, F., S. R. Driver and C. A. Briggs. 1955. *Hebrew and English Lexicon of the Old Testament*. Oxford: Oxford University Press.

Brueggemann, W. 1977. *The Land: Place as Gift, Promise and Challenge in Biblical Faith*. OBT. Philadelphia: Fortress.

—1982. *Genesis*. Interpretation. Atlanta: John Knox.

—1990. *First and Second Samuel*. Interpretation. Louisville, Ky.: Westminster John Knox.

Bundy, C. 1988. *The Rise and Fall of the South African Peasantry*. 2d ed. Cape Town: David Philip.

Bunimovitz, S. 1998. On the Edge of Empires: Late Bronze Age 1500–1200 BCE. Pages 320–31 in Levy 1998.

Bunimovitz, S., and Z. Lederman. 2001. The Iron Age Fortifications of Tel Beth Shemesh: A 1990–2000 Perspective. *IEJ* 51:121–47.

Bunimovitz, S., and A. Yasur-Landau. 1996. Philistine and Israelite Pottery: A Comparative Approach to the Question of Pots and People. *TA* 23:88–101.

Cahill, J. M. 1995. Rosette Stamp Seal Impressions from Ancient Judah. *IEJ* 45:230–52.

—1998. It is There: The Archaeological Evidence Proves it. *BARev* 24, no. 4:34–41, 63.

Callaway, J. 1976. Excavating Ai (Et-Tell): 1964–1972. *BA* 39:18–30.

Callender, D. E. 1998. Servants of God(s) and Servants of Kings in Israel and the Ancient Near East. *Semeia* 83/84:67–82.

Camara, H. 1971. *Spiral of Violence*. London: Sheed & Ward.

Campbell, E. F. 1976. Two Amarna Notes: The Shechem City-State and Amarna Administrative Terminology. Pages 39–54 in Cross, Lemke and Miller 1976.

Carney, T. F. 1975. *The Shape of the Past: Models and Antiquity*. Lawrence, Kans.: Coronado.

Carpenter, E. 1997. "*Abad.*" *NIDOTTE* 3:304–9.

Carroll, R. M. D. 1996. "*Dll.*" *NIDOTTE* 1:951–54.

Carroll, R. P. 1986. *Jeremiah: A Commentary*. OTL. Philadelphia: Westminster.

Cassuto, U. 1967. *A Commentary on the Book of Exodus*. Jerusalem: The Hebrew University/Magnes.

Chambers, R. 1997. Poor People's Realities. The Professional Challenge. Pages 39–76 in Atal and Øyen 1997.

Chance, J. K. 1994. The Anthropology of Honor and Shame: Culture, Values and Practice. *Semeia* 68:139–52.

Chaney, M. L. 1982. You Shall Not Covet Your Neighbor's House. *Pacific Theological Review* 15, no. 2:3–13.

—1983. Ancient Palestinian Peasant Movements and the Formation of Premonarchic Israel. Pages 39–90 in Freedman and Graf 1983.

—1985. The Tenth Commandment as a Proscription of Latifundialization. Paper presented at the United College, Bangalore, India.

—1986. Systemic Study of the Israelite Monarchy. *Semeia* 37:53–76.

—1991. Debt Easement in Israelite History and Tradition. Pages 127–39 in *The Bible and the Politics of Exegesis: Essays in Honor of Norman K. Gottwald on His Sixty-Fifth Birthday*. Edited by D. Jobling, P. L. Day and G. T. Sheppard. Cleveland, Ohio: Pilgrim.

Chayanov, A. V. 1986. *The Theory of Peasant Economy*. Madison: University of Wisconsin Press.

Childs, B. S. 1974. *The Book of Exodus: A Critical, Theological Commentary*. OTL. Philadelphia: Westminster.

Chirichigno, G. C. 1993. *Debt Slavery in Israel and the Ancient Near East*. JSOTSup 141. Sheffield: JSOT Press.

Cipolla, C. M. 1976. *Before the Industrial Revolution: European Society and Economy 1000–1700*. New York: W.W. Norton.

Claessen, H., and P. Skalnik, eds. 1978. *The Early State*. The Hague: Mouton.

Clancy, F. 1999. Shishak/Shoshenq's Travels. *JSOT* 86: 3–23.

Clark, D. R. 2003. Bricks, Sweat and Tears: The Human Investment in Constructing a "Four-Room" House. *NEA* 66:34–43.

Coggins, R. J. 1986–87. The Old Testament and the Poor. *ExpTim* 99:11–14.

Cogan, M., and H. Tadmor. 1988. *Second Kings: A New Translation with Introduction and Commentary*. AB 11. Garden City, N.Y.: Doubleday.

Cohen, A. 1965. *Arab Border Villages in Israel: A Study of Continuity and Change in Social Organization*. Manchester. Manchester University Press.

Cohen, R. 1985. The Fortresses King Solomon Built to Protect His Southern Border. *BARev* 11, no. 3:56–70.

Coogan, M., et al., eds. *Scripture and Other Artefacts: Essays in Honour of Philip J. King*. Louisville, Ky.: John Knox.

Coote, R. B. 1981. *Amos Among the Prophets: Composition and Theology*. Philadelphia: Fortress.

—1991. Early Israel. *SJOT* 2:35–46.

Coote, R. B., and K. W. Whitelam. 1987. *The Emergence of Early Israel in Historical Perspective*. SWBA 5. Sheffield: Sheffield University Press.

Cross, F. M., W. E. Lemke and P. D. Miller, eds. *Magnalia Dei, The Mighty Acts of God: Essays on the Bible and Archaeology in Memory of G. Ernest Wright*. New York: Doubleday.

Currid, J. D., and A. Navon. 1989. Iron Age Pits and the Lahav (Tell Halif) Grain Storage Project. *BASOR* 273:67–78.

Cutileiro, J. 1971. *A Portuguese Rural Society*. Oxford: Clarendon.

Cutler, B., and J. MacDonald. 1982. On the Origin of the Ugaritic text KTU. 1.23. *UF* 14:33–50.

Dahood, M. 1965. *Psalms*. Vol. 1, *Psalms 1–50: Introduction, Translation and Notes*. AB 16. Garden City, N.Y. Doubleday.

—1968. *Psalms*. Vol. 2, *Psalms 51–100: Introduction, Translation and Notes*. AB 17. Garden City, N.Y. Doubleday.

Dandamayev, M. A. 1979. State and Temple in Babylonia in the First Millennium BC. Pages 589–604 in Lipinski 1979b.

—1987. Free Hired Labor in Babylonia during the Sixth through Fourth Centuries B.C. Pages 271–80 in Powell 1987.

Danin, A. 1998. Man and the Natural Environment. Pages 4–39 in Levy 1998.

Dar, S. 1980. Khirbet Jemaʾin: A Village from the Period of the Monarchy. *Qad* 13:97–100 [Hebrew].

—1986. *Landscape and Pattern: An Archaeological Survey of Samaria 800 BCE–636 CE with an Historical Commentary by Shimon Applebaum*, Parts 1–2. BARev International Series 308. Oxford: British Archaeological Reports.

Daviau, P. M. M. 1997. Tell Jawu: A Case Study of Ammonite Urbanism during Iron Age II. Pages 156–71 in Aufrecht, Mirau and Gauley 1997.

Davies, E. W. 1993. The Inheritance of the First-born in Israel and the Ancient Near East. *JSS* 38: 175–91.

Davies, G. 2002. Hebrew Inscriptions. Pages 270–86 in vol. 1 of Barton 2002.

Davies, P. R. 1992. *In Search of "Ancient Israel"*. JSOTSup 148. Sheffield: Sheffield Academic Press.

—1994. The Society of Biblical Israel. Pages 22–33 in Eskenazi and Richards 1994.

Davis, J. 1977. *People of the Mediterranean*. London: Routledge & Kegan Paul.

Dawes, S. B. 1991. ANAWA in Translation and Tradition. *VT* 41:38–48.

Dayton, J. E. 1984. Sardinia, the Sherden and Bronze Age Trade Routes. *Annali* 44:353–71.

Dearman, J. A. 1988. *Property Rights in the Eighth Century Prophets. The Conflict and Its Background*. SBLDS 106. Atlanta: Scholars Press.

De Geus, C. H. J. 1975. The Importance of Archaeological Research into the Palestinian Agricultural Terraces with an Excursus on the Hebrew Word *Gbi*. *PEQ* 107:65–74.

—1986. The Profile of an Israelite City. *BA* 49:224–27.

—1993. Of Tribes and Towns: The Historical Development of the Israelite City. *ErIs* 24:70–76.

Deist, F. E. 2000. *The Material Culture of the Bible: An Introduction*. The Biblical Seminar 70. Sheffield: Sheffield Academic Press.

De Ste. Croix, G. E. M. 1981. *The Class Struggle in the Ancient Greek World from the Archaic Age to the Arab Conquests*. London: Duckworth.

De Vaux, R. 1973. *Ancient Israel: Its Life and Institutions*. 2d ed. London: Darton, Longman & Todd.

Dever, W. G. 1985. Solomonic and Assyrian Period "Palaces" at Gezer. *IEJ* 35:217–30.

—1987. The Middle Bronze Age: Zenith of the Urban Canaanite Era. *BA* 50:148–77.

—1991. Archaeological Data on the Israelite Settlement: A Review of Two Recent Works. *BASOR* 284:77–90.

—1993. Cultural Continuity, Ethnicity in the Archaeological Record and the Question of Israelite Origins. *ErIs* 24:22–23.

—1994. Archaeology, Texts, and History-Writing: Towards an Epistemology. Pages 105–17 in *Uncovering Ancient Stones: Essays in Memory of H. Neil Richardson*. Edited by L. M. Hopfe. Winona Lake, Ind.: Eisenbrauns.

—1995. Ceramics, Ethnicity and the Question of Israel's Origins. *BA* 58:200–213.

—1997. Archaeology, Urbanism, and the Rise of the Israelite State. Pages 172–93 in Aufrecht, Mirau and Gauley 1997.

—1998a. Social Structure in the Early Bronze IV Period in Palestine. Pages 282–96 in Levy 1998.

—1998b. Social Structure in Palestine in the Iron II Period on the Eve of Destruction. Pages 416–31 in Levy 1998.

—1998c. Archaeology, Ideology, and the Quest for an "Ancient" or "Biblical Israel." *NEA* 61:39–52.

—2000. Settlement: Archaeology. Pages 1190–92 in Freedman, Myers and Beck 2000.

—2001. *What Did the Biblical Writers Know and When Did They Know It?* Grand Rapids: Eerdmans.

—2005. *Who Were the Early Israelites and Where Did They Come from?* Grand Rapids: Eerdmans.

Dewalt, K. M., and G. H. Pelto. 1977. Food Use and Household Economy in a Mexican Community. Pages 79–139 in *Nutrition and Anthropology in Action*. Edited by T. K. Fitzgerald. Assen: Van Gorcum.

DeWitt Knauth, R. J. 2000. Jubilee. Pages 743 in Freedman, Myers and Beck 2000.

Diakonoff, I. M. 1972. Socio-economic Classes in Babylonia and the Babylonian Concept of Social Stratification. *AbhBAW* 75:41–52.

Domeris, W. R. 1990. Blessed are you... (Matt 5:1–12). *JTSoA* 73:67–76.

—1991a. God Cares for his Own: Prosperity Readings of the Bible. Pages 26–34 in Bosman, Gous and Spangenberg 1991.

—1991b. Reading the Bible Against the Grain. *Scriptura* 37:68–79.

—1993. Jews and Romans at the Outbreak of the Jewish Revolt. Pages 137–56 in *Judaism in the Context of Diverse Civilizations*. Edited by M. Sharon. Johannesburg: Maksim.

—1995. Wise Women and Foolish Men: Shame and Honour in Proverbs. *OTE* 8, no. 1:86–102.

—1997a. *"Ebyon." NIDOTTE*, 1:228–32.

—1997b. *"Bzz, baz, bizza." NIDOTTE* 1:630–34.

—1997c. *"Gsl, gezel." NIDOTTE* 1:844–45.

—1997d. *"Misken, miskenut." NIDOTTE* 2:1001–2.

—1997e. *"Nekasim." NIDOTTE* 3:107–8.

—1997f. *"Paris II, prs." NIDOTTE* 3:686–87.

—1997g. *"Hwn, Hon." NIDOTTE* 1:1020–21.

—1997h. *"Srl, Asir." NIDOTTE* 3:558–61.

—1997i. *Hrg, hereg." NIDOTTE* 1:1055–57.

—1997j. *"Rws, res." NIDOTTE* 3:1085–87.

—1999. When Metaphor Becomes Myth: A Socio-linguistic Reading of Jeremiah. Pages 250–68 in *Troubling Jeremiah*. Edited by A. R. P. Diamond, K. M. O'Connor and L. Stulman. JSOTSup 260. Sheffield: Sheffield Academic Press.

Dosch, G. 1987. Non-slave Labor in Nuzi. Pages 223–36 in Powell 1987.

Dothan, T. 1995. Tel Miqne-Ekron: The Aegean Affinities of the Sea Peoples' (Philistine's) Settlement in Canaan in the Iron Age I. Pages 41–59 in Gitin 1995b.

—1998. Initial Philistine Settlement: From Migration to Coexistence. Pages 148–61 in Gitin, Mazar and Stern 1998.

Dothan, T., and A. Zukerman. 2004. A Preliminary Study of the Mycenaean IIIC:1 Pottery Assemblages from Tel Miqne-Ekron and Ashdod. *BASOR* 333:1–54.

Driver, S. R. 1913. *Notes on the Hebrew Text and Topography of the Books of Samuel.* 2d ed. Oxford: Clarendon.

Drori, I., and A. Horowitz. 1988–89. Tel Lachish: Environment and Subsistence During the Middle Bronze, Late Bronze and Iron Ages. *TA* 15–16:206–11.

Dubisch, J. 1993. "Foreign Chickens" and Other Outsiders: Gender and Community in Greece. *American Ethnologist* 20:272–87.

Duby, G. 1974. *The Early Growth of the European Economy: Warriors and Peasants from the Seventh to the Twelfth Century.* Ithaca, N.Y.: Cornell University Press.

Dumbrell, W. J. 1997. *"Anaw." NIDOTTE* 3:454–64.

Edelstein, G., and Y. Gat. 1980–81. Terraces Around Jerusalem. *Israel, Land and Nature* 6:72–78.

Edelstein, G., and S. Gibson. 1982. Ancient Jerusalem's Rural Food Basket. *BARev* 8:46–54.

Edelstein, G., and I. Milevski. 1994. The Rural Settlement of Jerusalem Re-evaluated: Surveys and Excavations in the Rephʾaim Valley and Mevassereet Yerushalayim. *PEQ* 126:2–23.

Eichler, B. L. 1973. *Indenture at Nuzi: The Personal Tidennutu Contract and Its Mesopotamian Analogies.* YNER 5. New Haven: Yale University Press.

Eisenberg, E. 1989–90. Nahal Refaʾim. *Excavations and Surveys in Israel* 7–8:84–89.

Eisenstadt, S. N. 1963. *The Political Systems of Empires.* New York: Free Press.

Eisenstadt, S. N., and L. Roniger. 1984. *Patrons, Clients, and Friends: Interpersonal Relations and the Structure of Trust in Society.* Cambridge: Cambridge University Press.

Ephʾal, I. 1998. Changes in Palestine During the Persian Period in the Light of Epigraphic Sources. *IEJ* 48:106–19.

Eskenazi, T. C., and K. H. Richards, eds. 1994. *Second Temple Studies*, vol. 2. Sheffield: JSOT Press.

Evenari, M., L. Shanan and N. Tadmor. 1971. *The Negev: The Challenge of a Desert.* Cambridge, Mass.: Harvard University Press.

Fabry, H.-J. 1978. *"Dal." TDOT* 3:208–30.

Faust, A. 1999. Differences in Family Structure Between Cities and Villages in Iron Age II. *TA* 26:233–52.

—2000a. The Rural Community in Ancient Israel During Iron Age II. *BASOR* 317:17–39.

—2000b. Ethnic Complexity in Northern Israel During Iron Age II. *PEQ* 132:2–27.

—2003. Abandonment, Urbanization, Resettlement and the Formation of the Israelite State. *NEA* 66:147–61.

Faust, A., and S. Bunimovitz. 2003. The Four-Room House: Embodying Iron Age Israelite Society. *NEA* 66:22–31.

Fensham, F. C. 1962. Widow, Orphan, and the Poor in the Ancient Near Eastern Legal and Wisdom Literature. *JNES* 21:129–39.

Fenyves, K., S. Rule and D. Everatt. 1998. *Poverty and Religion: A Study of How Urban People Cope with Poverty in the Light of Their Religion.* Johannesburg: Community Agency for Social Enquiry.

Fiensy, D. 1987. Using the Nuer Culture of Africa in Understanding the Old Testament: An Evaluation. *JSOT* 38:73–83.

Finkelstein, I. 1988. *The Archaeology of the Israelite Settlement.* Jerusalem. Israel Exploration Society.

—1991a. The Central Hill Country in the Intermediate Bronze Age. *IEJ* 41:19–45.

—1991b. The Emergence of Israel in Canaan: Consensus, Mainstream and Dispute. *SJOT* 2:47–59.

—1992. Edom in the Iron I. *Levant* 24:159–66.

—1993. The Sociopolitical Organisation of the Central Hill Country in the Second Millennium B.C.E. Pages 110–31 in Biran and Aviram 1993.

—1994. The Archaeology of the Days of Manasseh. Pages 169–87 in Coogan et al. 1994.

—1995. The Date of the Settlement of the Philistines in Canaan. *TA* 22:213–39.

—1996. The Archaeology of the United Monarchy: An Alternative View. *Levant* 28:177–87.

—1997. Pots and People Revisited: Ethnic Boundaries in the Iron Age I. Pages 216–37 in *The Archaeology of Israel*. Edited by N. A. Silberman and D. Small. JSOTSup 237. Sheffield: Sheffield Academic Press.

—1998a. The Great Transformation: The "Conquest" of the Highlands Frontiers and the Rise of the Territorial States. Pages 349–67 in Levy 1998.

—1998b. Philistine Chronology: High, Middle or Low? Pages 140–47 in Gitin, Mazar and Stern 1998.

—1998c. Bible Archaeology or Archaeology of Palestine in the Iron Age? A Rejoinder. *Levant* 30:167–74.

—1998d. The Rise of Early Israel: Archaeology and Long-Term History. Pages 7–39 in *The Origin of Early Israel: Current Debate. Biblical, Historical and Archaeological Perspectives*. Edited by S. Ahituv and E. D. Oren. Irene Levi-Sala Seminar 1997. Beer-Sheva Studies by the Department of Bible and Ancient Near East 12. Beer-Sheva: Ben-Gurion University of the Negev Press.

—1999. Hazor and the North in the Iron Age: A Low Chronology Perspective. *BASOR* 314:55–70.

—2001. The Rise of Jerusalem and Judah: the Missing Link. *Levant* 33:105–15.

—2002. Gezer Revisited and Revised. *TA* 29:262–96.

—2004. Tel Rehov and Iron Age Chronology. *Levant* 36:181–88.

Finkelstein, I., and Z. Lederman, eds. 1997. *Highlands of Many Cultures: The Southern Samaria Survey. The Sites*. 2 vols. Monograph Series 14. Tel Aviv: Institute of Archaeology, Tel Aviv University Press.

Finkelstein, I., and A. Perevolotsky. 1990. Processes of Sedentarization and Nomadization in the History of Sinai and the Negev. *BASOR* 279:67–88.

Finkelstein, I., and N. A. Silberman. 2001. *The Bible Unearthed: Archaeology is Rewriting the Bible and Reshaping the Middle East*. New York: Free Press.

Finkelstein, I., and D. Ussishkin. 2000. Archaeological and Historical Conclusions. Pages 576–605 in Finkelstein, Ussishkin and Halpern 2000.

Finkelstein, I., D. Ussishkin and B. Halpern, eds. 2000. *Megiddo III: The 1992–1996 Seasons*. 2 vols. Sonia and Marco Nadler Institute of Archaeology Monograph Series 18. Tel Aviv: Emery and Claire Yass Publications in Archaeology.

Finkelstein, I., and Y. Zilberman. 1995. Site Planning and Subsistence Economy: Negev Settlements as a Case Study. Pages 213–26 in Holloway and Handy 1995.

Finkelstein, I., O. Zimhoni and A. Kafri. 2000. The Iron Age Pottery Assemblages from Areas F, K and H and Their Stratigraphic and Chronological Implications. Pages 244–324 in Finkelstein, Ussishkin and Halpern 2000.

Finkelstein, L. 1962. *The Pharisees*, vols. 1 and 2. Philadelphia: Jewish Publication Society of America.

Finley, M. I., ed. 1960. *Slavery in Classical Antiquity*. Cambridge: W. Heffer & Sons.

—1968. Slavery. Pages 307–13 in vol. 14 of *Encyclopaedia of Social Sciences*. Edited by E. R. Anderson and A. Johnson. New York: Macmillan.

—1980. *Ancient Slavery and Modern Ideology*. New York: Viking.

Fleishman, J. 1992. The Age of Legal Maturity in Biblical Law. *JANES* 21:35–48.

Foxhall, L., and H. A. Forbes. 1982. Sitometria: The Role of Grain as a Staple Food in Classical Antiquity. *Chiron* 12:41–90.

Free, J. P. 1960. The Seventh Season at Dothan. *BASOR* 160:6–15.

Freedman, D. N., ed. 2000. *Eerdmans Dictionary of the Bible*. Grand Rapids: Eerdmans.

Freedman, D. N., and D. F. Graf, eds. 1983. *Palestine in Transition: The Emergence of Ancient Israel*. Sheffield: Almond.

French, M. 1985. *Beyond Power*. New York: Summit.

Frick, F. S. 1977. *The City in Ancient Israel*. SBLDS 36. Missoula, Mont.: Scholars Press.

—1985. *The Formation of the State in Ancient Israel: A Survey of Models and Theories*. Sheffield: JSOT Press.

—1994a. *Cui Bono*? History in the Service of Political Nationalism: The Deuteronomistic History as Political Propaganda. *Semeia* 66:79–92.

—1994b. Widows in the Hebrew Bible: A Transactional Approach. Pages 139–51 in *A Feminist Companion to Exodus to Deuteronomy*. Edited by A. Brenner. The Feminist Companion to the Bible 6. Sheffield: Sheffield Academic Press.

—1999. "Oil from Flinty Rock" (Deuteronomy 32:13): Olive Cultivation and Olive Oil Processing in the Hebrew Bible. A Socio-materialist Perspective. *Semeia* 86:1–18.

Fritz, V. 1987. Conquest or Settlement? The Early Iron Age in Palestine. *BA* 50:84–100.

—1995. *The City in Ancient Israel*. The Biblical Seminar 29. Sheffield: Sheffield Academic Press.

—1996. Monarchy and Re-Urbanization: A New Look at Solomon's Kingdom. Pages 187–95 in Fritz and Davies 1996.

Fritz, V., and P. R. Davies, eds. 1996. *The Origins of the Ancient Israelite States*. JSOTSup 228. Sheffield: Sheffield Academic Press.

Gal, Z. 1988–89. The Lower Galilee in the Iron Age H: Analysis of Survey Material and its Historical Interpretation. *TA* 15–16:56–64.

Gallant, T. W. 1991. *Risk and Survival in Ancient Greece: Reconstructing the Rural Domestic Economy*. Stanford, Calif.: Stanford University Press.

Garbini, G. 1977. L'Inscrizione fenicia di Kilamuwa e il verbo *skr* in Semitico Nordoccidentale. *Bibbia e Oriente* 19:113–18.

Garnsey, P. 1988. *Famine and Food Supply in the Graeco-Roman World: Responses to Risk and Crisis*. Cambridge: Cambridge University Press.

Geertz C. 1973. *The Interpretation of Cultures*. New York: Basic.

Gelb, I. J. 1979. Household and Family in Early Mesopotamia. Pages 1–97 in Lipinski 1979b.

George, A. 1977. Poverty in the Old Testament. Pages 3–21 in *Gospel Poverty: Essays in Biblical Theology*. Edited by M. D. Guinan. Chicago: Franciscan.

Gerstenberger, E. 2001. "*ānâ*." *TDOT* 11:230–52.

Gibson, S. 1983–84. Ancient Jerusalem's Rural Landscape. *BAIAS* 3:30–35.

—2001. Agricultural Terraces and Settlement Expansion in the Highlands in Early Iron Age Palestine: Is There Any Correlation between the Two? Pages 113–46 in Mazar 2001.

Giddens, A. 1979. *Central Problems in Social Theory*. London: Macmillan.

—1984. *The Constitution of Society: Outline of the Theory of Structuration*. Berkeley: University of California Press.

GiPad, H. 1990–91. A Garden of Vegetables. *JBQ* 19:123–26.

Gilboa, A., and I. Sharon. 2003. An Archaeological Contribution to the Early Iron Age Chronological Debate: Alternative Chronologies for Phoenicia and Their Effects on the Levant, Cyprus and Greece. *BASOR* 332:7–80.

Gillingham, S. 1988–89. The Poor in the Psalms. *ExpTim* 100(1):15–19.

Gilmore, D. D. 1982. Anthropology of the Mediterranean Area. *Annual Review of Anthropology* 11:175–205.

Gitin, S. 1990. Ekron of the Philistines. Part 2, Olive-Oil Suppliers to the World. *BARev* 16, no. 2:32–42, 59.

—1995a. Tel Miqne-Ekron in the 7th Century B.C.E.: The Impact of Economic Innovation and Foreign Cultural Influences on a Neo-Assyrian Vassal City-State. Pages 61–79 in Gitin 1995b.

—, ed. 1995b. *Recent Excavations in Israel: A View of the West. Reports on Kabri, Nami, Miqne-Ekron, Dor and Ashkelon.* AIACCP 1. Dubuque, Iowa: Kendell/Hunt.

Gitin, S., and A. Golani. 2004. A Silver-based Monetary Economy in the Seventh Century BCE: A Response to Raz Kletter. *Levant* 36:203–5.

Gitin, S., A. Mazar and E. Stern, eds. *Mediterranean Peoples in Transition: Thirteenth to Early Tenth Centuries BCE.* Jerusalem: Israel Exploration Society.

Giveon, R. 1983–84. Archaeological Evidence for the Exodus. *BAIAS*: 42–44.

Glantz, M. H. 1987. *Drought and Hunger in Africa: Denying Famine a Future.* Cambridge: Cambridge University Press.

Goedicke, H. 1979. Cult-temple and "State" During the Old Kingdom in Egypt. Pages 113–31 in Lipinski 1979b.

Goldberg, P. 1998. The Changing Landscape. Pages 40–57 in Levy 1998.

Gonen, R. 1992a. The Late Bronze Age. Pages 211–57 in Ben-Tor 1992a.

—1992b. The Chalcolithic Period. Pages 40–80 in Ben-Tor 1992a.

Goodfriend, E. A., and K. Van Der Toorn. 1992. "Prostitution." *ABD* 5:505–13.

Gophna, R. 1992. The Intermediate Bronze Age. Pages 126–58 in Ben-Tor 1992a.

Gordis, R. 1950. Naʿalam and Other Observations on the Ain Feshka Scrolls. *JNES* 9:44–47.

Görg, M. 2001. Israel in Hieroglyphen. *BN* 106:21–27.

Gossai, H. 1993. *Justice, Righteousness and the Social Critique of the Eighth Century Prophets.* American University Studies 7. Theology and Religion 141. New York: Lang.

Gottwald, N. K. 1978. Were the Early Israelites Pastoral Nomads? *BARev* 4:2–7.

—1979. *The Tribes of Yahweh: A Sociology of the Religion of Liberated Israel 1250–1050 B.C.E.* Maryknoll, N.Y.: Orbis.

—1985. *The Hebrew Bible: A Socio-Literary Introduction.* Philadelphia: Fortress.

—1986. The Participation of Free Agrarians in the Introduction of Monarchy to Ancient Israel: An Application of H. A. Landsberger's Framework for the Analysis of Peasant Movements. *Semeia* 37:77–106.

—1993. *The Hebrew Bible in Its Social World and in Ours.* Atlanta: Scholars Press.

—1997. Triumphalist Versus Anti-Triumphalist Versions of Early Israel: A Response to Articles by Lemche and Dever in Volume 4. *CR:BS* 5:15–42.

—2001. *The Politics of Ancient Israel.* Louisville, Ky.: Westminster John Knox.

Goubert, P. 1987. *The French Peasantry in the Seventeenth Century.* Translated by I. Patterson. Cambridge: Cambridge University Press.

Gowan, D. E. 1986. *Eschatology in the Old Testament.* Philadelphia: Fortress.

—1987. Wealth and Poverty in the Old Testament: The Case of the Widow, the Orphan, and the Sojourner. *Int* 41:341–53.

Grabbe, L. L. 1995. *Priests, Prophets, Diviners, Sages: A Socio-historical Study of Religious Specialists in Ancient Israel.* Valley Forge, Pa.: Trinity.

—, ed. 1997. *Can a "History of Israel" be Written?* JSOTSup 245. European Seminar in Historical Methodology 1. Sheffield: Sheffield Academic Press.

—2002. Israel Under Persia and Greece. Pages 440–57 in vol. 1 of Barton 2002.

Granott, A. 1952. *The Land System in Palestine: History and Structure*. London: Eyre & Spottiswoode.

Gregory, J. R. 1975. Image of Limited Good or Expectation of Reciprocity? *Current Anthropology* 16:73–92.

Grelot, P. 1972. *Documents Araméens d'Egypte*. Paris: Cerf.

Grigson, C. 1998. Plough and Pasture in the Early Economy of the Southern Levant. Pages 245–68 in Levy 1998.

Gutierrez, G. 1973. *A Theology of Liberation: History, Politics and Salvation*. Maryknoll, N.Y.: Orbis.

Haan, R. 1991. *The Economics of Honour: Biblical Reflections on Money and Property*. Rev. ed. Geneva: WCC.

Haldane, C. W. 1990. Shipwrecked Plant Remains. *BA* 53:55–60.

Halliday, M. A. K. 1978. *Language as Social Semiotic: The Social Interpretation of Language and Meaning*. London: Edward Arnold.

—1985. *Language as Social Semiotic: Language, Context and Text*. Oxford: Oxford University Press.

Halligan, J. M. 1983. The Role of the Peasant in the Amarna Period. Pages 15–24 in Freedman and Graf 1983.

Halpern, B. 1988. *The First Historians: The Hebrew Bible and History*. San Francisco: Harper & Row.

—1994. The Stela from Dan: Epigraphic and Historical Considerations. *BASOR* 296:63–80.

Halpern, B., and D. W. Hobson. 1991. *Law and Ideology in Monarchic Israel*. JSOT Sup 124. Sheffield: Sheffield Academic Press.

Halstead, P. 1987. Traditional and Ancient Rural Economy in Mediterranean Europe: Plus ça Change? *JHS* 107:77–87.

Hamel, G. 1989. *Poverty and Charity in Roman Palestine, First Three Centuries C.E.* Near Eastern Studies 23. Berkeley: University of California Press.

Handy, L. K., ed. 1997. *The Age of Solomon: Scholarship at the Turn of the Millennium*. SHCANE 11. Leiden: Brill.

Hanks, T. D. 1983. *For God so Loved the Third World: The Biblical Vocabulary of Oppression*. Translated by J. C. Dekker. Maryknoll, N.Y.: Orbis.

Harris, M. 1979. *Cultural Materialism*. New York: Random.

Hasel, M. G. 1995. Israel in the Merneptah Stela. *BASOR* 296:45–61.

Hauck, F., and W. Kasch. 1968. "Riches and the Rich in the Old Testament." *TDNT* 6:323–25.

Hayes, J. H. 1987. On Reconstructing Israelite History. *JSOT* 39:5–9.

Hayes, J. H., and J. M. Miller, eds. 1977. *Israelite and Judaean History*. London: SCM Press.

Hellwing, S. 1988–89. Animal Bones for Tel Tsaf. *TA* 15–16:47–51.

Hellwing, S., and M. Sadeh. 1985. Animal Remains: Preliminary Report. *TA* 12:177–80.

Heltzer, M. 1982. *The Internal Organization of the Kingdom of Ugarit*. Wiesbaden: Ugarit.

—1987. Labour in Ugarit. Pages 237–50 in Powell 1987.

Hengel, M. 1986. *Earliest Christianity: Acts and the History of Earliest Christianity and Property and Riches in the Early Church*. London: SCM Press.

Hentschke, R. 1963. *Satzung und Setzender: ein Beitrag zur israelitischen Rechtsterminologie*. BWANT 5/3. Stuttgart: Kohlhammer.

Herrmann, S. 1981. *History of Israel in Old Testament Times*. 2d ed. Philadelphia: Fortress.

Herzfeld, M. 1980. Honour and Shame: Problems in the Comparative Analysis of Moral Systems. *Man* 15:339–51.

Herzog, Z. 1992a. Administrative Structure in the Iron Age. Pages 223–30 in Kempinski and Reich 1992.

—1992b. Settlement and Fortification Planning in the Iron Age. Pages 231–74 in Kempinski and Reich 1992.

—2002. The Fortress Mound at Tel Arad: An Interim Report. *TA* 29:3–109.

Hess, R. S. 2000. "Amarna Letters." Pages 50–51 in Freedman 2000.

Hilliers, D. R. 1984. *Micah*. Hermeneia. Philadelphia: Fortress.

Hilton, R. H. 1973. Peasant Society, Peasant Movements and Feudalism in Medieval Europe. Pages 67–94 in Landsberger 1973a.

Hjelm, I., and T. L. Thompson. 2002. The Victory Song of Merneptah, Israel and the People of Palestine. *JSOT* 27:3–18.

Hobbs, T. R. 1988–89. Reflections on "the Poor" and the Old Testament. *ExpTim* 100:291–94.

Hobsbawm, E. J. 1965. *Primitive Rebels*. New York: Norton.

—1969. *Bandits*. New York: Pantheon.

Hoffner, H. A. 1977. "*Almanah*." *TDOT* 1:287–91.

Holladay, J. S. 1991. The Use of Pottery and Other Diagnostic Criteria, from the Solomonic Era to the Divided Kingdom. Pages 86–101 in Biran and Aviram 1991.

—1998. The Kingdoms of Israel and Judah: Political and Economic Centralization in the Iron IIa–b (ca. 1000–750 BCE). Pages 368–98 in Levy 1998.

Holloway, S. W. 1997. Assyria and Babylonia in the Tenth Century B.C.E. Pages 202–16 in Handy 1997.

Holloway, S. W., and L. K. Handy, eds. 1995. *The Pitcher is Broken: Memorial Essays for Gösta W. Ahlström*. JSOTSup 190. Sheffield: Sheffield Academic Press.

Hopkins, D. C. 1985. *The Highlands of Canaan: Agricultural Life in the Early Iron Age*. SWBA 3. Sheffield: Almond.

—1987. Life on the Land: Subsistence Struggles of Early Israel. *BA* 50:178–91.

—1993. Pastoralists in Late Bronze Age Palestine: Which Way Did They Go? *BA* 56:200–11.

—1996. Bare Bones: Putting Flesh on the Economics of Ancient Israel. Pages 121–39 in Fritz and Davies 1996.

Hopkins, K. 1965. The Age of Roman Girls at Marriage. *Population Studies* 18:309–27.

Hoppe, J. L. 1987. *Being Poor: A Biblical Study*. GNS. Wilmington, Del.: Michael Glazier.

—2004. *There Shall be No Poor Among You: Poverty in the Bible*. Nashville: Abingdon.

Horwitz, L. K. 1986–87. Faunal Remains from the Early Iron Age Site on Mount Ebal. *TA* 13–14:173–89.

Humbert, P. 1952. Le Mot Biblique Ebyon. *RHPR* 32:1–6.

Hyatt, J. P. 1971. *Exodus*. NCB. Grand Rapids: Eerdmans.

Jacobs, M. R. 2003. Love, Honor and Violence: Socioconceptual Matrix in Genesis 34. *Semeia* 44:11–36.

Janssen, J. J. 1979. The Role of the Temple in the Egyptian Economy During the New Kingdom. Pages 505–15 in Lipinski 1979b.

Johnson, A. G. 1995. *The Blackwell Dictionary of Sociology. A Users' Guide to Sociological Language.* Oxford: Blackwell.

Jordan, L. S., and D. L. Shaner. 1979. Weed Control. Pages 266–296 in *Agriculture in Semi-arid Environments.* Edited by A. E. Hall, G. H. Cannell and H. W. Laweton. New York: Springer.

Kaiser, O. 1983. *Isaiah 1–12: A Commentary.* Translated by J. Bowden. 2d ed. OTL. London: SCM Press.

Kallai, Z. 1993. The King of Israel and the House of David. *IEJ* 43:248.

Katsnelson, J. 1971. "Dew." *EncJud* 5:1600–1602.

Kaufman, S. A. 1984. A Reconstruction of the Social Welfare System of Ancient Israel. Pages 277–86 in *In the Shelter of Elyon: Essays on Ancient Palestinian Life and Literature in Honour of G. W. Ahlström.* Edited by W. B. Barrick and J. R. Spencer. JSOTSup 31. Sheffield: JSOT Press.

Kautsky, J. H. 1982. *The Politics of Aristocratic Empires.* Chapel Hill: University of North Carolina Press.

Keefe, A. A. 1993. Rapes of Women/Wars of Men. *Semeia* 61:79–98.

Kempenski, A. 1992. The Middle Bronze Age. Pages 159–210 in Ben-Tor 1992a.

Kempinski, A., and R. Reich, eds. 1992. *The Architecture of Ancient Israel: From the Prehistoric to the Persian Periods.* Jerusalem: Israel Exploration Society.

Kenyon, K. M. 1976. Jericho. Pages 550–64 in vol. 2 of Avi-Yonah 1975–78.

—1978. *The Bible and Recent Archaeology.* London: Colonnade.

Key Indicators of Poverty in South Africa. 1995. The South African Reconstruction and Development Programme (RDP) and the World Bank. Southern African Labour and Research Development Research Unit [SALDRU] of the University of Cape Town. Pretoria: SA Communications Service.

Kessler, R. 1986. Silber und Gold, Gold und Silber zur Wertschätzung der Edelmetalle im Alten Israel. *BN* 31:57–69.

—1994. Frühkapitalismus, Rentenkapitalismus, Tributarismus, antike Klassengesell-schaft. Theorien zur Gesellschaft des Alten Israel. *EvT* 54:413–27.

Kevers, P. 1985. Het Recht van de Armen in de Schrift. *Coll* 15:264–83.

Khazanov, A. 1984. *Nomads and the Outside World.* Cambridge: Cambridge University Press.

King, P. J. 1988a. *Amos, Hosea, Micah: An Archaeological Commentary.* Philadelphia: Westminster.

—1988b. The Marzeah Amos Denounces. *BARev* 15, no. 4:34–44.

Klengel, H. 1987. Non-slave Labour in the Old Babylonian Period: The Basic Outlines. Pages 159–66 in Powell 1987.

Kletter, R. 1998. *Economic Keystones: The Weight System of the Kingdom of Judah.* JSOTSup 276. Sheffield: Sheffield Academic Press.

—2001. Between Archaeology and Theology: The Pillar Figurines from Judah and the Asherah. Pages 179–216 in Mazar 2001.

—2003. Iron Age Hoards of Precious Metals in Palestine: An "Underground Economy"? *Levant* 35:139–52.

—2004. Coinage Before Coins? A Response. *Levant* 36:207–10.

Knapp, A. B. 1989. Response: Independence, Imperialism, and the Egyptian Factor. *BASOR* 275:64–68.

Knight, D. A. 1994. Political Rights and Powers in Monarchic Israel. *Semeia* 66:93–118.

Knight, J. D. 2001. Israelites, Canaanites, and Barbeque Ribs: A Diachronic Study of Pig Remains as an Indicator of Ethnic Change in Palestine around 1200 B.C.E. *PCSSBLASSOR* 4:81–101.

Knoppers, G. N. 1997. The Vanishing Solomon: The Disappearance of the United Monarchy from Recent Histories of Ancient Israel. *JBL* 116:19–44.

Kuschke, A. 1939. Arm und Reich im Alten Testament mit besonderer Berücksichtigung der nachexilischen Zeit. *ZAW* 57:31–57.

Kutsch, E. 1978. *"Hon." TDOT* 3:364–68.

Lambton, A. K. S. 1953. *Landlord and Peasant in Persia.* London: Oxford University Press.

Landsberger, H. A. 1973a. Peasant Unrest: Themes and Variations. Pages 1–64 in Landsberger 1973b.

Lang, B. 1985. The Social Organisation of Peasant Poverty in Biblical Israel. Pages 83–99 in *Anthropological Approaches to the Old Testament.* Edited by B. Lang. IRT 8. Philadelphia, Fortress.

Leeb, C. S. 2000. *Away from the Father's House: The Social Location of Naʿar and Naʿarah in Ancient Israel.* JSOTSup 301. Sheffield: Sheffield Academic Press.

—2002. The Widow: Homeless and Post-Menopausal. *BTB* 32:160–62.

Lemaire, A. 1984. Sagesse et Ecoles. *VT* 34:270–81.

Lemche, N. P. 1985. *Early Israel: Anthropological and Historical Studies on the Israelite Society Before the Monarchy.* VTSup 37. Leiden: Brill.

—1991. *The Canaanites and Their Land: The Traditions of the Canaanites.* JSOTSup 110. Sheffield: JSOT Press.

—1993. The Old Testament: A Hellenistic Book? *SJOT* 7:163–93.

—1997. On Doing Sociology with "Solomon." Pages 312–35 in Handy 1997.

—1998. *The Israelites in History and Tradition.* Library of Ancient Israel. London: SPCK.

—1996. From Patronage Society to Patronage Society. Pages 106–20 in Fritz and Davies 1996.

Lemnche, N. P. 1998. *The Israelites in History and Tradition.* Library of Ancient Israel. London: SPCK.

Lemche, N. P., and T. L. Thompson. 1994. Did Biran Kill David? The Bible in the Light of Archaeology. *JSOT* 64:3–22.

Lenski, G. E. 1984. *Power and Privilege: A Theory of Social Stratification.* Rev. ed. Chapel Hill: University of North Carolina Press.

Lenski, G., J. Lenski and P. Nolan. 1991. *Human Societies: An Introduction to Macrosociology.* 3d ed. New York: McGraw–Hill.

Letsoalo, E. M. 1987. *Land Reform in South Africa: A Black Perspective.* Johannesburg: Skotaville.

Levenson, J. D. 1976. Poverty and State in Biblical Thought. *Judaism* 25:230–41.

Levinson, B. M., ed. 1994. *Theory and Method in Biblical and Cuneiform Law: Revision, Interpolation and Development.* JSOTSup 181. Sheffield: Sheffield Academic Press.

Levy, K. H., ed. 1998. *The Archaeology of Society in the Holy Land.* 2d ed. London: Leicester University Press.

Levy, T. E., and A. F. C. Holl. 1998. Social Change and the Archaeology of the Holy
    Land. Pages 1–20 in Levy 1998.
Liebowitz, H. 1989. Response: LB IIB Ivories and the Material Culture of the Late
    Bronze Age. *BASOR* 275:63–64.
Linville, J. R. 1998. *Israel in the Book of Kings: The Past as a Project of Social Identity.*
    JSOTSup 272. Sheffield: Sheffield Academic Press.
Lipinski, E. 1979a. Les temples Néo-Assyriens et les Origines du Monnayage. Pages
    565–88 in Lipinski 1979b.
—ed., 1979b. *State and Temple Economy in the Ancient Near East*, vols. 1 and 2. OLA.
    Leven: Department Oriëntalistiek.
Liverani, M. 1979b. Economia delle Fattorie Palatine Ugaritiche. *DdA* 2:57–72.
—1983. Political Lexicon and Political Ideologies in the Amarna Letters. *Berytus* 31:41–
    56.
Lohfink, N. 1986. "*Hopsi.*" *TDOT* 5:114–18.
—1990. "*Yāraš.*" *TDOT* 6:368–96.
—1991. Poverty in the Laws of the Ancient Near East and of the Bible. *TS* 52:34–50.
Lutfiyya, A. M. 1966. *Baytin: A Jordanian Village.* The Hague: Mouton.
MacPherson, S., and R. Silburn. 1998. The Meaning and Measuring of Poverty. Pages 1–
    19 in *Poverty: A Persistent Global Reality.* Edited by J. Dixon and D. Macarov.
    London: Routledge.
Maidman, M. 1976. A Socioeconomic Analysis of a Nuzi Family Archive. Ph.D. diss.,
    University of Pennsylvania. Michigan: University Microfilms.
Mair, L. 1977. *Primitive Government.* Rev. ed. London: Scholars Press.
Malchow, B. 1982. Social Justice in the Wisdom Literature. *BTB* 12:120–24.
Malina, B. J. 1981. *The New Testament World: Insights from Cultural Anthropology.*
    Atlanta: John Knox.
—1987. Wealth and Poverty in the New Testament and Its World. *Int* 41:354–67.
Maloney, R. P. 1973. The Old Testament Teaching on Usury. *Colloquium* 5:42–51.
—1974. Usury and Restrictions on Interest-taking in the Ancient Near East. *CBQ*
    36:1–20.
Mann, M. 1986. *The Sources of Social Power.* Vol. 1, *A History of Power from the
    Beginning to A.D. 1760.* Cambridge: Cambridge University Press.
Mantovani, P. A. 1988. La "conquista" di Israele. *RevB* 36:47–60.
Marcus, A. D. 2000. *The View from Nebo: How Archaeology is Rewriting the Bible and
    Reshaping the Middle East.* Boston: Little, Brown.
Marfoe, L. 1980. The Integrative Transformation: Patterns of Socio-political Organi-
    zation in Southern Syria. *BASOR* 234:1–42.
Marx, K. 1981. *Capital: A Critique of Political Economy*, vol. 3. Translated by D.
    Fernbach. Harmondsworth: Penguin.
Matthews, V. H. 1994. The Anthropology of Slavery in the Covenant Code. Pages 119–
    35 in Levinson 1994.
—1999a. The Unwanted Gift: Implications of Obligatory Gift Giving in Ancient Israel.
    Semeia 87:91–104.
—1999b. Treading the Winepress: Actual and Metaphorical Viticulture in the Ancient
    Near East. *Semeia* 86:19–32.
Matthews, V. H. E., and D. C. Benjamin. 1991. The Stubborn and the Fool: A Question
    of Labels. *TBT* 29:222–26.
—1993. *Social World of Ancient Israel: 1250–587 BCE.* Peabody, Mass.: Hendrickson.

Maxwell, S. 1999. Meaning and Measurement of Poverty. No Pages. Cited 14 April 2003. Online: http://www.odi.org.uk/publications/briefing/pov3.htm.

May, J. 1998. An Elusive Definition: Definitions, Measurements and Analysis of Poverty. No pages. Cited 16 May 2005. Online: http://www.undp.org/dpa/publications/choicesforthepoor/English/chap02.pdf.

Mayes, A. D. H. 1979. *Deuteronomy*. NCB. London: Nelson.

Mays, J. L. 1969a. *Amos: A Commentary*. OTL. London: SCM Press.

—1969b. *Hosea: A Commentary*. OTL. London: SCM Press.

—1976. *Micah. A Commentary*. OTL. Philadelphia. Westminster.

—1983. Justice: Perspectives from the Prophetic Tradition. *Int* 37:5–17.

Mazar, A. 1990. *Archaeology of the Land of the Bible*. ABRL. New York: Doubleday.

—1992. The Iron Age I. Pages 258–301 in Ben-Tor 1992.

—1993. Beth Shean in the Iron Age: Preliminary Report and Conclusions of the 1990–91 Excavations. *IEJ* 43:201–29.

—1998. On the Appearance of Red Slip in the Iron Age I Period in Israel. Pages 368–78 in Gitin, Mazar and Stern 1998.

—ed., 2001. *Studies in the Archaeology of the Iron Age in Israel and Jordan*. JSOTSup 331. Sheffield: Sheffield Academic Press.

Mazar, E. 1987. Ophel Excavations, Jerusalem, 1986. *IEJ* 37:60–63.

—1989. Royal Gateway to Ancient Jerusalem Uncovered. *BARev* 15, no. 3:38–51.

McCarter, P. K. 1980. *I Samuel: Notes, Translation and Commentary*. AB 8. New York: Doubleday.

McClenney-Sadler, M. 2003. Cry Witch! The Embers Still Burn. *SemeiaSt* 44:117–42.

McKane, W. 1970. *Proverbs: A New Approach*. OTL. London: SCM Press.

Meier, S. 1997. "*Hsr.*" *NIDOTTE* 2:225–27.

Meillassoux, C. 1991. *The Anthropology of Slavery: The Womb of Iron and Gold*. Translated by A. Dasnois. Chicago: University of Chicago Press.

Mendelsohn, I. 1949. *Slavery in the Ancient Near East: A Comparative Study of Slavery in Babylon, Assyria, Syria and Palestine from the Middle of the Third Millennium to the End of the First Millennium*. Oxford: Oxford University Press.

—1962. Slavery in the Old Testament. *IDB* 4:383–91.

Mendenhall, G. E. 1962. The Hebrew Conquest of Palestine. *BA* 25:66–87.

—1975. The Monarchy. *Int* 29:155–70.

—1983. Ancient Israel's Hyphenated History. Pages 95–103 in Freedman and Graf 1983.

Mercer, S. A. B. 1939. *The Tell El-Amarna Tablets*. 2 vols. Toronto: Macmillan.

Mettinger, T. N. D. 1971. *Solomonic State Officials: A Study of the Civil Government Officials of the Israelite Monarchy*. Lund: Gleerup.

Meyers, C. 1978. The Roots of Restriction: Women in Early Israel. *BA* 41:91–103.

—1988. *Discovering Eve: Ancient Israelite Women in Context*. Oxford: Oxford University Press.

—1997. The Family in Early Israel. Pages 1–47 in Perdue 1997.

Meyers, E. M., ed. 1997. *The Oxford Encyclopaedia of Archaeology in the Near East*. Oxford: Oxford University Press.

Mildenberg, L. 1996. *Yehud* and *smryn*. Über das Geld der persischen Provinzes Juda und Samaria im 4.Jahrhundert. Pages 119–46 in *Geschichte-Tradition-Reflexion: Festschrift für Martin Hengel zum 70. Geburstag*, vol. 1. Judentum. Tübingen: Mohr (Siebeck).

—2000. On Fractional Silver Issue in Palestine. *Transeu* 20:90–100.

Milgrom, J. 1995. The Alien in Your Midst. *BRev* 11, no. 6:18, 48.

Millard, A. 1986–87. Archaeology and the World of the Bible. *BAIAS* 6:46–48.

Miller, J. M. 1977. The Israelite Occupation of Canaan. Pages 213–84 in Hayes and Miller 1977.

—1989. Recent Archaeological Explorations on the El-Kerak Plateau. *JNSL* 15:143–53.

Miller, R. D., II. 2004. Identifying Earliest Israel. *BASOR* 333:55–68.

Miller, S. M. 1996. The Great Chain of Poverty Explanation. Pages 569–86 in Øyen, Miller and Samad 1996.

Milson, D. 1986. The Design of the Royal Gates of Megiddo, Hazor and Gezer. *ZDPV* 102:87–92.

Mirau, N. A. 1997. The Social Context of Early Iron Working in the Levant. Pages 99–115 in Aufrecht, Mirau and Gauley 1997.

Misch-Brandl, O. 1985. Ancient Seafarers Bequeath Unintended Legacy. *BARev* 11, no. 6:40–43.

Moore, B. 1966. *Social Origins of Dictatorship and Democracy: Lord and Peasant in the Making of the Modern World*. Boston: Beacon.

Morley, S. G., and G. W. Brainert. 1956. *The Ancient Maya*. 3d ed. Stanford, Calif.: Stanford University Press.

Mosala, I. J. 1989. *Biblical Hermeneutics and Black Theology in South Africa*. Grand Rapids: Eerdmans.

Moxnes, H. 1988. *The Economy of the Kingdom: Social Conflict and Economic Relations in Luke's Gospel*. OBT. Philadelphia: Fortress.

Moynihan, D. P., ed. 1968–69. *On Understanding Poverty: Perspectives from the Social Sciences*, vol. 1. Perspectives on Poverty. New York: American Academy of Arts and Sciences Library, Basic Books.

Muhly, J. D. 1984. The Beginning of Iron Metallurgy in Antiquity. *Qad* 17:2–11 [Hebrew].

Mullen E. T. 1993. *Narrative History and Ethnic Boundaries: The Deuteronomistic Historian and the Creation of Israelite National Identity*. SemeiaSt. Atlanta: Scholars Press.

Myers, J. M. 1965. *Ezra, Nehemiah: Introduction, Translation and Notes*. AB 14. Garden City, N.Y.: Doubleday.

Na'aman, N. 1986a. Habiru and Hebrews: The Transfer of a Social Term to the Literary Sphere. *JNES* 45:271–88.

—1986b. Hezekiah's Fortified Cites and the LMLK Stamps. *BASOR* 261:5–21.

Nakanose, S. 1993. *Josiah's Passover: Sociology and the Liberating Bible*. Maryknoll, N.Y.: Orbis.

Narayan, D., with R. Patal, K. Schafft, A. Rademacher and S. Koch-Schulte. 2000.*Voices of the Poor: Can Anyone Hear Us?* World Bank. New York: Oxford University Press.

Nash, Manning. 1966. *Primitive and Peasant Economic Systems*. San Francisco: Chandler.

Navone, J. 2001. Famine, Hunger, and Thirst in the Bible. *TBT* 39:155–59.

Negev, A., ed. 1972a. *Archaeological Encyclopaedia of the Holy Land*. Jerusalem. Jerusalem Publishing.

—1972b. Agriculture. Pages 13–17 in Negev 1972a.

—1972c. Food and Drink. Pages 111–12 in Negev 1972a.

Netting, R. M., R. R. Wilk and E. J. Arnould. 1984. Introduction. Pages iii–xxiii in *Households: Comparative and Historical Studies of the Domestic Group.* Edited by R. M. Netting, R. R. Wilk and E. J. Arnould. Berkeley: University of California Press.

Netzer, E. 1992. Domestic Architecture in the Iron Age. Pages 193–201 in Kempinski and Reich 1992.

Neufeld, E. 1960. The Emergence of a Royal-Urban Society in Ancient Israel. *HUCA* 31:31–53.

Neumann, J., and S. Parpola. 1987. Climatic Change and the Eleventh–Tenth Century Eclipse of Assyria and Babylonia. *JNES* 46:161–82.

Niditch, S. 1993. War, Women and Defilement in Numbers 31. *Semeia* 61:39–58.

North, R. 1954. *Sociology of the Biblical Jubilee.* AnBib 4. Rome: Pontifical Biblical Institute.

Norton, A., D. Owen and J. Milimo. 1994. *Zambia Participatory Poverty Assessment.* Vol. 5, *Participatory Poverty Assessment.* Washington, D.C.: Southern Africa Department, World Bank.

Noth, M. 1962. *Exodus: A Commentary.* Translated by J. S. Bowden. London: SCM Press.

Novak, M. 1996. Concepts of Poverty. Pages 47–61 in Øyen, Miller and Samad 1996.

Oakman, D. E. 1986. *Jesus and the Economic Questions of His Day.* Studies in the Bible and Early Christianity 8. New York: Edwin Mellen.

Oded, B. 2000. The Settlements of the Israelite and the Judean Exiles in Mesopotamia in the 8th–6th Centuries BCE. Pages 91–103 in *Studies in Historical Geography and Biblical Historiography: Presented to Zecharia Kallai.* Edited by G. Galil and M. Weinfeld. VTSup 81. Leiden: Brill.

Olivier, J. P. J. 1983. In Search of a Capital for the Northern Kingdom. *JNSL* 11:117–32.

—1994a. Kantaantekeninge ten Opsigte van die Sosioekonimiese Opset tydens die Regering van Koning Manasse van Juda. *NGTT* 35:174–85.

—1994b. Money Matters: Some Remarks on the Economic Situation in the Kingdom of Judah during the Seventh Century B.C. *BN* 73:90–100.

—1998. Restitution as Economic Redress: The Fine Print of the Old Babylonian *mesarum* Edict of Ammisaduqa. *JNSL* 24:83–99.

Oppenheim, A. L. 1977. *Ancient Mesopotamia: A Portrait of a Dead Civilization.* Rev. ed. Chicago: University of Chicago Press.

Oredsson, D. 1998. Jezreel: Its Contribution to Iron age Chronology. *SJOT* 12:86–101.

Oswalt, J. N. 1986. *The Book of Isaiah Chapters 1–39.* NICOT. Grand Rapids: Eerdmans.

Øyen, E. 1996. Poverty Research Rethought. Pages 3–17 in Øyen, Miller and Samad 1996.

—1997. The Act of Building Bridges between the World of the Poor and the World of the Non-poor. Pages 123–42 in Atal and Øyen 1997.

Øyen, E., S. M. Miller and S. A. Samad, eds. 1996. *Poverty: A Global Review. Handbook on International Poverty Research.* Oslo: Scandinavian University Press.

Palmer, C. 1998. "Following the Plough": The Agricultural Environment of Northern Jordan. *Levant* 30:129–65.

Parsons, T. 1968. *The Structure of Social Action.* New York: Free Press.

Patella, M. 1988. Olives: Mediterranean Treasure. *TBT* 26:293–97.

Patterson, O. 1982. *Slavery and Social Death: A Comparative Study.* Cambridge, Mass.: Harvard University Press.

Piers, G., and M. B. Singer. 1963. *Shame and Guilt.* Springfield: Addison.

Pilch, J. J. 1993. The Necessities of Life: Drinking and Eating. *TBT* 31:231–37.

—2002a. A Window into the Biblical World: Marriage. *TBT* 40:314–19.

—2002b. A Window into the Biblical World: The Family; Status and Roles. *TBT* 40:386–91.

Pitt-Rivers, J. 1968. Honor. Pages 503–11 in vol. 6 of *Encyclopaedia of the Social Sciences.* 2d ed. London: Routledge & Kegan Paul.

—1977. *The Fate of Shechem or the Politics of Sex: Essays in the Anthropology of the Mediterranean.* Cambridge: Cambridge University Press.

Pixley, G. V. 1987. *On Exodus: A Liberation Perspective.* Maryknoll, N.Y.: Orbis.

Pleins, J. D. 1987. Poverty in the Social World of the Wise. *JSOT* 37:61–78.

—1992. Poor, Poverty. *ABD* 5:402–14.

Polanyi, K. 1957. The Economy as Institutional Process. Pages 243–69 in *Trade and Market in the Early Empires: Economics in History and Theory.* Edited by K. Polanyi, C. M. Arensberg and H. W. Pearsons, Glencoe, Ill.: Free Press.

Pons, J. 1981. *L'Oppression dans l'Ancien Testament.* Paris: Letouzey et Ané.

Pope, M. H. 1965. *Job: Introduction, Translation and Notes.* AB 15. Garden City, N.Y.: Doubleday.

Popkin, S. L. 1979. *The Rational Peasant: The Political Economy of the Rural Society in Vietnam.* Berkeley: University of California Press.

Postgate, J. N. 1987. Employer, Employee and Employment in the Neo-Assyrian Empire. Pages 257–70 in Powell 1987.

Premnath, D. N. 1988. Latifundialization and Isaiah 5:8–10. *JSOT* 40:49–60.

Preobrazhensky, E. 1971. Peasantry and the Political Economy of the Early Stages of Industrialization. Pages 219–25 in Shanin 1971a.

Pritchard, J. B., ed. 1969. *Ancient Near Eastern Texts Relating to the Old Testament.* 3d ed with Supplement. Princeton, N.J.: Princeton University Press.

Rackham, O. 1983. Observations in the Historical Ecology of Boiotia. *Annual of the British School at Athens* 78:291–352.

Rainey, A. F. 1982. Wine from the Royal Vineyards. *BASOR* 245:57–62.

—1996. Who is a Canaanite? A Review of the Textual Evidence. *BASOR* 304:1–15.

Redfield, R. 1956. Peasant Studies and Culture: An Anthropological Approach. Chicago: University of Chicago Press.

Redman, C. L. 1978. *The Rise of Civilization: From Early Farmers to Urban Society in the Ancient Near East.* San Francisco: W. H. Freeman.

Reich, R., and E. Shukron. 2000a. The System of Rock-cut Tunnels near Gihon in Jerusalem Reconsidered. *RB* 107:5–17.

—2000b. The Excavations at the Gihon Spring and Warren's Shaft System in the City of David. Pages 327–39 in Geva 2000.

—2004. The History of the Gihon Spring in Jerusalem. *Levant* 36:211–23.

Rendtorff, R. 1984. The Future of Pentateuchal Criticism. *Hen* 6:1–14.

Ringgren, H. 1982. "*Yatom.*" *ThWAT* 3:1075–79.

—1999. "*Abad.*" *TDOT* 10:376–405.

Robinson, S. 2005. The Road to Recovery. *Time Magazine* 165, no. 11:40–41.

Rock, J. 1997. Making Widows: The Patriarchal Guardian at Work. *BTB* 27:10–15.

—1998. When is a Widow not a Widow? Guardianship Provides the Answer. *BTB* 28:4–6.

Rodinson, M. 1973. Islam and Capitalism. New York: Pantheon.

Rogerson, J. W. 1986. Was Israel a Segmentary Society? *JSOT* 36:17–26.

Ron, Z. 1966. Agricultural Terraces in the Judean Mountains. *IEJ* 16:33–49, 111–22.

Ronen, Y. 1996. The Enigma of the Shekel Weights of the Judean Kingdom. *BA* 59:122–25.

Rosen, B. 1986–87. Wine and Oil Allocations in the Samaria Ostraca. *TA* 13–14:39–45.

Rosen, S. A. 1988. Finding Evidence of Ancient Nomads. *BARev* 14, no. 5:46–53, 58–59.

Rossi, P. H., and Z. D. Blum. 1968–69. Class, Status and Poverty. Pages 36–63 in vol. 1 of Moynihan 1968–69.

Roth, M. T. 1995. *Law Collections from Mesopotamia and Asia Minor*. SBLWAW. Atlanta: Scholars Press.

Routledge, B. 1997. Learning to Love the King: Urbanism and the State in Iron Age Moab. Pages 130–44 in Aufrecht, Mirau and Gauley 1997.

Rowton, M. B. 1977. Dimorphic Structure and the Parasocial Element. *JNES* 36:181–98.

Ruether, R. R. 1999. Prophetic Tradition and the Liberation of Women: Premise and Betrayal. *JTSoA* 73:24–33.

Ruggles, P. 1990. *Drawing the Line: Alternative Poverty Measures and Their Implications for Public Policy*. Washington, D.C.: Urban Institute.

Ruggles, S. 1987. *Prolonged Connections: The Rise of the Extended Family in Nineteenth-Century England and America*. Madison: University of Wisconsin Press.

Sachs, J. 2005. The End of Poverty: Exclusive Book Excerpt. *Time Magazine* 165, no. 11:26–32.

Sahlin, G. 1974. "*Chera.*" *TDNT* 9:445–47.

Sahlins, M. D. 1960. Political Power and the Economy in Primitive Society. Pages 400–15 in *Essays in the Science of Culture, in Honour of Leslie A. White*. Edited by G. E. Dole and R. L. Caneiro. New York: Thomas Y. Crowell.

—1972. *Stone Age Economics*. Chicago: Aldine.

Saller, R. P. 1987. Men's Age at Marriage and Its Consequences in the Roman Family. *Classical Philology* 82:21–34.

Samad, S. A. 1996. The Present Situation in Poverty Research. Pages 33–46 in Øyen, Miller and Samad 1996.

Sanderson, J. 1992. Amos. Pages 205–9 in *The Women's Bible Commentary*. Edited by C. A. Newsom and S. H. Ringe. London: SPCK.

Sasson, A. 1998. The Pastoral Component in the Economy of Hill Country Sites in the Intermediate Bronze and Iron Ages: Archaeo-Ethnographic Case Studies. *TA* 25:3–51.

Saul, J. S., and R. Woods. 1971. African Peasantries. Pages 103–14 in Shanin 1971a.

Schaar, K. W. 1991. An Architectural Theory for the Origin of the Four-Room House. *SJOT* 2:75–98.

Schaper, J. 1995. The Jerusalem Temple as an Instrument of the Achaemenid Fiscal Administration. *VT* 45:528–39.

Scheff, T. J. 1987. Shame and Conformity: The Deference–Emotion System. *American Sociological Review* 53:395–406.

Schmidt, T. E. 1987. *Hostility to Wealth in the Synoptic Gospels*. JSOTSup 15. Sheffield: JSOT Press.

Schneider, J. 1971. Of Vigilance and Virgins. *Ethnology* 9:1–24.

Schottroff, L., and W. Stegemann. 1986. *Jesus and the Hope of the Poor*. Translated by M. J. O'Connell. Maryknoll, N.Y.: Orbis.

Schottroff, W. 1989. Der Zugriff des Königs auf die Töchter. *EvT* 49:268–85.

Schram, S. F. 1995. *Words of Welfare: The Poverty of Social Science and the Social Science of Poverty*. Minneapolis: University of Minnesota Press.

Schwantes, M. 1977. *Das Recht der Armen*. BBET 4. Frankfurt: P. Lang.

Schwienhorst-Schömberger, L. 1990. *Das Bundesbuch (Ex 20,22–23,33). Studien zu seiner Enstehung und Theologie*. BZAW. Berlin: de Gruyter.

Scott, J. C. 1976. *The Moral Economy of the Peasant: Rebellion and Subsistence in Southeast Asia*. New Haven: Yale University Press.

—1985. *Weapons of the Weak: Everyday Forms of Peasant Resistance*. New Haven: Yale University Press.

Scott, R. B. Y. 1959. Weights and Measures of the Bible. *BA* 22, no. 2:22–39.

—1965. *Proverbs, Ecclesiastes: Introduction, Translation and Notes*. AB 18. Garden City, N.Y.: Doubleday.

Scoones, I. 1995. Investigating Difference: Applications of Wealth Ranking and Household Survey Approaches Among Farming Households in Southern Zimbabwe. *Development and Change* 26:67–88.

Sen, A. 1977. Starvation and Exchange Entitlements: A General Approach and its Application to the Great Bengal Famine. *Cambridge Journal of Economics* 1:33–59.

—1981. *Poverty and Famines: An Essay on Entitlement and Deprivation*. Oxford: Oxford University Press.

—1999. *Development as Freedom*. New York: Anchor.

Shanin, T., ed. 1971a. *Peasants and Peasant Societies*. Selected Readings. London: Penguin.

—1971b. Peasantry as a Political Factor. Pages 238–63 in Shanin 1971a.

Shanks, H., R. R. Stieglitz and B. Lang. 2003. Real or Fake? *BARev* 29:40–45.

Shaw, B. D. 1987. The Age of Roman Girls at Marriage: Some Reconsiderations. *Journal of Roman Studies* 77:30–46.

Shaw, C. S. 1993. *The Speeches of Micah: A Rhetorical-Historical Analysis*. JSOTSup 145. Sheffield: Sheffield Academic Press.

Shiloh, Y. 1970. The Four-Room House: Its Situation and Function in the Israelite City. *IEJ* 20:180–90.

—1973. The Four-Space House: The Israelite House Type. *ErIs* 11:277–85 [Hebrew].

—1980. The Population of Iron Age Palestine in the Light of a Sample Analysis of Urban Plans, Areas and Population Density. *BASOR* 239:25–35.

—1984. *Excavations at the City of David. I. 1978–1982: Interim Report of the First Five Seasons*. Qedem 19. Jerusalem: Institute of Archaeology/Hebrew University of Jerusalem.

—1985–86. Biblical Jerusalem: A Canaanite City and an Israelite Capital. *BAIAS* 5:27–31.

—1986. A Group of Hebrew Bullae from the City of David. *IEJ* 36:16–38.

—1987. The Casemate Wall, the Four Room House, and Early Planning in the Israelite City. *BASOR* 268: 3–15.

Silverman, S. 1986. Anthropology and History: Understanding the Boundaries. *Historical Methods* 19:123–26.

Simkins, R. A. 1999. Patronage and the Political Economy of Monarchic Israel. *Semeia* 87:123–44.

Singer, I. 1988. Merneptah's Campaign to Canaan and the Egyptian Occupation of the Southern Coastal Plain of Palestine in the Ramesside Period. *BASOR* 269:1–10.

Singer-Avitz, L. 1999. Beersheba: A Gateway Community in Southern Arabian Long-Distance Trade in the Eighth Century BCE. *TA* 26:3–74.

Sjoberg, G. 1960. *The Preindustrial City: Past and Present*. New York: Free Press.

Skotte, P. 1988. The Problem of Poverty and the Old Testament. *TBT* 26:87–93.

Smith, P. 1998. People of the Holy Land from Pre-History to the Recent Past. Pages 58–75 in Levy 1998.

Snaith, N. H. 1967. *Leviticus and Numbers*. New Century Bible Commentary. London: Nelson.

Sneed, M. 1999. Israelite Concern for the Alien, Orphan and Widow: Altruism or Ideology? *ZAW* 111:498–507.

Soares-Prabhu, G. M. 1991. Class in the Bible: The Biblical Poor a Social Class? Pages 147–71 in *Voices from the Margins: Interpreting the Bible in the Third World*. Edited by R. S. Sugirtharajah. Maryknoll, N.Y.: Orbis.

Sœbø, M. 2004. *"Rws." TDOT* 13:422–26.

Soggin, J. A. 1977. The Davidic-Solomonic Kingdom. Pages 332–80 in Hayes and Miller 1977.

—1987. *The Prophet Amos: A Translation and Commentary*. Translated by J. Bowden. London: SCM Press.

Speiser, E. A. 1940. Of Shoes and Shekels. *BASOR* 77:15–20.

Spencer, J. E., and G. N. Hale. 1961. The Origin, Nature and Distribution of Agricultural Terracing. *Pacific Viewpoint* 2:1–40.

Stager, L. E. 1976. Agriculture. *IDB Supplement*: 11–13.

—1982. The Archaeology of the East Slope of Jerusalem and the Terraces of the Kidron. *JNES* 41:111–21.

—1985. The Archaeology of the Family in Ancient Israel. *BASOR* 260:1–35.

—1990. Shemer's Estate. *BASOR* 277, no. 8:93–107.

Stansell, G. 1999. The Gift in Ancient Israel. *Semeia* 87:65–90.

Steiner, M. 2000. Jerusalem in the Tenth and Seventh Centuries BCE: From Administrative Town to Commercial City. Pages 280–88 in Geva 2000.

Stern, E. 1998. Between Persia and Greece: Trade, Administration and Warfare in the Persian and Hellenistic Periods (539–63 BCE). Pages 432–45 in Levy 1998.

—2000. The Settlement of Sea Peoples in Northern Israel. Pages 197–212 in *The Sea Peoples and Their World: A Reassessment*. Edited by E. D. Oren. University Museum Monograph 108. University Symposium 11. Philadelphia: The University of Pennsylvania Museum of Archaeology and Anthropology.

Stern, E., A. Gilboa and I. Sharon. 1989. Tel Dor, 1987: Preliminary Report. *IEJ* 39:32–42.

Stiebing, W. H. 1983. The Amarna Period. Pages 1–14 in Freedman and Graf 1983.

—1994. Climate and Collapse: Did the Weather Make Israel's Emergence Possible? *BRev* 10:18–27, 54.

Stirling, P. 1971. A Turkish Village. Pages 37–48 in Shanin 1971a.

Stone, K. 1996. *Sex, Honour, and Power in the Deuteronomistic History*. JSOTSup 234. Sheffield: Sheffield Academic Press.

Streeten, P. 1995. Human Development: The Debate about the Index. *International Social Science Journal* 143:25–38.

Stuhlmueller, C. 1989. Sickness and Disease: An Old Testament Perspective. *TBT* 27:5–9.

Szubin, H. Z., and B. Porten, 1988. A Life Estate of Usufruct: A New Interpretation of Kraeling 6. *BASOR* 269:29–45.

Tamez, E. 1982. *The Bible of the Oppressed*. Maryknoll, N.Y.: Orbis.

—ed., 1989. *Through Her Eyes: Women's Theology from Latin America*. Maryknoll, N.Y.: Orbis.

Thistlethwaite, S. B. 1993. "You May Enjoy the Spoil of Your Enemies": Rape as a Biblical Metaphor for War. *Semeia* 61:59–78.

Thompson, E. A. 1965. *The Early Germans*. Oxford: Clarendon.

Thompson, J. A. 1984. Farming in Ancient Israel. *BurH* 20:53–60.

Thompson, T. L. 1992. *Early History of the Israelite People: From the Written and Archaeological Sources*. Leiden: Brill.

—1995. The Intellectual Matrix of Early Biblical Narrative. Pages 107–24 in D. V. Edelman, ed., *The Triumph of Elohim: From Yahwisms to Judaisms*. Biblical Exegesis and Theology 13. Kampen: Kok Pharos.

—1999. *The Mythic Past: Biblical Archaeology and the Myth of Israel*. New York: Basic.

Timmerman, P. 1981. *Vulnerability, Resilience and the Collapse of Society: A Review of Models and Possible Climatic Applications*. Toronto: Institute for Environmental Studies, University of Toronto.

Townsend, T. P. 1988. The Poor in Wisdom Literature. *BibBh* 14:5–25.

Tsiakolos, G., and D. Kongidou. 1991. Definitions of Poverty. No pages. Cited 11 December 2005. Online: http://www.eled.auth.gr/reds/p3/p3keimena/definition_poverty.htm..

Turkowski, L. 1969. Peasant Agriculture in the Judean Hills. *PEQ* 101:21–33, 101–12.

Ussishkin, D. 1987. Lachish: Key to the Israelite Conquest of Canaan? *BARev* 13, no. 1:18–39.

—1994. Gate 1567 at Megiddo and the Seal of Shema, Servant of Jeroboam. Pages 410–28 in Coogan et al. 1994.

—1995. The Destruction of Megiddo at the End of the Late Bronze Age and Its Historical Significance. *TA* 22:240–67.

—2000. The Credibility of the Tel Jezreel Excavations: A Rejoinder to Amnon Ben-Tor. *TA* 27:248–56.

Uyal, B. 2003. The Mosaic of Time. *JBQ* 31:226–29.

Vallely, P. 1990. *Bad Samaritans: First World Ethics and Third World Debt*. Maryknoll, N.Y.: Orbis.

Van der Ploeg, J. 1950. Les Pauvres d'Israel et leur Piété. *OTS* 7:236–70.

Van Wyk, C. 1999. Collar Rim Jars: Terminological and Methodological Dilemmas. *Sahmyook University Journal* 31:101–47.

Von Rad, G. 1966. *Deuteronomy: A Commentary*. Philadelphia: Westminster.

—1972. *Wisdom in Israel*. Nashville: Abingdon.

Von Waldow, H. E. 1970. Social Responsibility and Social Structure in Early Israel. *CBQ* 32:182–204.

Waetzoldt, H. 1987. Compensation of Craft Workers and Officials in the Ur III Period. Pages 117–42 in Powell 1987.

Wagstaff, M., and C. Gamble. 1982. Island Resources and Limitations. Pages 95–105 in *An Island Polity: The Archaeology of Exploitation in Melos.* Edited by C. Renfrew and M. Wagstaff. Cambridge: Cambridge University Press.

Wakely, R. 1997. "*Hayil.*" *NIDOTTE* 2:116–26.

Waldbaum, J. C. 1978. *From Bronze to Iron: The Transition from the Bronze Age to the Iron Age in the Eastern Mediterranean.* Studies in Mediterranean Archaeology 54. Gothenberg: Paul Aströms.

Warriner, D. 1957. *Land Reform and Development in the Middle East: A Study of Egypt, Syria, and Iraq.* London: Royal Institute of International Affairs. Oxford University Press.

Washington, H. C. 1994. *Wealth and Poverty in the Instruction of Amenemope and the Hebrew Proverbs.* SBLDS. Atlanta: Scholars Press.

Watts, M. 1983. *Silent Violence: Food, Famine and Peasantry in Northern Nigeria.* Berkeley: University of California Press.

Weber, M. 1952. *Ancient Judaism.* Glencoe, Ill.: Free Press.

—1964. *The Theory of Social and Economic Organization.* Translated by A. M. Henderson and T. Parsons. New York: Free Press of Glencoe, Collier-Macmillan.

Webster, J., ed. 1986. *Desmond Tutu: Crying in the Wilderness. The Struggle for Justice in South Africa.* London: Mobray.

Weinfeld, M. 1988. Historical Facts Behind the Israelite Settlement Pattern. *VT* 38:324–32.

—1995. *Social Justice in Ancient Israel and in the Ancient Near East.* Jerusalem: Magnes/The Hebrew University.

Weippert, H. 1971. *The Settlement of the Israelite Tribes in Palestine: A Critical Survey of the Recent Scholarly Debate.* SBT, 2d Series 21. Naperville, Ill.: Alec R. Allenson.

—1988. *Palästina in vorhellenistischer Zeit.* Munich: Beck.

Wenham, G. J. 1979. *The Book of Leviticus.* NICOT. Grand Rapids: Eerdmans.

Westbrook, R. 1971. Jubilee Laws. *Israel Law Review* 6:209–26.

—1988. *Studies in Biblical and Cuneiform Law.* CahRB 26. Paris: Gabalda.

—1991. *Property and the Family in Biblical Law.* JSOTSup 113. Sheffield: Sheffield Academic Press.

Wevers, J. W., and D. B. Redford, eds. 1972. *Studies on the Ancient Palestine World: For Professor F. V. Winnett.* Toronto Semitic Texts and Studies 2. Toronto: University of Toronto Press.

Whitelam, K. W. 1986. Recreating the History of Israel. *JSOT* 35:45–70.

—1989. Israel's Traditions of Origin: Reclaiming the Land. *JSOT* 44:19–42.

—1996. *The Invention of Ancient Israel: The Silencing of Palestinian History.* London: Routledge.

—2000. "Israel is Laid Waste: His Seed is No More": What if Merneptah's Scribes Were Telling the Truth? *BibInt* 8:8–22.

—2002. Palestine During the Iron Age. Pages 391–415 in vol. 1 of Barton 2002.

Whybray, R. N. 1974. *The Intellectual Tradition of the Old Testament.* BZAW 135. Berlin: de Gruyter.

—1988–89. Poverty, Wealth, and Point of View in Proverbs. *ExpTim* 100:332–36.

—1990. The Sage in the Israelite Royal Court. Pages 133–39 in *The Sage in Israel and the Ancient Near East*. Edited by J. G. Gammie and L. G. Perdue. Winona Lake, Ind: Eisenbrauns.

Wightman, G. J. 1990. The Myth of Solomon. *BASOR* 277–28:5–22.

Wikan, U. 1984. Shame and Honour: A Contestable Pair. *Man* 19:35–52.

Wilk, R. R., and R. M. Netting. 1984. Households: Changing Forms and Functions. Pages 1–28 in Netting, Wilk and Arnold.

Willett, E. A. R. 2002. Infant Mortality and Family Religion in the Biblical Periods. *DavarLogos* 1:27–42.

Wilson, F., and M. Ramphele. 1989. *Uprooting Poverty: The South African Challenge*. New York: Norton.

Wittenberg, G. 1986. The Lexical Context of the Terminology for the "Poor" in the Book of Proverbs. *Scriptura* 2:40–85.

Wittfogel, K. A. 1957. *Oriental Despotism: A Comparative Study of Total Power*. New Haven: Yale University Press.

Wolf, C. U. 1962a. Poor. *IDB* 3:843–44.

—1962b. Poverty. *IDB* 3:853–54.

Wolf, E. R. 1966. *Peasants*. Foundations of Modern Anthropology Series. Englewood Cliffs, N.J.: Prentice–Hall.

Wolff, H. W. 1977. *Joel and Amos*. Hermeneia. Philadelphia: Fortress.

—1990. *Micah: A Commentary*. Translated by G. Stansell. Minneapolis: Augsburg.

World Bank.1978. *World Development Report*. Washington, D.C.: World Bank.

—1980. *Poverty and Human Development*. Oxford: Oxford University Press.

—2000. *Development Report: Knowledge, Information and Development. Attacking Poverty*. Oxford: Oxford University Press.

Wright, C. J. H. 1984. What Happened Every Seven Years in Israel? Old Testament Sabbatical Institutions for Land, Debts and Slaves. *EvQ* 56:129–38, 193–201.

Wyatt, N. 2001. The Mythic Mind. *SJOT* 15:3–56.

Wylie, A. 1989. Archaeological Cables and Tacking: The Implications of Practise for Bernstein's "Options Beyond Objectivism and Relativism." *PhilSocSci* 19:1–18.

Yadin, Y. 1975. *Hazor: The Rediscovery of a Great Citadel of the Bible*. Jerusalem: Weidenfeld & Nicolson.

Yee, G. A. 2003. *Poor Banished Children of Eve: Woman as Evil in the Hebrew Bible*. Minneapolis: Fortress.

Zaccagnini, C. 1976. Osservazioni sur contratti di "anticresi" a Nuzi. *Or Ant* 15:191–207.

Zeder, M. A. 1996. The Role of Pigs in Near Eastern Subsistence: A View from the Southern Levant. Pages in *Retrieving the Past: Essays on Archaeological Research and Methodology in Honour of Gus W. Van Beek*. Edited by J. D. Seger. Winona Lake, Ind.: Eisenbrauns.

Zohary, D. 1966. *Flora Palestina*, Part 1. Jerusalem: The Israel Academy of Sciences and Humanities.

—1972. *Flora Palestina*, Part 2. Jerusalem: The Israel Academy of Sciences and Humanities.

Zorn, J. R. 1994. Estimating the Population Size of Ancient Settlements: Methods, Problems, Solutions and a Case Study. *BASOR* 295:31–48.

Zwickel, W. 1999. Die Wirtschaftsreform des Hiskia und die Sozialkritik der Propheten des 8. Jahrhunderts. *EvT* 59:356–77.

INDEXES

INDEX OF REFERENCES

INDEX OF AUTHORS